PSYCHOPATHOLOGY:
Contributions from the Biological, Behavioral, and Social Sciences
edited by Muriel Hammer, Kurt Salzinger, and Samuel Sutton

ABNORMAL CHILDREN AND YOUTH:
Therapy and Research
by Anthony Davids

PRINCIPLES OF PSYCHOTHERAPY WITH CHILDREN
by John M. Reisman

AVERSIVE MATERNAL CONTROL:
A Theory of Schizophrenic Development
by Alfred B. Heilbrun, Jr.

INDIVIDUAL DIFFERENCES IN CHILDREN
edited by Jack C. Westman

EGO FUNCTIONS IN SCHIZOPHRENICS, NEUROTICS, AND NOR-
MALS:
A Systematic Study of Conceptual, Diagnostic, and Therapeutic Aspects
by Leopold Bellak, Marvin Hurvich, and Helen A. Gediman

INNOVATIVE TREATMENT METHODS IN PSYCHOPATHOLOGY
edited by Karen S. Calhoun, Henry E. Adams, and Kevin M. Mitchell

THE CHANGING SCHOOL SCENE: CHALLENGE TO PSYCHOLOGY
by Leah Gold Fein

TROUBLED CHILDREN: THEIR FAMILIES, SCHOOLS, AND
TREATMENTS
by Leonore R. Love and Jaques W. Kaswan

RESEARCH STRATEGIES IN PSYCHOTHERAPY
by Edward S. Bordin

THE VOLUNTEER SUBJECT
by Robert Rosenthal and Ralph L. Rosnow

INNOVATIONS IN CLIENT-CENTERED THERAPY
by Wexler and Rice

RORSCHACH:
A Comprehensive System
by John Exner

D1503017

THE VOLUNTEER SUBJECT

DATE DUE

About the Authors

ROBERT ROSENTHAL is Professor of Social Psychology at Harvard University. He previously served on the faculties of Boston University, Ohio State University, University of North Dakota, University of California, Los Angeles, and University of Southern California. Dr. Rosenthal received his B.A. (1953) and his Ph.D. (1956) from the University of California, Los Angeles. He is the author or co-author of several books and has also written numerous articles for professional journals.

RALPH L. ROSNOW is Professor of Psychology at Temple University. He has taught at Harvard University and Boston University and in 1973 was a Visiting Professor at London School of Economics. He received his B.S. in 1957 from the University of Maryland, his M.A. in 1958 from The George Washington University, and his Ph.D. in 1962 from The American University. He has co-authored and co-edited several other books, as well as authoring a variety of articles.

Rosenthal and Rosnow have collaborated on another John Wiley & Sons book, *Primer of Methods for the Behavioral Sciences* (1974).

THE VOLUNTEER SUBJECT

ROBERT ROSENTHAL   and   **RALPH L. ROSNOW**
Harvard University   *Temple University*

A WILEY-INTERSCIENCE PUBLICATION

JOHN WILEY & SONS, New York · London · Sydney · Toronto

Library of Congress Cataloging in Publication Data

Rosenthal, Robert, 1933-
    The volunteer subject.

    (Wiley series on personality processes)
    "A Wiley-Interscience publication."
    Bibliography: p.
    1. Human experimentation in psychology. I. Rosnow,
Ralph L., joint author, II. Title.
BF181.R67   150'.7'24   74-16378
ISBN 0-471-73670-8

Printed in the United States of America

10–9 8 7 6 5 4 3 2 1

To Our Parents

and to Nancy Pearl, Lottie, Trude

Ginny, David, and Roberta

Series Preface

This series of books is addressed to behavioral scientists interested in the nature of human personality. Its scope should prove pertinent to personality theorists and researchers as well as to clinicians concerned with applying an understanding of personality processes to the amelioration of emotional difficulties in living. To this end, the series provides a scholarly integration of theoretical formulations, empirical data, and practical recommendations.

Six major aspects of studying and learning about human personality can be designated: personality theory, personality structure and dynamics, personality development, personality assessment, personality change, and personality adjustment. In exploring these aspects of personality, the books in the series discuss a number of distinct but related subject areas: the nature and implications of various theories of personality; personality characteristics that account for consistencies and variations in human behavior; the emergence of personality processes in children and adolescents; the use of interviewing and testing procedures to evaluate individual differences in personality; efforts to modify personality styles through psychotherapy, counseling, behavior therapy, and other methods of influence; and patterns of abnormal personality functioning that impair individual competence.

IRVING B. WEINER

Case Western Reserve University
Cleveland, Ohio

Preface

The idea is not new that persons volunteering for behavioral research may not be fully adequate models for the study of human behavior in general. Anthropologists, economists, political scientists, psychologists, sociologists, and statisticians are by now well aware of the problem of volunteer bias. In Bill McGuire's (1969) terms, we have almost passed out of the ignorance stage in the life of this particular artifact. Our purpose in writing this book was to tell what is known about the volunteer subject so that:

1. The complete passing of the stage of ignorance of this artifact would be hastened,

2. We might dwell more productively on McGuire's second stage in the life of an artifact, the coping stage, and

3. A beginning might be made in nudging our knowledge of volunteering as an artifact to McGuire's final stage, the stage of exploitation.

We hope our book will help ensure that the problem of the volunteer subject will not only be recognized and dealt with but also that volunteering for research participation may come to be seen as behavior of interest in its own right and not simply as a source of artifact.

To the extent that volunteers differ from nonvolunteers, the employment of volunteer subjects can have serious effects on estimates of such parameters as means, medians, proportions, variances, skewness, and kurtosis. In survey research, where estimation of such parameters is the principal goal, biasing effects of volunteer subjects could be disastrous. In a good deal of behavioral research, however, interest is centered less on such statistics as means and proportions and more on such statistics as differences between means and proportions. The experimental investigator is ordinarily interested in relating such differences to the operation of his independent variable. The fact that volunteers differ from nonvolunteers in their scores on the dependent variable may be of little interest to the behavioral experimenter. He may want more to know whether the magnitude of the difference between his experimental and control group means would be affected if he used volunteers. In other words, he may be interested in knowing whether volunteer status interacts with his experimental variable. In due course, we shall see that such interactions do indeed occur, and that their occurrence does not depend upon the main effects of volunteering.

The audience to whom this book is addressed is made up of behavioral and social scientists, their graduate students, and their most serious undergraduate students. Although psychologists and sociologists may be the primary readers we believe that anthropologists, economists, political scientists, statisticians, and others of, or friendly to, the behavioral sciences may be equally interested.

One way in which this book differs from most other empirically oriented works in the behavioral and social sciences is in its strong emphasis on effect sizes. Only rarely have we been content to specify that a relationship was "significant." Whenever practical we have tried to include estimates of the size of various effects. Quite apart from the particular topic of this book we believe that routinely specifying effect sizes may be a generally useful procedure in the behavioral sciences.

When specifying effect sizes we have most often employed r or σ as the unit of measurement. To give a rough indication of whether a particular effect was "large," "medium," or "small" we follow Cohen's (1969) guidelines: Large effects are defined as $r \geqslant .50$ or $\sigma \geqslant .80$; medium effects are defined as $r \cong .30$ or $\sigma \cong .50$; and small effects are defined as $r \cong .10$ or $\sigma \cong .20$.

Our research on the volunteer subject was supported by grants from the Division of Social Sciences of the National Science Foundation, which provided us the flexibility to pursue leads to whatever ends seemed most promising. Both of us were on leave from our home institutions during the academic year in which this book was written, 1973–1974, and we express our appreciation to Harvard University and Temple University for this time that was given us. One of us (RR) was on sabbatical leave for the full academic year and supported in part by a fellowship from the Guggenheim Foundation; the other (RLR) was on study leave during the first term while an academic visitor at the London School of Economics and then on leave of absence while a visiting professor at Harvard University during the second term. We are grateful for the support provided by these institutions and especially to the following individuals: Hilde Himmelweit, Brendan Maher, and Freed Bales.

For permission to reprint figures and other copyright data, we thank *American Psychologist, Educational and Psychological Measurement, Journal of Experimental Research in Personality, Journal of Experimental Social Psychology, Journal of Personality and Social Psychology,* and *Psychological Reports.*

For their devoted and expert typing we thank Donna DiFurio and Mari Tavitian.

We are also grateful to Zick Rubin for his helpful suggestions.

And finally, we thank our best friends Mary Lu and Mimi for the many ways in which they improved the book—and its authors.

ROBERT ROSENTHAL

RALPH L. ROSNOW

June 1974

Contents

CHAPTER 1

Introduction

There is a growing suspicion among behavioral researchers that those human subjects who find their way into the role of research subject may not be entirely representative of humans in general. McNemar put it wisely when he said, "The existing science of human behavior is largely the science of the behavior of sophomores" (1946, p. 333). Sophomores are convenient subjects for study, and some sophomores are more convenient than others. Sophomores enrolled in psychology courses, for example, get more than their fair share of opportunities to play the role of the research subject whose responses provide the basis for formulations of the principles of human behavior. There are now indications that these "psychology sophomores" are not entirely representative of even sophomores in general (Hilgard, 1967), a possibility that makes McNemar's formulation sound unduly optimistic. The existing science of human behavior may be largely the science of those sophomores who both enroll in psychology courses and volunteer to participate in behavioral research. The extent to which a useful, comprehensive science of human behavior can be based upon the behavior of such self-selected and investigator-selected subjects is an empirical question of considerable importance. It is a question that has received increasing attention in recent years, (e.g., Adair, 1973; Bell, 1961; Chapanis, 1967; Damon, 1965; Leslie, 1972; Lester, 1969; London and Rosenhan, 1964; Maul, 1970; Ora, 1965; Parten, 1950; Rosenhan, 1967; Rosenthal, 1965; Rosenthal and Rosnow, 1969; Rosnow and Rosenthal, 1970; Schappe, 1972; Silverman and Margulis, 1973; Straits and Wuebben, 1973; Wells and Schofield, 1972; Wunderlich and Becker, 1969.)

Some of this recent interest has been focused on the actual proportion of human research subjects that are drawn from the collegiate setting. Table 1-1 shows the results of six studies investigating this question during the 1960s. The range is from 70% to 90%, with a median of 80%. Clearly, then, the vast majority of human research subjects have been sampled from populations of convenience, usually the college or university in which the investigator is

Table 1-1. College Students as a Percentage of Total Subjects Employed

Author	Source	Years	% College Students
Smart (1966) I	*Journal of Abnormal and Social Psychology*	1962–1964	73
Smart (1966) II	*Journal of Experimental Psychology*	1963–1964	86
Schultz (1969) I	*Journal of Personality and Social Psychology*	1966–1967	70
Schultz (1969) II	*Journal of Experimental Psychology*	1966–1967	84
Jung (1969)	Psychology Department Survey	1967–1968	90
Higbee and Wells (1972)	*Journal of Personality and Social Psychology*	1969	76
Median			80

employed. The studies shown in Table 1-1 span only an eight-year period, a period too short for the purpose of trying to discern a trend. Nevertheless, there is no reason for optimism based on a comparison of the earliest with the latest percentages. If anything, there may have been a rise in the percentage of human subjects who were college students. The concern over the use of college students as our model of persons in general is based not only on the very obvious differences between college students and more representative persons in age, intelligence, and social class but also on the suspicion that college students, because of their special relationship with the teacher-investigator, may be especially susceptible to the operation of the various mechanisms that together constitute what has been called the social psychology of behavioral research (e.g., Adair, 1973; Fraser and Zimbardo, n.d.; Haas, 1970; Lana, 1969; Lester, 1969; McGuire, 1969a; Orne, 1969, 1970; Rosenberg, 1969; Straits and Wuebben, 1973; Straits, Wuebben, and Majka, 1972.)

Although most of the interest in, and concern over, the problem of subject selection biases has been centered on human subjects, we should note that analogous interests and concerns have been developing among investigators employing animal subjects. Just as the college student may not be a very good model for the "typical" person, so the laboratory rat may not be a very good model for the typical rodent nor for a wild rat, nor even for another laboratory rat of a different strain (e.g., Beach, 1950, 1960; Boice, 1973; Christie, 1951; Ehrlich, 1974; Eysenck, 1967; Kavanau, 1964, 1967; Richter, 1959; Smith, 1969.)

VOLUNTEER BIAS

The problem of the volunteer subject has been of interest to many behavioral researchers and evidence of their interest will be found in the chapters to follow. Fortunately for those of us who are behavioral researchers, however, mathematical statisticians have also devoted attention and effort to problems of the volunteer subject (e.g., Cochran, 1963; Cochran, Mosteller, and Tukey, 1953; Deming, 1944; Hansen and Hurwitz, 1946.) Their work has shown the effects of the proportion of the population who select themselves out of the sample by not volunteering or responding, on the precision of estimates of various population values. These results are depressing to say the least, showing as they do how rapidly the margin of error increases as the proportion of nonvolunteers increases even moderately. In the present volume we shall not deal with the technical aspects of sampling and "nonresponse" theory, but it will be useful at this point to give in quantitative terms an example of volunteer bias in operation.

The basic data were presented by Cochran (1963) in his discussion of nonresponse bias. Three waves of questionnaires were mailed out to fruit growers, and the number of growers responding to each of the three waves was recorded, as was the remaining number of growers who never responded. One of the questions dealt with the number of fruit trees owned, and for just this question, data were available for the entire population of growers. Because of this fortunate circumstance, it was possible to calculate the degree of bias due to nonresponse, or nonvolunteering, present after the first, second, and third waves of questionnaires. Table 1-2 summarizes these calculations and gives the formal definition of volunteer bias. The first three rows of Table 1-2 give the basic data provided by Cochran: (1) the number of respondents to each wave of questionnaires and the number of nonrespondents, (2) the percentage of the total population represented by each wave of respondents and by the nonrespondents, and (3) the mean number of trees actually owned by each wave of respondents and by the nonrespondents. Examination of this row reveals the nature of the volunteer bias: the earlier responders owned more trees, on the average, than did the later responders. The remaining five rows of data are based on the cumulative number of respondents available after the first, second, and third waves. For each of these waves, five items of information are provided: (1) the mean number of trees owned by the respondents up to that point in the survey (Y_1); (2) the mean number of trees owned by those who had not yet responded up to that point in the survey (Y_2); (3) the difference between these two values ($Y_1 - Y_2$); (4) the percentage of the population that had not yet responded up to that point in the survey (P); and (5) the magnitude of the bias up to that point in the survey, defined as $P \times (Y_1 - Y_2)$. Examination of this last row shows that with each successive wave of respondents there was an appreciable decrease in the magnitude of the bias. This appears to be a fairly typical result of studies of this kind: increasing the effort to recruit the nonvolunteer decreases the bias in the sample estimates. Cochran gives considerable advice on how to minimize bias, given the usually greater cost of trying to recruit a nonvolunteer compared to the cost of recruiting a more willing respondent. Before leaving the present example of the calculation of bias, we should note again that in most circumstances of behavioral research we can compute the proportion of our population who fail to participate (P) and the statistic of interest for those who volunteer their data (Y_1); but we cannot compute the statistic of interest for those who do not volunteer (Y_2) so that it is often our lot to be in a position to suspect bias but to be unable to give an accurate quantitative statement about its magnitude.

Put most simply, then, the concern over the volunteer problem has had for its goal the reduction of bias, or unrepresentativeness, of volunteer samples so that investigators might increase the generality of their research results (e.g., Ferber, 1948–1949; Ford and Zeisel, 1949; Hyman and Sheatsley, 1954; Locke, 1954). The magnitude of the problem is not trivial. The potential biasing effects of using volunteer samples has been illustrated recently and clearly. At one large university, rates of volunteering varied from 100% down to 10%. Even within the same course, different recruiters visiting different sections of the course obtained rates of volunteering varying from 100% down to 50% (French, 1963). At another university, rates of volunteering varied from 74% down to 26% when the same recruiter, extending the same invitation to participate in the same experiment, solicited female volunteers from different floors of the same dormitory (Marmer, 1967). A fuller picture of the rates of volunteering obtained in various kinds of studies will be presented in Chapter 2 (e.g., Tables 2-1, 2-2, and 2-3).

Some reduction of the volunteer sampling bias might be expected from the

Table 1-2.   Example of Volunteer Bias in Survey Research

	Response to Three Mailings				
	First	Second	Third	Nonrespondents	Total Population
Basic data					
Number of respondents	300	543	434	1839	3116
% of population	10	17	14	59	100
Mean trees per respondent	456	382	340	290	329
Cumulative data					
Mean trees per respondent (Y_1)	456	408	385	—	—
Mean trees per nonrespondent (Y_2)	315	300	290	—	—
Difference ($Y_1 - Y_2$)	141	108	95	—	—
% of nonrespondents (P)	90	73	59	—	—
Bias [(P) $\times$ ($Y_1 - Y_2$)]	127	79	56	—	—

fairly common practice of requiring psychology undergraduates to spend a certain number of hours serving as research subjects. Such a requirement gets more students into the overall sampling urn, but without making their participation in any given experiment a randomly determined event (e.g., Johnson, 1973b; King, 1970; MacDonald, 1972b.) Students required to serve as research subjects often have a choice between alternative experiments. Given such a choice, will brighter (or duller) students sign up for an experiment on learning? Will better (or more poorly) adjusted students sign up for an experiment on personality? Will students who view their consciousness as broader (or narrower) sign up for an experiment that promises an encounter with "psychedelicacies"? We do not know the answers to these questions very well, nor do we know whether these possible self-selection biases would necessarily make any difference in the inferences we want to draw.

If the volunteer problem has been of interest and concern in the past, there is good evidence to suggest that it will become of even greater interest and concern in the future. Evidence of this comes from the popular press and the technical literature, and it says to us that in the future investigators may have less control than ever before over the kinds of human subjects who find their way into research. The ethical questions of humans' rights to privacy and to informed consent are more salient now than ever before (Adair, 1973; Adams, 1973; Bean, 1959; Clark et al., 1967; Etzioni, 1973; Katz, 1972; Martin, Arnold, Zimmerman, and Richart, 1968; May, Smith, and Morris, 1968; Miller, 1966; Orlans, 1967; Rokeach, 1966; Ruebhausen and Brim, 1966; Sasson and Nelson, 1969; Steiner, 1972; Sullivan and Deiker, 1973; Trotter, 1974; Walsh, 1973; Wicker, 1968; Wolfensberger, 1967; Wolfle, 1960). One possible outcome of this unprecedented soul-searching is that the social science of the future may, because of internally and perhaps externally imposed constraints, be based upon propositions whose tenability will come only from volunteer subjects who have been made fully aware of the responses of interest to the investigator. However, even without this extreme consequence of the ethical crisis of the social sciences, we still will want to learn as much as we can about the external circumstances and the internal characteristics that bring any given individual into our sample of subjects or keep him out.

Our purpose in the chapters to follow will be to say something about the characteristics that serve to differentiate volunteers for behavioral research from nonvolunteers and to examine in some detail what is known about the motivational and situational determinants of the act of volunteering. Subsequently we shall consider the implications of what is now known about volunteers and volunteering for the representativeness of the findings of behavioral research. We shall give special attention to experimental research that suggests that volunteer status may often interact with the independent variables employed in a variety of types of research studies. There is increasing reason to believe that such interactions may well occur, although the effects will not always be very large (Cope and Kunce, 1971; Cox and Sipprelle, 1971; Marlatt, 1973; Oakes, 1972; Pavlos, 1972; Short and Oskamp, 1965.) Finally, an artifact influence model will be described that will help to provide an integrative overview.

THE RELIABILITY OF VOLUNTEERING

Before we turn to a consideration of characteristics differentiating volunteers from nonvolunteers, it will be useful to consider the evidence for the reliability of the act of volunteering. If volunteering were a purely random event (i.e., completely unreliable), we could not expect to find any stable relationships between volunteering and various personal characteristics. As we shall see in the next chapter, however, there are a good many characteristics that have been found to relate predictably to the act of volunteering. The reliability of volunteering, then, could not reasonably be expected to be zero on psychometric grounds alone. To check these psychometric expectations, Table 1-3 was constructed. In some of the studies listed, the reliabilities had been computed, while in the remaining studies sufficient data were provided for us to be able to estimate the reliabilities ourselves.

Table 1-3.   The Reliability of Volunteering Behavior

Author	Index	Magnitude	p	Type of Study
1. Barefoot (1969) I	r_{pb}	.45	.001	Various experiments
2. Barefoot (1969) II	r_{pb}	.42	.001	Various experiments
3. Dohrenwend and Dohrenwend (1968)	ϕ	$.24^{a,\,b}$	.02	Interviews
4. Laming (1967)	ρ	$.22^b$	.05	Choice-reaction
5. Martin and Marcuse (1958) I	r_t	$.91^a$	.001	Learning
6. Martin and Marcuse (1958) II	r_t	$.80^a$	.001	Personality
7. Martin and Marcuse (1958) III	r_t	$.67^a$	.001	Sex
8. Martin and Marcuse (1958) IV	r_t	$.97^a$	.001	Hypnosis
9. Rosen (1951)	ϕ	.34	.05	Personality
10. Wallace (1954)	C	.58	.001	Questionnaires
Median		.52	.001	

[a] In these studies the second request was to volunteer for the same research as the first request.
[b] All subjects had been volunteers at one time, so that the reliabilities were probably lowered by a restriction of range of the volunteering variable.

Table 1-3 shows that the empirical evidence is consistent with our psychometric expectations. For the 10 studies shown, the median reliability coefficient was .52, with a range going from .97 to .22. As a standard against which to compare these reliability coefficients, we examined the subtest intercorrelations for what is perhaps the most widely used and carefully developed test of intelligence, the Wechsler Adult Intelligence Scale (WAIS) (Wechsler, 1958). Repeated factor analyses of this test have shown that there is a very large first factor, g, that in its magnitude swamps all other factors extracted, typically accounting for 10 times more variance than other factors. The full-scale WAIS, then, is an excellent measure of this first factor, or g. The range of subtest intercorrelations for the WAIS is reported by Wechsler to go from .08 to .85, with a median of .52, which, by coincidence, is the median value of the reliabilities of volunteering shown in Table 1-3.

Of the 10 studies shown in Table 1-3, 8 requested volunteering for studies to be conducted in the laboratory, while only 2 requested cooperation in survey research conducted in the field. The median reliability of the laboratory studies was .56, while the median for the field studies was .41. Because there were only 2 studies in the latter group, however, we can draw no conclusions about this difference. The types of studies for which volunteering had been requested were quite variable for the samples shown in Table 1-3 and there were not enough studies in any one category to permit inferences about the type of research task for which volunteering was likely to be particularly reliable or unreliable.

Also, as indicated in the footnote to Table 1-3, 5 of the studies requested people to volunteer a second time for the same task. In the remaining 5 studies the second and subsequent requests were for volunteering for a different study. If there are propensities to volunteering, then surely these propensities should be more stable when persons are asked to volunteer for the same, rather than a different, type of research experience. The data of Table 1-3 bear out this plausible inference. The median reliability for studies requesting volunteers for the same task is .80, while the median reliability for studies requesting volunteers for different tasks is only .42. Both these median reliabilities are very significantly different from zero, however (p much less than .001). Although 10 studies are not very many upon which to base such a conclusion, these results suggest that volunteering may have both general and specific predictors. Some people volunteer reliably more than others for a variety of tasks, and these reliable individual differences may be further stabilized when the particular task for which volunteering was requested is specifically considered.

CHAPTER 2

Characteristics of the Volunteer Subject

In this chapter we consider the evidence that volunteer subjects differ from their reluctant peers in more or less systematic ways. We shall proceed attribute by attribute from those that are regarded as biosocial through those that are regarded as psychosocial, to those that must be seen as geosocial. Our inventory of attributes was developed inductively rather than deductively. Our question, put to the archives of social science (i.e., the "literature"), was, in what ways have volunteers been found to differ or not to differ from nonvolunteers?

Volunteers have been compared to nonvolunteers in many ways, but there is to be found in these hundreds of comparisons an underlying strategy: to discover those attributes in which volunteers differ from nonvolunteers that have a special likelihood of being related to the respondents' or subjects' responses on the dependent variable of ultimate interest. Thus, in survey research, return rates of questionnaires by males and females have been compared not simply because sex is easy to define but because males and females have often been found to have different attitudes, opinions, and beliefs. If they did not, it would make little difference in terms of survey results that women may be overrepresented at least in the early waves of response to a mailed questionnaire. In psychological research on the effects of sensory restriction, volunteers have been compared to nonvolunteers on the attribute of sensation-seeking, precisely because sensation-seekers may plausibly be regarded as likely to respond differently to sensory restriction than those less in search of new sensations. We return to these implications of volunteer status for the interpretation of research findings in Chapter 4.

ASSESSING THE NONVOLUNTEER

A general question may occur to those readers not familiar with the specific literatures of volunteer effects or response bias: How does one find out the attributes of those who do not volunteer to participate in psychological experiments, those who do not answer their mail or their telephone or their doorbell? It seems difficult enough to determine the sex and age of the person not answering the doorbell; how does one get his or her score on the California F Scale?

A number of procedures have been found useful in comparing characteristics of those more or less likely to find their way into the role of data producer for the social or behavioral scientist. These methods can be grouped into one of two types, the exhaustive and the nonexhaustive. In the exhaustive method, all potential subjects or respondents are identified by their status on all the variables on which volunteers and nonvolunteers are to be compared. In the nonexhaustive method, data are not available for all potential subjects or respondents, but they are available for subjects or respondents differing in likelihood of finding their way into a final sample. There follow some examples of each of these classes of methods.

Exhaustive Methods

Archive Based Sampling Frames (Test, then Recruit)

In this method, the investigator begins with an archive containing for each person listed all the information desired for a comparison between volunteers and nonvolunteers. Requests for volunteers are then made some time later, sometimes years later, and those who volunteer are compared to those who do not volunteer, on all the items of information in the archive in which the investigator is interested. Many colleges, for example, administer psychological tests and questionnaires to all incoming freshmen during an orientation period. These data can then be used not only to compare those who volunteer with those who do not volunteer for a psychological experiment later that same year, but also to compare respondents with nonrespondents to an alumni-organization questionnaire sent out 10 years later.

Sample Assessment (Recruit, then Test)

In this method, volunteers for behavioral research are solicited, usually in a college classroom context, so that volunteers and nonvolunteers can be identified. Shortly thereafter, a test and/or a questionnaire is administered to the entire class by someone ostensibly unrelated to the person who recruited the volunteers. Volunteers can then be compared to nonvolunteers on any of the variables measured in the classwide testing or surveying.

Nonexhaustive Methods

Second-Level Volunteering (The Easy to Recruit)

In this method all the subjects or respondents are volunteers to begin with, and any required data can easily be obtained from all. From this sample of volunteers, volunteers for additional research are then recruited and these second-level, or second-stage, volunteers can be compared to second-level nonvolunteers on the data available for all. Differences between the second-level volunteers and nonvolunteers are likely to underestimate the differences between volunteers and true nonvolunteers, however, since even the second-level nonvolunteers had at least been first-level volunteers. This problem of underestimation of volunteer–nonvolunteer differences is generally characteristic of all the nonexhaustive methods. These methods, by virtue of their not including true nonvolunteers, all require extrapolation on a gradient of volunteering. The underlying assumption, not unreasonable yet no doubt often wrong, is that those who volunteer repeatedly, those who volunteer with less incentive, or those who volunteer more quickly are further down the curve from those who volunteer less often, with more incentive, or more slowly, and still further down the curve from those who do not volunteer at all. Thus, two or more levels of volunteering eagerness are employed to extrapolate roughly to the zero level of volunteering. If, for example, repeated volunteers were higher in the need for social approval than one-time volunteers, it might be guessed that the nonvolunteers would be lower still in need for social approval. Fig. 2-1 shows such a theoretical extrapolation.

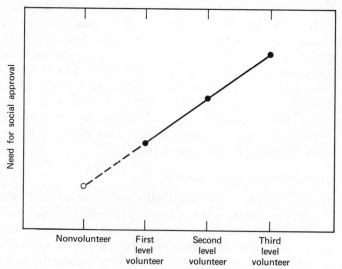

Fig. 2-1. Hypothetical illustration of extrapolating probable characteristics of nonvolunteers from characteristics of volunteers found at various levels of volunteering.

Increasing the Incentive (The Hard to Recruit)

In this method, volunteers are solicited from some sampling frame or list. After a suitable interval, another request for volunteers is made of those who were identified originally as nonvolunteers, and this process of repeated requesting may be repeated five or six times. Characteristics of those volunteering at each request are then plotted as data points from which a tentative extrapolation may be made to the characteristics of those who never respond. This method is frequently employed in survey research, and, in general, it is possible to get an increasingly sharper picture of the nonrespondent with successive waves of requests for participation in the survey. This method, it may be noted, is something like the reverse of the method of second-level volunteering. The latter method generates its data points by finding those more and more willing to participate, while the method of increasing the incentive generates its data points by finding those more and more unwilling to participate. An example of the successful application of the method of increasing the incentive was the case of volunteer bias described in Chapter 1. The data shown in Table 1-2 are plotted in Fig. 2-2. In this case the mean number of

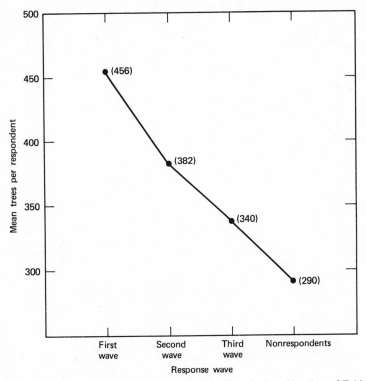

Fig. 2-2. Illustration of the method of increasing the incentive based on data of Table 1-2.

trees owned by nonrespondents would have been quite accurately extrapolated from the date provided by the respondents to the earlier waves.

Latency of Volunteering (The Slow to Reply)

In this method only a single request for volunteers is issued but the latency of the volunteering response is recorded. Characteristics of those responding at each of two or more levels of latency are then employed as data points from which to extrapolate to the characteristics of those who do not volunteer at all. This method has been used primarily in survey research, and it appears to have some promise. Nevertheless, it is probably less effective as a basis for extrapolating to nonvolunteers or nonrespondents than the method of increasing the incentive. This method can be combined with the method of increasing the incentive, and the trends within waves or requests can be compared with the trends between waves or requests. Figure 2-3 shows a theoretical extrapolation to the nonrespondent from an analysis of both the between and within wave variation of respondent characteristics. Figure 2-3 was drawn in such a way as to suggest that the within-first-wave latency could give as good an extrapolation to the nonrespondent, or to the very late respondent, as the

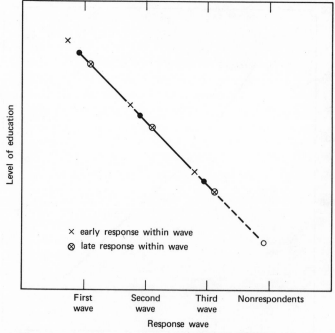

Fig. 2-3. Hypothetical illustration of extrapolating probable characteristics of nonvolunteers from characteristics of volunteers responding early and late within each of three waves of requests for participation.

between-wave data. That is surely an unduly optimistic view of the situation, but it illustrates the principle involved. In a real-life example it is entirely possible for the within-wave slopes to be opposite in sign from the between-wave slopes.

We turn now to a consideration of the various characteristics that have been found to be associated with volunteering in studies employing some of the methods described. In our review of the literature we have tried to identify the main threads of the literatures that differentiate volunteers from nonvolunteers.

SEX

It will become readily apparent that there are few characteristics that un-equivocally differentiate volunteers from nonvolunteers. The first attribute we consider, sex, will serve as an illustration. There are studies showing that females volunteer more than males; there are studies showing that males volunteer more than females; and there are studies showing no difference between the sexes in their likelihood of volunteering for participation in behavioral research. Table 2-1 shows the results of studies in which females showed a significantly greater likelihood of volunteering than did males. Some of these were series of studies, in which cases the table shows the overall results of the series as well as the results of each of the independent studies. Thus, the first entry in Table 2-1, research by Barker and Perlman (1972), found that for two studies employing questionnaires, 76% of the women and 62% of the men responded ($p < .03$). One of the questionnaires dealt with parent–child relations, and one dealt with sexual behavior standards. In the first of these studies, there was a difference of 22% in response rates favoring women, while in the second study, the response rate favored women by only 9%. As it turns out, this second study is one of the few in which there was a higher rate of responding or volunteering for women in a study investigating sexual behavior, and even here there was an appreciable drop in the difference between female and male volunteer rates compared to that difference for the non–sex-behavior questionnaire. In several cases in this table and elsewhere exact probabilities much higher than the conventional .05 level are shown instead of symbolizing such probabilities in the perhaps more familiar way simply as *ns* (for nonsignificant at .05). We provided these exact probabilities to facilitate the estimation of power by interested readers (Cohen, 1969) and to enable interested readers to combine probabilities should they wish to do so (Mosteller and Bush, 1954).

In the research by Hill, Rubin and Willard (1973), students at four colleges were invited to participate in a study of dating couples. Overall, women replied more often than did men to the first request (53% versus 40%), but there were important differences in response rate differences between males and females, between the four colleges. Thus, at a state college the volunteering rate among

Table 2-1.   Studies Showing Higher Overall Rates of Volunteering by Females

Author	Task	Percentage Volunteering		Two-Tail p of Difference
		Females	Males	
Barker and Perlman (1972)	Questionnaire (overall)	76	62	.03
	a. Parent–child relations	80	58	.03
	b. Sexual behavior	73	64	.38
Ellis, Endo, and Armer (1970)	Questionnaire	50	32	.001
Gannon, Nothern, and Carroll (1971)	Questionnaire	66	57	.04
Hill, Rubin, and Willard (1973)	Questionnaire (overall)	53	40	.003
	a. State college	39	35	.22
	b. Small private univ.	52	41	.001
	c. Catholic univ.	46	34	.001
	d. Large private univ.	63	45	.001
Himelstein (1956)	Psychology experiment	65	43	.02
MacDonald (1972a)	Psychology experiment (overall)	74	59	.001
	a. Pay incentive	73	48	.002
	b. Love of science	61	56	.52
	c. Extra credit	89	73	.04
Mann (1959)	Questionnaire	78	70	.05
Mayer and Pratt (1966)	Questionnaire	78	73	.003
Newman (1956)	Psychology experiments (overall)	60	41	.001
	a. Perception experiment	60	39	.001
	b. Personality experiment	59	45	.13
Ora (1966)	Psychology experiments	66	54	.001
Philip and McCulloch (1970)	Questionnaire	71	47	.05
Pucel, Nelson, and Wheeler (1971)	Questionnaire (overall)	60	42	.001
	a. No incentives	49	28	.08
	b. One incentive	59	38	.001
	c. Two incentives	62	41	.001
	d. Three incentives	66	58	.36
Rosnow, Holper, and Gitter (1973)	Psychology experiment	47	34	.006
Rosnow and Rosenthal (1966)	Perception experiment	48	13	.02

Author	Task	Percentage Volunteering		Two-tail p of Difference
		Females	Males	
Rosnow, Rosenthal, McConochie, and Arms (1969)	Psychology experiments	27	10	.002
Rothney and Mooren (1952)	Questionnaire	62	49	.001
Schubert (1964)	Psychology experiment	60	44	.001
Sheridan and Shack (1970)	Sensitivity training research	42	20	.06
Weiss (1968)	Psychology experiment	81	61	.02
Wicker (1968b)	Questionnaire	56	38	.12

females was only 4% higher than among males, while at a large private university the volunteering rate was 18% higher among females than among males. In this study, a number of students replying to the initial inquiry were invited to participate further, along with their dating partner. Of these students, however, only 46% of the females actually did participate, while 56% of the males did so. At first glance this result might appear to be a reversal of the finding that females are more willing to participate in behavioral research. Such a conclusion might be premature, however. All the students invited to participate had already agreed to do so; therefore, their actual participation as a couple may have depended primarily upon their partner's willingness to participate. The response rate favoring males, then, may have been caused by their female partner's greater willingness to participate compared to the female students' male partners' willingness to participate.

We have seen now that even when the overall results show women more likely than men to volunteer, the magnitude of the difference can be affected both by the nature of the task for which volunteering is solicited and by characteristics of the target sample. The study by MacDonald (1972a) shows that, in addition, these magnitudes can be affected by the nature of the incentives offered to the potential volunteers. Thus, when volunteers were solicited only on the basis of their "love of science," women were only slightly more likely (5%) to volunteer than men, but when pay was offered, women were very much more likely (25%) to volunteer than men.

There are a number of other studies that also show women more likely than men to volunteer for behavioral research. These studies are not included in Table 2-1, because the percentages of females or of males responding were not given or because the significance of the difference between percentages was not available.

Studies by Lowe and McCormick (1955), Thistlethwaite and Wheeler (1966), and Tiffany, Cowan, and Blinn (1970) show higher rates of responding (or responding earlier) by females to survey questionnaires, while research by May, Smith, and Morris (1968) showed higher rates of volunteering by females for psychological research. Related to these results are those obtained by Rosen (1951) and Schubert (1964), both of whom found males more likely to volunteer for standard experiments if they showed greater femininity of interests.

Table 2-2 shows the results of studies in which males showed a significantly greater likelihood of volunteering than did females. The study by Britton and Britton (1951) is unusual in that it is one of the few studies showing that in a mailed questionnaire survey, men respond more than women. Their study surveyed retired teachers and found that those who had held administrative positions or who had taught at the college level were more likely to respond than those who had taught at the high school or elementary school level. It seems likely that men were overrepresented in the administrator and college-teacher categories so that it may have been this higher preretirement status rather than their gender per se that led to the overrepresentation of men. Later we shall see that persons of higher occupational status are generally more likely to respond to questionnaires than their colleagues of lower occupational status.

The study by Wilson and Patterson (1965) is also unusual in that males volunteered more than females in response to a somewhat nonspecific request

Table 2-2. Studies Showing Higher Overall Rates of Volunteering by Males

Author	Task	Percentage Volunteering Females	Males	Two-Tail p of Difference
Britton and Britton (1951)	Questionnaire	34	57	.006
Howe (1960)	Electric shock	67	81	.05
MacDonald (1969)	Electric shock (overall)	78	92	.04
	a. Firstborns	69	97	.006
	b. Laterborns	85	87	1.00
Schopler and Bateson (1965)	High temperature (overall)	33	61	.01
	a. Recruiter less dependent	25	71	.004
	b. Recruiter more dependent	40	50	.68
Schultz (1967b)	Sensory deprivation	56	76	.06
Siegman (1956)	Sex interview	17	42	.02
Wilson and Patterson (1965)	Psychology experiment	60	86	.005

for volunteers made to New Zealand undergraduate students. In the vast majority of studies of volunteering for general or unspecified psychological experiments, females volunteer more than do males. The fact that this unusual result was obtained in New Zealand may help to explain it, but one wonders how.

The remaining studies of Table 2-2 have in common that the task for which volunteers were solicited was physically or psychologically stressful and relatively unconventional. These tasks required tolerance of electric shocks, high temperatures, sensory deprivation, and personally asked questions about sex behavior. These are all tasks that give the (ordinarily fairly young) male volunteer an opportunity to assert what the culture defines for him as "his masculinity." Additional evidence for this interpretation can be found in the research of Siess (1973), who discovered that compared to females, males significantly preferred experiments requiring them to withstand changes in gravitational pressure, deprivation of oxygen, rapid temperature changes, fatigue, sensory deprivation, and drug effects. Similarly, Wolf and Weiss (1965) found males expressing greater preference than females for isolation experiments. Some further support may be found, too, in the research of Martin and Marcuse (1958), who solicited volunteers for four experiments in the areas of learning, personality, hypnosis, and sex. Female volunteers were overrepresented in the first three of these areas (approximately 30%, 51%, and 43% volunteering rates for females versus 27%, 35%, and 27% volunteering rates for males respectively), while male volunteers were overrepresented in the fourth area, the study of sex behavior (approximately 25% of females and 52% of males volunteered). The studies by Martin and Marcuse are not listed in our tables since the percentages calculable from their data could only be quite approximate.

In addition to the studies shown in Table 2-2, three others were discovered in which males found their way more easily into behavioral research. Crossley and Fink (1951) found that women refused to be interviewed more often than men, and Katz and Cantril (1937) found that mail returns overrepresented men rather than women. This latter study, however, also showed that persons of higher socioeconomic status responded more, and it may be that, for this sample, males were of higher socioeconomic status than women (e.g., listed in Who's Who versus being on relief). Thus, socioeconomic status rather than sex per se may have accounted for the results.

Finally, Teele (1967) found that among relatives of former mental patients, males were slightly more likely than females ($r = .13$) to participate in voluntary associations. Listing this study as in support of the proposition that males volunteer more than females requires that we view participation in such associations as related to volunteering for participation in behavioral research.

Table 2-3.   Studies Showing No Reliable Sex Differences in Volunteering

Author	Task	Percentage Volunteering Females	Males
Back, Hood, and Brehm (1963); Hood (1963)	Psychology experiments	57	54
Bergen and Kloot (1968–1969)	Psychology experiment (overall)	66	73
	a. More personal appeal	76	71
	b. Less personal appeal	56	76
Diamant (1970)	Sex survey	35	51
Ebert (1973)	Questionnaire	79	75
Francis and Diespecker (1973)	Sensory deprivation	47	48
London (1961)	Hypnosis research	42	40
Loney (1972)	Sex survey (overall)	66	72
	a. Heterosexual persons	92	100
	b. Homosexual persons	50	56
Olsen (1968)	Psychology experiments	26	25
Poor (1967)	Questionnaire	36	23
Raymond and King (1973)	Research participation	42	41
Rosnow and Suls (1970)	Psycholinguistic experiment	40	30
Rubin (1973a; in press)	Airport interviews (overall)	67	63
	a. Handwriting sample	67	71
	1. Female experimenter	77	71
	2. Male experimenter	57	70
	b. Self-description	67	56
	1. Female experimenter	78	67
	2. Male experimenter	56	45
Tune (1968)	Sleep research	84	84
Tune (1969)	Sleep research	88	90
Wicker (1968a)	Church survey (overall)	87	78
	a. First request	50	61
	b. Second request	74	45
Wolf (1967)	Psychology experiments (overall)	48	44
	a. Summer session	36	40
	b. Regular term	64	52
Wolfgang (1967)	Learning experiment	48	47

Table 2-3 shows the results of studies in which there was no reliable difference in volunteering rates between males and females. As we would expect, the
average absolute difference between volunteering rates of males and females is
smaller in this table than are the average absolute differences to be found in
Tables 2-1 and 2-2. But we should note that there are some substantial absolute
differences to be found in this table, nevertheless. When that occurs, it is
because the sample sizes on which the percentages are based are too small for
the differences in percentages to reach statistical significance. That was the
situation, for example, in the study by Bergen and Kloot (1968–1969). When

a less personal appeal for volunteers was made, 56% of the 39 women, but 76% of the 29 men, agreed to participate, a difference that, while not significant, can hardly be considered small. Cohen (1969) provides useful guidelines for the interpretation of the magnitude of differences between proportions. The detectability of differences between proportions depends not only upon the difference between the proportions but on the absolute value of the two proportions as well. However, when proportions are transformed by the relationship $\phi = 2 \arcsin \sqrt{\text{Proportion}}$, the differences between the values ϕ are equally detectable, regardless of their absolute level. Cohen regards a difference between two ϕ values as small when its value is .2, medium when its value is .5, and large when its value is .8. The difference between the arcsin transformed proportions of .56 and .76 is .43, or approximately a medium-size effect. We should note that a good many of the significant differences in volunteering rates between males and females shown in Tables 2-1 and 2-2 represent effects smaller than this effect size simply because those smaller effects were based on larger sample sizes.

Another nontrivial difference in volunteering rates between males and females can be noted in the study by Diamant (1970). In that study, volunteers were recruited for a sex survey, and 51% of the males and 35% of the females agreed to participate. Thus, although the difference was not significant statistically, it seems to agree with other results, reported earlier, showing men to be more willing to participate in sex research. The magnitude of this effect (51%–35%) in arcsin units is .32, about halfway between a small and a medium-size effect. Loney's (1972) results were quite similar. Among both heterosexual and homosexual persons, males were more willing to participate in a survey of sex behavior. Arcsin transformed or not, the difference in volunteering rates was quite small for the homosexual sample but not at all trivial for the heterosexual sample. The 8-percentage-point difference between 92% and 100% is much larger in arcsin units (.57) than the 6-percentage-point difference between 50% and 56% (.12 arcsin units).

A very informative study was conducted by Rubin 1973a; in press), who sought his volunteers in airport departure lounges. He employed male and female interviewers to solicit volunteering either for a study of handwriting or for a study of self-descriptions. Although Rubin found no important overall differences in volunteering rates between males and females, he found the equivalent of a three-way interaction between type of task for which volunteering was solicited, sex of interviewer, and sex of subject. When requests were for handwriting samples, subjects volunteered for an experimenter of the same sex more than when requests were for self-descriptions. In the latter case, both male and female subjects volunteered more for a female experimenter. To a lesser extent subjects also volunteered more for female experimenters when the request was for handwriting samples. Rubin's study is one of the few to have investigated simultaneously the effects on volunteering rates of both type of task and sex of recruiter. His results suggest that it was a good idea. Actually, Coffin (1941) cautioned long ago that there might be complicating effects of the experimenter's sex, and we might wonder along with Coffin and Martin and Marcuse (1958) about the differential effects on volunteer rates among male and female subjects of being confronted with a male versus a female Kinsey interviewer, as well as the differential effects on eagerness to be hypnotized of being confronted with a male versus a female hypnotist.

In addition to the studies listed in Table 2-3, several others were found in which there were no reliable differences between males and females in rates of volunteering. Belson (1960), Bennet and Hill (1964), Fischer and Winer (1969; two different studies), Sirken, Pifer, and Brown (1960), and Wallin (1949) reported no sex differences in volunteering rates in their survey research projects, nor did Hilgard, Weitzenhoffer, Landes, and Moore (1961), Hood (1963), MacDonald (1972b), Mackenzie (1969), Mulry and Dunbar (n.d.), Rosen (1951), Schachter and Hall (1952), and Stein (1971) in their laboratory or clinic projects. One more study appears to be at least tangentially relevant, that by Spiegel and Keith-Spiegel (1969). These investigators asked for college student volunteers not for a psychological experiment but for participation in a companionship program in which students would spend time with psychiatric patients over a 10-week period. No significant differences were found in rates of volunteering by female (39%) versus male (33%) students.

Summarizing the Data

Tables 2-1, 2-2, and 2-3 contain quite a lot of information and it will be useful to recast that information into more manageable forms. The strategy adopted here is based on the "stem-and-leaf" technique developed by John Tukey (1970). Stem-and-leaf plots look like histograms and indeed they are that, but they permit retention of all the raw data at the same time so that no information need be lost in the grouping process.

Table 2-4 shows four parallel stem-and-leaf displays, two for studies requesting volunteering for physically or psychologically stressful studies (e.g. electric shock, high temperature, sensory deprivation, sex behavior) and two for all other studies, Within each type of study, there are two parallel stem-and-leaf plots, one showing the distribution of percentages of females volunteering and the other showing the distribution of percentages of males volunteering. For each of our stem and leaf plots, the numbers to the left of the dividing line (the stems) represent the leading digit(s) of the percentage, while the digits to the right of the dividing line (the leaves) represent the final digit of the percentage. In the leftmost plot of Table 2-4 there are no leaf entries for the stems of 10 or 9. That means that no percentages of 90% or above were found for females in general studies of volunteering. In that same plot the stem of 8 is followed by leaves of 0, 1, 4, 8, and 9 (by convention not separated by commas.) We

Table 2-4. Stem-and-Leaf Plots of Volunteering Rates in Percentage Units

General Studies

Stem	Females (N = 51)	Males (N = 51)
10		
9		0
8	0 1 4 8 9	4 6
7	1 3 4 6 7 8 8 8 9	0 0 1 1 3 5 6
6	0 0 0 1 2 2 3 4 5 6 6 6	1 1 7
5	0 0 2 6 6 6 7 7 9 9	2 4 4 6 7 7 8 8
4	0 2 2 2 6 7 8 8 9	0 0 1 1 1 3 4 5 5 5 5 7 7 8 9
3	4 6 6 9	0 2 4 4 5 5 8 8 9
2	6 7	0 3 5 8
1		0 3

Stress Studies

Stem	Females (N = 12)	Males (N = 12)
10		0
9	2	7
8	5	1 7
7	3	1 6
6	7 9	4
5	0 6	0 1 6
4	0 7	2 8
3	5	
2	5	
1	7	

Summary statistics

	General Studies Females (N = 51)	General Studies Males (N = 51)	Stress Studies Females (N = 12)	Stress Studies Males (N = 12)
Maximum	89	90	92	100
Quartile$_3$	73	61	71	84
Median	60	45	53	67.5
Quartile$_1$	48	38	37.5	50.5
Minimum	26	10	17	42
$Q_3 - Q_1$	25	23	33.5	33.5
$\hat{\sigma}$	19	17	25	25
S	15.8	18.3	23.3	19.8
Mean	59.1	49.1	54.7	68.6

read those five leaves as representing a recording of the following scores: 80, 81, 84, 88, and 89.

Coarse examination of the parallel stem-and-leaf displays for studies in general shows the heavy center region to be higher for females (modal stem = 6) than for males (modal stem = 4), while somewhat the opposite is true for the displays for studies involving stress (n too small to use modal stems). A more formal summary of each stem-and-leaf display is given below each plot. There we find the highest percentage obtained; the percentages corresponding to the third, second (median), and first quartiles; and the lowest percentage obtained. In addition, the difference between the third and first quartiles is given, the rough estimate $\hat{\sigma}$ $[(Q_3 - Q_1) (.75)]$, the unbiased estimate of σ, and the mean.

Skews, bobbles, and bunchings can be found and described employing the plots themselves and/or the summaries given below the plots. For our present purpose, and for most readers, it may be sufficient to note that for studies in general, the median rate of volunteering is 60% for women and 45% for men. For studies involving stress, however, the median rate of volunteering is only 53% for women but over 67% for men. Considering the rates of volunteering by women for the two types of studies suggests that the median rates are not so very different ($\chi^2 = 0.10$), although there is a hint that volunteering rates of women may be more variable in the stress studies than in the general studies (interquartile range and S are both larger for the stress studies, the latter nearly significantly: $F = 2.17$, $df = 11,50$, $p < .07$). When we consider the rates of volunteering by men for the two types of studies, however, we find a substantial difference with the greater likelihood of volunteering occurring for the stress studies (median of 67.5% versus 45%). Such a difference in arcsin units (.46) corresponds to what Cohen considers a medium-size effect, and it is significant ($p < .025$, $\chi^2 = 5.06$) despite the small sample size of the stress studies. Relative to females (median volunteer rate for all 63 studies = 59%), then, males are likely to overvolunteer somewhat for stressful studies (67.5%) and to undervolunteer quite a lot for all other kinds of studies (45%).

Although Table 2-4 has been useful, it does not preserve the information that for each of the 63 studies listed, there was both a male and female volunteering rate (i.e., that there was blocking by studies). Table 2-5 preserves this information by showing stem-and-leaf plots of the differences between volunteering rates with the male percentage always subtracted from the female percentage. Comparison of the plots for studies in general and for studies involving stress shows that they are virtually mirror images of one another. For studies in general, females volunteer more than males 84% of the time, while in studies involving stress, males volunteer more than females 92% of the time ($\chi^2 = 24.7$, $df = 1$, p very small). Before leaving our discussion of studies involving stress versus studies not involving stress, we should note that the latter studies can be readily divided into those involving questionnaires and

Table 2-5. Stem-and-Leaf Plots of Differences in Volunteering Rates Between Females and Males

	General Studies (N = 51)	Stress Studies (N = 12)
+3	5	
+3		
+2	5 9	
+2	0 1 1 1 1 2 2 2 4	
+1	6 6 7 8 8 8	
+1	0 1 1 1 2 2 2 3 3 3 4	
+0	5 5 5 6 8 8 9	9
+0	1 1 1 2 3 4 4	
0	0	
−0	2 4	1 2
−0		6 8
−1	1 3	0 4
−1		6
−2	0 3	0
−2	6	▸ 5 8
−3		
−3		
−4		
−4		6
−5		
Maximum	+35	+ 9
Quartile₃	+18	− 4
Median	+11	−12
Quartile₁	+ 3	−22
Minimum	−26	−46
$Q_3 - Q_1$	+15	+18
$\hat{\sigma}$	11	14
S	12.6	14.6
Mean	+ 9.4	−13.9

those involving the more typical behavioral laboratory research. Sex differences in volunteering rates were examined as a function of this breakdown. The median difference in volunteering rate (percent of women volunteering minus percent of men volunteering) was 13 for the 21 questionnaire studies and 10.5 for the 30 remaining studies, a difference that did not approach significance ($\chi^2 = 0.13$).

Pseudovolunteering

Our interest in volunteers is based on the fact that only they can provide us with the data that the nonvolunteers have refused us. But not all volunteers, it usually turns out, provide us with the data we need. To varying degrees in different studies there will be those volunteers who fail to keep their experimental appointment. These "no-shows" have been referred to as "pseudovolunteers" by Levitt, Lubin, and Brady (1962), who showed that on a variety of personality measures, pseudovolunteers are not so much like volunteers as they are like the nonvolunteers who never agreed to come in the first place. Other studies also have examined characteristics of experimental subjects who fail to keep their appointments, but somewhat surprisingly, there is no great wealth of data bearing on the rates of pseudovolunteering one may expect to find in one's research. What makes this data dearth surprising is that every investigator obtains such data routinely in every study conducted. One suspects, however, that experienced investigators have a fairly adequate sense of the proportion of no-shows to expect for any given type of study conducted at any given time of year. Knowing approximately how many subjects will not appear is very useful in planning the number of sessions required to fill the sampling quotas. Speaking from experience, the present authors can offer the suggestion, however, that this "adequate sense" can be quite inadequate. In a variety of studies we have found pseudovolunteering rates to range from perhaps 50% to −5%. The −5% occurred in a rather large-size study in which every subject appeared on schedule, with several bringing along friends who had not volunteered but wanted either to earn the $1.00 offered as compensation or to keep their friends company. Table 2-6 gives the results of 20 more formal studies of pseudovolunteering. For these studies considered as a set, we might guess that as many as a third of our volunteers might never appear as promised. No claim is made, however, that these studies are in any way representative. There appears to be no systematic research on variables affecting rates of pseudovolunteering, but there are procedures widely employed for keeping those rates at a minimum, such as reminder letters and telephone calls. There is some likelihood, however, based on the survey research literature that it is the potential pseudovolunteer who is less likely to be at home, to read his or her mail, or answer his or her telephone.

There is also little information available to suggest whether males or females are more likely not to show. In their research, Frey and Becker (1958) found no sex differences between subjects who notified the investigator that they would be absent versus those who did not notify him. Although these results argue against a sex difference in pseudovolunteering, it should be noted that the entire experimental sample was composed of extreme scorers on a test of introversion–extraversion. Furthermore, no comparison could be made of either group of no-shows with the parent population from which the samples were drawn.

Leipold and James (1962) also compared the characteristics of shows and no-shows among a random sample of introductory psychology students who

Table 2-6. Some Rates of Pseudovolunteering

Author	% Failing to Appear
Belson (1960)	16
Bergen and Kloot (1968-69)	10
Craddick and Campitell (1963)	42
Dreger and Johnson (1973)	36
Kirby and Davis (1972)	41
Leipold and James (1962)	36
Levitt, Lubin, and Brady (1962)	30
MacDonald (1969) I	14
MacDonald (1969) II	32
Minor (1967)	37
Tacon (1965)	40
Valins (1967) I	37
Valins (1967) II	3
Waters and Kirk (1969) I	24
Waters and Kirk (1969) II	31
Waters and Kirk (1969) III	30
Waters and Kirk (1969) IV	37
Wicker (1968a)	12
Wicker (1968b)	38
Wrightsman (1966)	19
Median	31.5

had been requested to serve in an experiment in order to satisfy a course requirement. Again, no sex differences were found. Interestingly enough, however, about half of Frey and Becker's no-shows notified the experimenter that they would be absent, while only one of Leipold and James's 39 no-shows did so. Finally, there are the more recent studies by Belson (1960) and Wicker (1968b), in which it was possible to compare the rates of pseudovolunteering by male and female subjects for a questionnaire study. These results also yielded no sex differences. Hence, four studies out of four suggest that failing to provide the investigator with data promised him may not be any more the province of males than of females. Four studies, however, are not very many, and it would be premature to defend staunchly the null hypothesis on the basis of so little data.

BIRTH ORDER

Ever since the seminal work of Schachter (1959) there has been an increased interest in birth order as a useful independent variable in behavioral research (Altus, 1966; Belmont and Marolla, 1973; Warren, 1966; Weiss, 1970). A

Table 2-7.   **Studies Comparing Rates of Volunteering by Firstborns and Laterborns**

| Author | Results Showing Greater Volunteering by: | | |
	Firstborns (FB)	Laterborns (LB)	Number Significant
Altus (1966)	2	0	1 FB
Capra and Dittes (1962)	1	0	1 FB
Diab and Prothro (1968)	1	1	0
Ebert (1973)	1	0	1 FB
Eisenman (1965)	0	1	1 LB
Fischer and Winer (1969)	1	2	0
Lubin, Brady, and Levitt (1962b)	—[a]	—[a]	0
MacDonald (1969)	1	1	0
MacDonald (1972a)	2	1	0
MacDonald (1972b)	—[a]	—[a]	0
Myers, Murphy, Smith, and Goffard (1966)	—[a]	—[a]	0
Olsen (1968)	2	0	2 FB
Poor (1967)	1	0	0
Rosnow, Rosenthal, McConochie, and Arms (1969)	0	1	0
Schultz (1967a)	0	1	0
Stein (1971)	0	1	1 LB
Suedfeld (1964)	1	0	1 FB
Suedfeld (1969)	0	1	0
Varela (1964)	1	0	1 FB
Wagner (1968)	0	1	0
Ward (1964)	4	2	1 LB
Wilson and Patterson (1965)	1	0	0
Wolf (1967)	1	1	0
Wolf and Weiss (1965); Weiss, Wolf, and Wiltsey (1963)	1	3	0
Zuckerman, Schultz, and Hopkins (1967)	0	2	0
Sum	21	19	10

[a] Unable to determine direction of difference.

number of studies have investigated the question of whether firstborns or only children are more likely than laterborns to volunteer for behavioral research. Table 2-7 lists the authors of such studies and tabulates for each author the number of results showing firstborns to volunteer more and the number of results showing laterborns to volunteer more. The final column of the table lists the number of results by each investigator that were significant at approximately the 5% level and whether it was the firstborns or laterborns that had volunteered more. The most striking finding is that about half the studies listed show firstborns to have volunteered more and about half show laterborns to have volunteered more. Of the studies showing significant differences in volunteering rates, seven show firstborns to have volunteered more and three show laterborns to have volunteered more. It seems clear, then, that no overall conclusion can be drawn as to which ordinal position is likely to be overrepresented in a sample of volunteers. However, it would probably be unwise to conclude that there is no relationship between birth order and volunteering, since, disregarding direction of outcome, there are too many studies showing some significant relationship to make the null hypothesis defensible.

Perhaps we can gain a better understanding of these results by considering the type of research for which volunteering was requested as a function of the type of results obtained. Table 2-8 shows such a listing. Ward (1964) found laterborns to volunteer more (55%) than firstborns (32%) for an optional experiment in which subjects were to work on a task while alone. However, Suedfeld (1964) found firstborns to volunteer more than laterborns for an experiment in sensory deprivation which was also optional and also involved the subject's being alone. Given a significant relationship between birth order and volunteering, then, the direction of the difference cannot very well be dependent exclusively on either (a) the required nature of the experiment or (b) the solitary nature of the subject's participation.

Capra and Dittes (1962) found that among their Yale University undergraduates 36% of the firstborns, but only 18% of the laterborns, volunteered for an experiment requiring cooperation in a small group. Varela (1964) found

Table 2-8. Types of Research for Which Volunteering Was Requested for Each Type of Outcome

Firstborns Volunteer Significantly More	No Significant Difference	Laterborns Volunteer Significantly More
Sensory deprivation	General experiments	Optional experiment, working alone
Small-group research	Hypnosis	Psychotherapy research
Psychological testing	Interview	Strong electric shock
Questionnaire	Psychoacoustic research	
	Questionnaire	
	Sensory deprivation	
	Small-group research	
Number of results in each outcome		
7	30	3

that among his Uruguayan male and female high school students 70% of the firstborns, but only 44% of the laterborns, volunteered for a small-group experiment similar to that of Capra and Dittes. Altus (1966) and Olsen (1968) reported that firstborn males were overrepresented relative to laterborn males when subjects were asked to volunteer for testing. Altus as well as Olsen obtained similar results when the subjects were female undergraduates, but in Altus' study the difference in volunteering rates was not significant statistically. In his survey of college students, Ebert (1973) found that only-children were significantly more likely to respond than were children with siblings. Thus, for studies requesting volunteers for small-group research, for psychological testing, and for mailed questionnaires, when there is a significant difference, it seems to favor the greater participation of the firstborn.

The remaining studies showing a significant relationship between birth order and volunteering are those by Stein (1971) and Eisenman (1965). Stein studied psychotherapy patients drawn from a psychological clinic and found that his laterborns were more cooperative in completing the required pre- and posttests than were the firstborns. Eisenman studied student nurses and found that more laterborns than firstborns were willing to participate in a study involving severe electric shock. In both these studies there appears to be an element of unusually high stress. In the study by Stein, we can assume that the clinic patients were under considerable stress simply by virtue of their having required psychological assistance. In the study by Eisenman, we can assume that persons confronted with very strong electric shock would also be under considerable stress or threat. Perhaps, then, when the experiment involves a very high level of stress either as a trait of the subject or as a characteristic of the task, and when there is a significant relationship between birth order and volunteering, it is the laterborns who will volunteer more. An apparent weakening of this hypothesis may be noted in the first column of Table 2-8. There we find that an experiment in sensory deprivation obtained significantly higher rates of volunteering by firstborn rather than laterborn subjects. We are inclined to think of sensory deprivation as a stressful experience—hence, the weakening of the stress hypothesis. In this particular study of volunteering for sensory deprivation (Suedfeld, 1964), however, Suedfeld's recruiting technique was quite reassuring in tone. Suedfeld (1968) has shown further that a reassuring orientation toward sensory deprivation specifically lowers the anticipated stress in firstborn as compared to laterborn subjects. Indeed, there is an indication from the research of Dohrenwend, Feldstein, Plosky, and Schmeidler (1967) that when recruitment specifically tries to arouse anxiety about sensory deprivation, laterborns may tend to volunteer significantly more than firstborns. Taken together, then, the Suedfeld results and those of Dohrenwend et al. actually tend to strengthen the hypothesis that when great stress is involved, firstborns will volunteer significantly less than laterborns.

In several of the studies relating birth order to volunteering the focus was less on whether a subject would volunteer and more on the type of experiment for which he would volunteer. That was the case in a study by Brock and Becker (1965), who found no differences between first- and laterborns in their choices of individual or group experiments. Studies reported by Weiss, Wolf, and Wiltsey (1963) and by Wolf and Weiss (1965) suggest that preference for participation in group experiments by firstborn versus laterborn subjects may depend on the form in which the subject is asked to indicate his volunteer status. When a ranking of preferences was employed, firstborns more often volunteered for a group experiment. However, when a simple yes–no technique was employed, firstborns volunteered relatively less for group than for individual or isolation experiments.

Just as the nature of the research for which volunteering is requested may moderate the relationship between birth order and volunteering, so there are other variables that have been suggested as serving potential moderating functions in this relationship. Thus, MacDonald (1969) has shown that sex may operate interactively with birth order and volunteering such that firstborn females are most likely to avoid an electric shock, while firstborn males are least likely to avoid an electric shock, with male and female laterborns falling in between. MacDonald (1972a) has also found the nature of the incentive to volunteer to interact with birth order and volunteering behavior. Firstborns were appreciably more likely to volunteer for extra credit than for either pay or "love of science." Several investigators (MacDonald, 1969; Fischer and Winer, 1969) have also suggested that the degree of intimacy or face-to-faceness of the recruiting situation might affect the relationship between birth order and volunteering. One suspects that the hypotheses put forward by all these authors could well be investigated simultaneously. Male and female firstborns and laterborns could be recruited under more versus less intimate conditions and offered extra credit or not. If a really large population of subjects was available, the degree of stressfulness of the task for which recruitment is solicited could also be varied orthogonally to the group versus individual nature of subjects' interaction in the experiment. One suspects that a doctoral dissertation lurks here.

Before summing up what we think we may know about the relationship between birth order and volunteering, we must consider the possible relationship between birth order and pseudovolunteering. Even if there were no differences between firstborns and laterborns in volunteering rates, if one of these were more likely to be a no-show, then the other would be overrepresented in the subject pool that finally produced data. MacDonald (1969) has investigated the matter. He found that 86% of the firstborns kept their appointments for an experiment ostensibly involving painful electric shock, while only 68% of the laterborns appeared. If further research were to support this direction and magnitude of effect for a variety of experimental situations, one might infer that the final subject sample may overrepresent the more docile, less suspicious type of subject. MacDonald (1969) found that while 22% of the laterborns were suspicious about the true purpose of the experiment, only 8% of the firstborns were suspicious ($p < .01$).

To sum up the state of the evidence bearing on the relationship between volunteering and birth order, we can begin by saying that most of the studies conducted found no significant relationship between these variables. Still, there were many more studies that did find a significant relationship than we could easily ascribe to the operation of chance. For those studies in which firstborns volunteered significantly more, there was perhaps a more intimate recruitment style and a greater likelihood that the request was for participation in an experiment requiring group interaction. For those studies in which firstborns volunteered significantly less, there was perhaps a greater degree of stress experienced by those approached for participation.

SOCIABILITY

The bulk of the evidence seems to suggest that those persons more likely to volunteer for participation in behavioral research are more sociable than those less likely to volunteer. Table 2-9 summarizes this evidence by listing, separately for the more experimental studies and for the studies employing questionnaires, those results showing volunteers to be more sociable, those studies finding no difference in sociability between volunteers and nonvolunteers, and those studies showing volunteers to be less sociable.

Of the 19 studies listed in Table 2-9, only 1 found that volunteers could be considered significantly less sociable than nonvolunteers. Abeles, Iscoe, and Brown (1954–1955) reported a study in which male undergraduates were invited by the president of their university to complete questionnaires concerning the draft, the Korean conflict, college life, and vocational aspirations. Results showed that members of fraternities, who might be regarded as more sociable, were significantly less likely to reply spontaneously to the questionnaire. In a subsequent session, which followed both a letter "ordering" the students to participate as well as a personal telephone call, fraternity members were significantly more likely to participate. Reuss (1943), in his earlier research, had found fraternity and sorority members to be more responsive to requests for participation in behavioral research.

The three questionnaire studies showing no differences in volunteering as a function of sociability had in common only that all three sampled college, or former college, students. The five questionnaire studies showing volunteers to be more sociable also included studies of college students but were not re-

Table 2-9. Studies of the Relationship Between Volunteering and Sociability

	Psychological Experiments	Questionnaires
Volunteers found more sociable	Hayes, Meltzer, and Lundberg (1968) London, Cooper, and Johnson (1962) MacDonald (1972a) MacDonald (1972b) Martin and Marcuse (1957, 1958) Poor (1967) Schubert (1964)	Abeles, Iscoe, and Brown (1954-1955) Kivlin (1965) Lehman (1963) Reuss (1943) Tiffany, Cowan, and Blinn (1970)
($n = 12$)	($n = 7$)	($n = 5$)
No difference	Myers, Smith, and Murphy (1967) Martin and Marcuse (1958) I Martin and Marcuse (1958) II	Bennett and Hill (1964) Ebert (1973) Poor (1967)
($n = 6$)	($n = 3$)	($n = 3$)
Volunteers found less sociable		Abeles, Iscoe, and Brown (1954–1955)
($n = 1$)	($n = 0$)	($n = 1$)

stricted to them. Thus Kivlin (1965) sampled Pennsylvania dairy farmers; and Tiffany, Cowan, and Blinn (1970) surveyed former psychiatric patients. Considering only the questionnaire studies, then, it appears that respondents are likely to be more sociable than nonrespondents, a relationship possibly stronger for noncollege than for college samples.

When we consider the relationship between volunteering and sociability for more laboratory-oriented behavioral research, we find a similar picture. Again, three studies reported no positive relationship between sociability and volunteering. Perhaps one of these exceptions (Myers, Smith, and Murphy, 1967) can best be understood in terms of the task for which volunteers were recruited —sensory deprivation. It seems reasonable to think that, while in general sociable subjects will volunteer more than unsociable subjects, in an experiment in which their sociability will be specifically frustrated sociable subjects will be less likely to volunteer. The other exceptions are results reported by Martin and Marcuse (1958), who found no differences in sociability between volunteers and nonvolunteers for sex research or, for males only, for hypnosis research.

In the research relating sociability to volunteering, a variety of measures of sociability have been employed. Employing as subjects male and female college freshmen, Schubert (1964) observed that volunteers ($n = 562$) for a psychological experiment scored higher in sociability than nonvolunteers ($n = 443$) on the Social Participation Scale of the MMPI. Poor (1967) employed the California Psychological Inventory Scale of Sociability and obtained the same results and MacDonald (1972a,b) found that both those more likely to volunteer at all and those who volunteer earlier had made more new friends since coming to college. In their experiment on social participation, Hayes, Meltzer, and Lundberg (1968) found undergraduate volunteers to be more talkative than undergraduate (nonvolunteer) conscripts. Talkativeness appears to be related to sociability, but in this case talkativeness was measured after the volunteering or nonvolunteering occurred, so that it may have been situationally determined. Perhaps volunteers talked more because they were engaged in an experiment for which they had volunteered and nonvolunteers talked less because they had been coerced into participation. Although it seems reasonable to think so, we cannot be certain that conscripts would have been less talkative than volunteers even before the recruitment procedures were begun.

In their research, London, Cooper, and Johnson (1962) found serious volunteers for hypnosis to be somewhat more sociable than those less serious about serving science, with sociability defined by the California Psychological Inventory, the 16 PF, and the MMPI. Martin and Marcuse (1957, 1958) found female volunteers for hypnosis to score higher on sociability than female nonvolunteers as measured by the Bernreuter Personality Inventory.

Another study of volunteers for hypnosis research appears relevant to the discussion of the variable of sociability, although it was not listed in Table 2-9 because its results were too difficult to interpret. Lubin, Brady, and Levitt (1962a) asked student nurses to volunteer for hypnosis and found volunteers to score higher on dependency than nonvolunteers on a measure based on Rorschach content. Dependency may be positively related to sociability and so this result appears to support the general results showing volunteers to be more sociable. However, Lubin et al. also found that these same volunteers were significantly less friendly than the nonvolunteers, as defined by scores on the Guilford–Zimmerman Temperament Survey. Friendliness may also be positively related to sociability, and so this result appears not to support the general conclusion that volunteers tend to be more sociable. It is possible, of course, that there is more than one kind of sociability and that it is the dependency aspects of sociability rather than the friendliness aspects that may predispose persons to volunteer for hypnosis. This interpretation still would not account for the significant negative relationship between friendliness and volunteering for hypnosis, although it would account for the absence of a positive relationship.

There is another study that investigated the relationship between volunteering and dependency. In their questionnaire study of student nurses, Lubin, Levitt, and Zuckerman (1962) found that those who responded were more dependent than those who did not, the measure of dependency having been based on several subscores of the Edwards Personal Preference Schedule (EPPS). Thus, for two requests for volunteering (hypnosis and questionnaire) and for two measures of dependency (Rorschach and EPPS), volunteers were found to be more dependent than nonvolunteers.

Finally, there is a surprising result relating sociability to thoughtfulness among a sample of pseudovolunteers. Frey and Becker (1958) found that those of their pseudovolunteers who notified the investigator that they would be unable to attend had lower sociability scores on Guilford's scale than did the pseudovolunteers who simply never appeared. It is difficult to explain this somewhat paradoxical finding that presumably more thoughtful pseudovolunteers were in fact less sociable than their less thoughtful counterparts.

To summarize, now, the evidence bearing on the relationship between volunteering and sociability, it seems safe to conclude that when a significant relationship does occur, it is much more likely to be positive than negative. Furthermore, whether the request is for participation in a psychological experiment or in a survey study, the probability is good that a positive relationship will be found at a significant or nearly significant level. No very powerful moderating variables were found, although sex remains a usual candidate, as does the nature of the task for which volunteering was solicited. Sociable persons who normally volunteer most may not volunteer much for unsociable tasks.

EXTRAVERSION

The variable of extraversion would seem to be related conceptually to the variable of sociability, so that we might expect to find volunteers more extraverted than nonvolunteers, since volunteers appear to be more sociable than nonvolunteers. That expectation is not supported by the evidence. Table 2-10 shows that two studies found volunteers to be more extraverted, two studies found volunteers to be more introverted, and four studies found volunteers not to differ from nonvolunteers in extraversion. There are not enough studies in Table 2-10 to permit strong inferences about characteristics of those studies showing volunteers to be more extraverted versus more introverted, versus those studies showing no differences, but we should consider at least the types of instruments employed and the nature of the tasks for which volunteering was solicited as a source of clues.

Inspection of the last column of Table 2-10 suggests no very clear differences between the three sets of instruments employed to measure extraversion. Per-

Table 2-10.   Studies of the Relationship Between Volunteering and Extraversion

	Author	Instrument
Volunteers found more extraverted	Jaeger, Feinberg, and Weissman (1973)[a]	Omnibus Personality Inventory
	Schubert (1964)[b]	MMPI
No difference	Francis and Diespecker (1973) I[c]	Eysenck Personality Inventory
	Francis and Diespecker (1973) II[c]	16 PF
	Martin and Marcuse (1958)[b]	Bernreuter Personality Inventory
	Rosen (1951)[b]	MMPI
Volunteers found more introverted	Ora (1966)[b]	Self-report
	Tune (1968)[d]	Heron Inventory

[a] Group experience
[b] Psychological experiment
[c] Sensory deprivation
[d] Sleep research

haps the nature of the tasks for which volunteering was requested may provide some clues to help differentiate the three classes of outcomes. One of the studies finding volunteers to be more extraverted and one of those finding volunteers to be more introverted requested volunteers for general psychological experiments. The other study finding volunteers to be more extraverted requested volunteers for participation in an extracurricular group experience, a finding that makes good sense. More extraverted persons should be more likely to want to interact in groups than less extraverted persons. The remaining study finding volunteers to be more introverted requested volunteers to participate in a 56-day study of sleep patterns in which subjects were to record their hours of sleep each day in the privacy of their own home. That such a solitary task should be preferred by more introverted persons also makes good sense. The remaining studies, those finding no differences between volunteers and nonvolunteers, requested either participation in general psychological research or in studies of sensory deprivation.

No very clear summary of the relationship between volunteering and extraversion is possible. Although there is no net difference in outcomes favoring either the view that volunteers are more introverted or the view that they are more extraverted, there are probably too many studies showing some significant relationship to permit a conclusion of "no relationship." The task for the future is to learn what types of studies are likely to find significant positive relationships and what types of studies are likely to find significant negative relationships. We do have a hint, at least, that when the task for which volunteering is requested involves group interaction, volunteers may tend to be more extraverted, while when the task involves no interaction either with other subjects or even with the experimenter, volunteers may tend to be more introverted.

SELF-DISCLOSURE

Sydney Jourard (1971) has done for the variable of self-disclosure what Stanley Schachter has done for the variable of birth order. In both cases a large volume of research has followed upon the integrative work of these scholars. We have already considered the relationship between birth order and volunteering; we consider now the relationship between volunteering and the predisposition to be self-disclosing.

Hood and Back (1971) solicited volunteers for one or more experiments varying in the degree to which the situation would be (1) competitive, (2) under the strong control of the experimenter, (3) affiliative, or (4) self-revealing. The Jourard measure of self-disclosure had been administered to all subjects, and results showed very clearly for male subjects that those scoring higher on self-disclosure were more likely to volunteer. The magnitude of this effect was very large, with volunteers scoring 1.42 standard deviation units higher than nonvolunteers ($p < .001$).For female subjects, the relationship between volunteering and self-disclosure was complicated by the nature of the experiments for which volunteering occurred and not in any predictable manner. Females generally, however, scored very much higher than males in self-disclosure, and there is a possibility that the complexity of the results for females may have been partially caused by problems of ceiling effects.

Sheridan and Shack (1970) invited 81 undergraduates enrolled in a personal-adjustment type of course to volunteer for a seven-session program in sensitivity training, and 23 agreed to do so. As measured by Shack's Epistemic Orientation Inventory, those who volunteered were higher in self-exploration by over half a standard deviation than those who did not volunteer. In addition, volunteers scored more than two-thirds of a standard deviation higher than nonvolunteers on the Spontaneity Scale of Shostrom's Personal Orientation Inventory. These results, too, seem consistent with the hypothesis that volunteers are more likely to be self-disclosing than their nonvolunteering peers.

Alm, Carroll, and Welty (1972) and Welty (n.d.) reported the results of a study in which 56 students of introductory sociology were asked to volunteer for an experiment in psycholinguistics. The 16 students who volunteered were then compared on the Twenty Statements Test to the 40 students who did not.

Volunteers told significantly more about their beliefs, aspirations, and preferences than did nonvolunteers, with a median p level of .05 and a median effect size of two-thirds of a standard deviation. In addition, volunteers had fewer omissions than did nonvolunteers (p < .05, effect size = .57σ).

Finally, Aiken and Rosnow (1973) asked 374 high school students to describe how they thought subjects in psychological research were expected to behave. A majority felt that subjects should be frank and trustful, a combination that suggests proneness to self-disclosure.

Although there is as yet no very large literature dealing with the relationship of volunteering to self-disclosure, the evidence that is available points to the probability of such a relationship. It might be hypothesized further that particularly for studies requiring subjects to reveal something personal about themselves, those who volunteer may be considerably more self-disclosing than those who do not volunteer.

ALTRUISM

Although there are many motives operating that lead subjects to volunteer for behavioral research, at least some of these motives are altruistic in nature (Orne, 1969). It is reasonable, therefore, to expect that people who are highly altruistic may be more willing to volunteer to serve science or to help the recruiter than people who are not so highly altruistic, but there are surprisingly few studies that have directly investigated that hypothesis.

Wicker (1968a) surveyed 105 members of liberal Protestant churches and found that those who responded sooner to his questionnaire contributed about 80% more financially to their church than did those more reluctant to reply. Although this result is consistent with the hypothesis that more altruistic persons are more likely to contribute their data to the behavioral data pool, alternative interpretations are plausible. Thus, as we shall see later, those higher in socioeconomic status are also more likely to participate in behavioral research. In Wicker's study, therefore, the more generously contributing early responders may simply have been more able to afford larger contributions than the less generously contributing later responders. We cannot be sure, then, whether Wicker's earlier responders were actually more altruistic or whether they merely had greater financial resources.

Raymond and King (1973) solicited volunteers for research in a variety of undergraduate classes and then administered the Rokeach Instrumental Value Scale to volunteers and nonvolunteers. Results showed that volunteers rated "helpful" as significantly more important than did nonvolunteers (effect size = .38σ). Valuing helpfulness appears to be related conceptually to altruism, although surely it is not quite the same thing. In a general way, however, this study does seem to support the hypothesis that more altruistic persons are more likely to volunteer.

Barker and Perlman (1972) administered Jackson's Personality Research Form (PRF) to all the students enrolled in introductory psychology. Some time later, questionnaires dealing with parent–child relationships were sent to some of the subjects, and respondents were compared with nonrespondents on PRF variables. Respondents were found to score higher on the nurturance measure than nonrespondents, a result consistent with the hypothesis that more altruistic persons are more likely to volunteer. Here again, however, an alternative interpretation is possible. It may be that the content of the questionnaire, parent–child relations, simply was of greater interest to more nurturant subjects, and it appears generally to be the case that questionnaires of greater interest to a particular person are more likely to be filled in and returned.

In a scaling study reported in detail in Chapter 5, Aiken and Rosnow (1973) identified students enrolled in introductory psychology as volunteers or nonvolunteers. Subjects were then asked to assess the similarity of various types of activities including "being a subject in a psychology experiment." For both volunteers and nonvolunteers, serving in an experiment was seen as significantly more related to altruism than to any other class of experience described (being obedient, being evaluated, being relaxed, being inconvenienced). In addition, this relationship was more marked for volunteers than for nonvolunteers in the sense that there was a greater difference between the similarity between serving as a subject and altruism and the similarity between serving as a subject and the next most similar experience for volunteers (.65 of a standard deviation) than for nonvolunteers (.35 of a standard deviation).

Aiken and Rosnow also asked high school students to describe the expected behavior of the subject in a psychological experiment. More than half (56%) of these respondents, none of whom had ever before participated in psychological research, felt that subjects should behave in a "helpful" way.

To summarize now what is known about the relationship between volunteering and altruism, we can only say that the evidence is indirect and suggestive rather than direct and strongly supportive. Direct evidence might show that altruistic persons are more likely to volunteer for behavioral research.

ACHIEVEMENT NEED

A rich network of relationships has been developed relating the need for achievement to a great variety of other variables (e.g. McClelland, 1961). A close-up of this network should surely reveal research conducted on the relationship between need for achievement and volunteering for behavioral research, and so it does. Atkinson (1955) has, for example, suggested that the

Table 2-11.   Studies of the Relationship Between Volunteering and Need for Achievement

Greater Volunteering Among Subjects:	
High in Nach	Low in Nach
Bass (1967)[a]	Heckhausen Boteram, and Fisch (1970)[a]
Burdick (1956) (Atkinson, 1955)[a]	Spiegel and Keith-Spiegel (1969)[a, c]
Cope (1968)[a]	
Lubin, Levitt, and Zuckerman (1962)	
Myers, Murphy, Smith, and Goffard (1966)	
Neulinger and Stein (1971)[a]	
Spiegel and Keith-Spiegel (1969)[b]	

[a] Significant at $p < .05$
[b] Male subjects
[c] Female subjects

fear of failure of persons low in need for achievement should prevent them from volunteering for psychological research, research in which their performance might be evaluated and found wanting. Persons high in need for achievement, on the other hand, should perhaps find the opportunity to perform and be evaluated a challenging opportunity. On the whole, this formulation seems to be supported by the evidence. Table 2-11 summarizes the results of nine studies investigating the relationship between volunteering and need for achievement. Seven of the nine studies showed those higher in need for achievement to be more likely to volunteer for behavioral research.

The two studies reporting unpredicted results are different in several ways from those reporting the theoretically more expected outcomes. Thus, the research by Heckhausen, Boteram, and Fisch (1970) was presumably conducted at a German university, while the research by Spiegel and Keith-Spiegel (1969) solicited volunteers not for psychological research but for a companionship program in which volunteers were to spend one hour per week for 10 weeks with a psychiatric patient. In this study, too, it was only the female subjects for whom the volunteers scored lower in attraction to fame and power than did the nonvolunteers. Among the male subjects of this same research, however, volunteers scored higher on the test measuring attraction to wealth, power, or fame (the Spiegel Personality Inventory). Thus, all of the studies requesting volunteers for behavioral research and presumably conducted in the United States found those higher in need for achievement to be more willing to volunteer, and four of the six studies in this set showed effects significant at the .05 level. Effect sizes ranged from small (one-sixth of a standard deviation) in the study by Cope (1968) to large in the study by Neulinger and Stein (1971) (a difference of .77 between percentages transformed to arcsin units).

Adding to the generality of the results is the fact that need for achievement was defined in a variety of ways for the studies summarized. In the research reported by Bass (1967) and Bass, Dunteman, Frye, Vidulich, and Wambach (1963), subjects were administered Bass's Orientation Inventory, which permitted grouping of the subjects into those who were task-oriented, interaction-oriented, or self-oriented. Among the task-oriented subjects, whom we may regard as more likely to be high in need for achievement, 71% volunteered for an unspecified research study, while only 60% of the subjects classifiable into the alternative categories did so. When more standard measures of need for achievement were employed by Burdick (1956), 77% of those scoring above the median in achievement motivation volunteered for an experiment, while only 58% of those scoring below the median volunteered.

A still different definition of need for achievement was involved in the study by Cope (1968). In his research, students who had dropped out of college were surveyed and early responders were compared to late responders on their fears of academic failure. As expected, later responders experienced significantly greater fear of failure than did earlier responders, although, as indicated before, the magnitude of the effect was small.

Neulinger and Stein studied women undergraduates who had scored as either intellectually oriented or as socially oriented on the Stein Self-Description Questionnaire. Subjects were then invited to participate in a psychological experiment. Of the intellectually oriented women, those presumably more achievement-motivated, 87% agreed to participate; while among the more socially oriented women, those presumably less achievement-motivated, only 53% agreed to participate. The difference in volunteering rates obtained in this study, although large, may nevertheless have been attenuated by the fact that all subjects—volunteers and nonvolunteers—had actually been volunteers in the first instance, volunteers for taking the Stein Self-Description Questionnaire. Earlier we noted that in the study by Spiegel and Keith-Spiegel, female volunteers for a companionship program scored lower in attraction to fame and power than did the female nonvolunteers. The finding by Neulinger and Stein that their female undergraduates volunteered more when they were presumably higher in need for achievement suggests that the opposite result obtained by Spiegel and Keith-Spiegel may have been caused more by the nature of the task for which volunteering was solicited than by the sex of the subjects.

In the two remaining studies finding volunteers to score higher on need for achievement, those by Lubin, Levitt, and Zuckerman (1962) and by Myers, Murphy, Smith, and Goffard (1966), need for achievement was defined by scores on the Edwards Personal Preference Schedule. In both of these studies, however, the differences between volunteers and nonvolunteers were not significant statistically.

We have seen earlier that the act of volunteering is a necessary, but not sufficient condition, for the volunteer actually to find his way into the behavioral researcher's data set. Also necessary for that outcome is that the volunteer actually appear for his or her appointment with the data collector. Two of the studies summarized in Table 2-11 made special note of the rates of pseudovolunteering by volunteers high and low in need for achievement. Burdick (1956; Atkinson, 1955) found that of those who volunteered, 58% of the high-scorers, but only 42% of the low scorers, actually showed up for their research appointment. The difference was not trivial, but it was also not significant ($\chi^2 = 1.12$). In their study, Neulinger and Stein (1971) found that 92% of the presumably more achievement-motivated and 88% of the presumably less achievement-motivated volunteers kept their appointments with the experimenter. Although neither of these two studies found a significant difference between the pseudovolunteering rates of presumably high versus presumably low achievement-motivated volunteers, the trends suggest that higher scorers on "need for achievement" (Nach) may better keep their promise to participate.

From an overview of the results of the research relating volunteering to achievement motivation, the indications are strong that, for American samples at least, volunteers for behavioral research are likely to show higher levels of achievement motivation than their less achievement-motivated colleagues.

APPROVAL NEED

Crowne and Marlowe (1964) have elegantly elaborated the empirical and theoretical network that surrounds the construct of approval motivation. Employing the Marlowe–Crowne Scale as their measure of need for social approval, they have shown that high-scorers are more easily influenced than low-scorers in a variety of situations. Directly relevant to this section is their finding that high-scorers report a significantly greater willingness to serve as volunteers in an excruciatingly dull task, and the difference they obtained was substantial in magnitude (about two-thirds of a standard deviation). Table 2-12 shows that there were 10 additional studies in significant support of the result reported by Crowne and Marlowe, while another 8 studies did not find a significant difference between volunteering rates by subjects high or low in need for approval.

Craddick and Campitell (1963) asked all of their research subjects to return for an additional session one month later. Those of their subjects scoring higher in need for approval were considerably more likely to return (73%) than were their subjects scoring lower in need for approval (43%). Employing a different measure of need for approval, the Christie–Budnitzky measure, Hood and Back (1971) found the same result for their male subjects, while for

Table 2-12.   Studies of the Relationship Between Volunteering and Need for Approval

Significantly Greater Volunteering by Subjects Higher in Need for Approval	No Significant Difference
Craddick and Campitell (1963)	Bennett and Hill (1964)
Crowne and Marlowe (1964)	Edwards (1968a)
Hood and Back (1971)[a]	Hood and Back (1971)[b]
Horowitz and Gumenik (1970)	MacDonald (1972a) I
MacDonald (1972a)	MacDonald (1972a) II
McDavid (1965)	MacDonald (1972b)
Mulry and Dunbar (undated)	Poor (1967) I
Olsen (1968) I	Poor (1967) II
Olsen (1968) II	
Olsen (1968) III	
Olsen (1968) IV	

[a] Male Subjects.
[b] Female subjects.

their female subjects the relationship between volunteering and approval-need appeared to depend on the task for which volunteering was requested.

Still another measure of approval motivation was employed in the studies by McDavid (1965) and by Horowitz and Gumenik (1970). In both studies McDavid's Social Reinforcement Scale (SRS) was employed, and in both studies volunteers scored higher than did nonvolunteers. In McDavid's study there were actually two kinds of volunteers, those who volunteered for extra grade credit and those who had already earned their maximum allowable extra grade credit, the dedicated volunteers. The mean SRS scores were significantly higher for the bonus-seeking volunteers than for the nonvolunteers, and they were significantly higher for the dedicated volunteers than for the bonus-seeking volunteers. The magnitude of the difference in SRS scores between nonvolunteers and dedicated volunteers was nearly a full standard deviation $(.95\sigma)$. The SRS scores of the less dedicated volunteers fell about halfway between the scores of the nonvolunteers and those of the dedicated volunteers. In the experiment by Horowitz and Gumenik, the magnitude of the difference in SRS scores between nonvolunteers and volunteers who had been offered no reward for volunteering was almost as large $(.80\sigma)$.

In the research by McDonald (1972a) volunteers were solicited under three different conditions: for pay, for extra credit, and for love of science. Only in the condition in which pay was offered were subjects high in need for approval on the Marlowe–Crowne Scale more willing to volunteer (77%) than subjects low in need for approval (57%). Under both other conditions of recruitment, there was essentially no difference in volunteering rates as a function of approval need.

Mulry and Dunbar (n.d.) employed a subset of the Marlowe–Crowne Scale items, but their comparison was not of volunteers with nonvolunteers but of those who volunteer earlier within a semester with those who volunteer later in a semester. Subjects volunteering early in the term earned modified Marlowe–Crowne Scale scores nearly half a standard deviation higher ($.45\sigma$) than those of subjects volunteering late in the term.

In her research, Olsen (1968) examined the relationship between volunteering and need for approval (Marlowe–Crowne) under conditions in which male or female subjects expected to be more versus less favorably evaluated by the experimenter. In all four groups the relationship was positive, but it was significantly greater (point biserial $r = .57$) under conditions of favorable expectations than under conditions of unfavorable expectations (point biserial $r = .26$). As the theory of approval motivation predicts, those high in need approval should be relatively less eager to volunteer for experiments in which they are likely to be evaluated unfavorably.

When we examine the studies reporting no significant difference in volunteering between those high or low in approval need, we find no systematic factors that might serve to differentiate these studies from those that did find significant differences. Six of the eight studies employed as their measure of approval motivation the Marlowe–Crowne Scale, an instrument that, as we have seen, has often revealed significant differences. The remaining two studies employed as their measures the California Psychological Inventory's Good Impression Scale (Bennett and Hill, 1964) and the Christie–Budnitzky measure (Hood and Back, 1971). The latter study had found a significant positive correlation between volunteering and approval need, but only for male subjects. The sex difference per se cannot account for the difference in outcomes, since many studies employing female subjects had found a significant relationship between volunteering and approval motivation. It is possible, however, that sex and a particular instrument may serve as co-moderator variables, but we simply lack the data to evaluate the plausibility of this hypothesis.

The nature of the incentives to volunteer also does not appear to differentiate the studies showing significant versus insignificant relationships between approval need and volunteering. In the two studies by MacDonald (1972a) showing no significant relationship, the incentives were extra credit and love of science, but there were also studies showing quite significant relationships that employed similar incentives.

Although the overall results were not significant, a closer look at the studies by C. Edwards (1968a) and by Poor (1967) may be instructive. In one of his studies, Poor solicited volunteers for a psychological experiment and found that volunteers scored half a standard deviation higher on the Marlowe–Crowne Scale than did the nonvolunteers. In his other study, Poor compared respondents with nonrespondents to a mailed questionnaire. In this study respondents scored about a quarter of a standard deviation higher in need for approval than did the nonrespondents. Neither of these studies, however, reached statistical significance as commonly defined, but both did reach the .07 level (one-tailed).

Carl Edwards (1968a) invited student nurses to volunteer for an hypnotic dream experiment and found no relationship between need for approval and volunteering. If this study were the only one to find no relationship, we might suppose it could have been caused by either the special nature of the task for which volunteers were solicited or the special nature of the subject population. There are other studies, however, also finding no relationship between volunteering and approval motivation in which more common tasks and more typical subjects were employed. It seems unlikely, therefore, that we can readily ascribe Edwards' finding to either his task or his population. Edwards reported some intriguing additional results, however. The need for approval scores of the volunteers' best friends were significantly higher than the need for approval scores of the nonvolunteers' best friends. In addition, the student nurses' instructors rated the volunteers as significantly more defensive than the nonvolunteers. If we were to reason that people chose people like themselves as their best friends, then we might conclude that at least in their choice of best friends, as well as in their instructors' judgment, Edwards' volunteers may have shown a higher need for approval not reflected in their own test scores.

Edwards went further in his analysis of subjects' scores on the Marlowe–Crowne Scale. He found a nonlinear trend suggesting that the volunteers were more extreme scorers than the nonvolunteers—that is, either too high (which one would have expected) or too low (which one would not have expected). Edwards' sample size of 37 was too small to establish the statistical significance of the suggested curvilinear relationship. However, Poor (1967), in both of the samples mentioned earlier, also found a curvilinear relationship, and in both samples the direction of curvilinearity was the same as in Edwards' study. The more extreme scorers on the Marlowe–Crowne Scale were those more likely to volunteer. In Poor's smaller sample of 40 subjects who had been asked to volunteer for an experiment, the curvilinear relationship was not significant. However, in Poor's larger sample of 169 subjects who had been asked to return a questionnaire, the curvilinear relationship was significant. None of the magnitudes of these curvilinear relationships was very great, however. Employing r as an index of relationship as suggested by Friedman (1968), we find the curvilinear correlations to be .19, .12, and .30 for the study by Edwards, the experiment by Poor, and the survey by Poor, respectively—effects that range from small to medium in Cohen's (1969) definition of effect magnitudes.

Before concluding our discussion of the relationship between volunteering and approval motivation, two other studies must be mentioned, one dealing with choice of subject role, the other with pseudovolunteering. Efran and

Boylin (1967) found in a sample of male undergraduate students, all of whom had volunteered for some form of participation, that volunteers higher in need for approval were less willing to serve as discussants in groups than were volunteers lower in approval need ($r = .39, p < .01$). Presumably the more approval-motivated volunteers felt they were more likely to be evaluated in a negative way when they were "on display" in an experiment rather than performing the less conspicuous role of observer.

Finally, in their study of pseudovolunteering, Leipold and James (1962) compared (on the Marlowe–Crowne Scale) subjects who appeared for their research appointments with those who did not appear. For female subjects there was essentially no difference, but for male subjects those who appeared tended to be higher in approval motivation. This result, while not significant statistically, was of moderate size ($.41\sigma$).

A summary of the research investigating the relationship between volunteering and approval motivation is not unduly complicated. When a significant linear relationship was obtained, and more than half the time it was, it always showed that volunteering was more likely among persons high rather than low in approval motivation. In three of the studies finding no significant linear relationship, there were indications of a curvilinear trend such that medium-scorers on the measure of approval need were least likely to volunteer. In trying to understand the reasons why the remaining studies showing no significant relationship failed to do so, it seems unlikely that any single moderator variable can bear the burden of responsibility. However, it is possible that the joint effects of two or more moderator variables may account for the obtained differences in outcomes. Our best candidates for playing the role of co-moderator variables are (1) the type of task for which volunteering is solicited, (2) the incentives offered to the potential volunteer, (3) the instrument employed to measure approval motivation, and (4) the sex of the prospective volunteers.

CONFORMITY

At first glance it would appear to be essentially tautological to consider the relationship between volunteering and conformity, since the act of volunteering is itself an act of conformity to some authority's request for participation. We shall see, however, that conforming to a request to volunteer is by no means identical with, and often not even related to, other definitions of conformity. Indeed, Table 2-13 shows that when there is a significant relationship between conformity and volunteering, and that occurs about 30% of the time, the relationship is found to be negative. Subjects lower in conformity, or higher in autonomy, are more likely to volunteer than their more conforming, or less autonomous, colleagues. We should note that although most of the studies

Table 2-13.   Studies of the Relationship Between Volunteering and Conformity

Significantly Greater Volunteering by Subjects Lower in Conformity	No Significant Difference
Fisher, McNair, and Pillard (1970)	Edwards (1968a, 1968b)
MacDonald (1972a)	Fisher, McNair, and Pillard (1970)
MacDonald (1972b)	Foster (1961)
Martin and Marcuse (1957)[a]	Frye and Adams (1959)
Newman (1956)	Lubin, Levitt, and Zuckerman (1962)
	Martin and Marcuse (1957)[b]
	Martin and Marcuse (1958) I
	Martin and Marcuse (1958) II
	Martin and Marcuse (1958) III
	McConnell (1967)
	Newman (1956)
	Spiegel and Keith-Spiegel (1969)

[a] Male subjects
[b] Female subjects

listed in Table 2-13 found no significant relationship between volunteering and conformity, there are far more studies that did find a significant relationship than we would expect if there were, in fact, no relationship between these variables in nature.

Fisher, McNair, and Pillard (1970) studied subjects high or low in physiological awareness. Among those high in such awareness, there was no relationship between volunteering and social acquiescence scores. Among those low in physiological awareness, however, only 29% of the highly acquiescent subjects volunteered for a drug study, compared to 80% of the less acquiescent subjects ($p < .02$). All of the subjects in this study had volunteered earlier for psychological testing, so, as is usually the case in a study of second level volunteers, the effects obtained may have been diminished in magnitude by the absence of a sample of true nonvolunteers.

In his study, MacDonald (1972a) employed two measures of conformity: MacDonald's own conformity scale (the C-20) and Barron's Independence of Judgment Scale. On both measures, volunteers were found to be significantly less conforming than nonvolunteers ($p < .005; p < .015$), although the magnitude of the effects was not large ($.24\sigma$ and $.21\sigma$, respectively.) In his other study, MacDonald (1972b) found that those who signed up for an experiment earlier in the semester were significantly less conforming than their more dilatory colleagues ($p = .01$, effect size $= .32\sigma$).

In their research, Martin and Marcuse (1957, 1958) requested four different samples of subjects to volunteer, each for a different psychological experiment. For three of these studies (learning, personality, and sex research) there was no relationship between volunteering and dominance as defined by the Bernreuter Personality Inventory. For the fourth study, however, that requesting volunteers for hypnosis research, male volunteers were found to score as significantly more dominant than nonvolunteers ($p < .05$), and the magnitude of the effect was substantial ($.62\sigma$). Among the female subjects of this hypnosis study, however, the relationship between volunteering and dominance was not only not significant but, indeed, was in the opposite direction.

Employing as his measure the Edwards Personal Preference Schedule, Newman (1956) found volunteers to be significantly more autonomous than nonvolunteers ($p = .01$) when the request was for volunteering for a perception experiment. When the request was for volunteering for a personality experiment, however, no significant relationship was obtained.

Three studies, listed in Table 2-13 as showing no significant relationship between volunteering and conformity, also employed the Edwards Personal Preference Schedule; those were studies by Carl Edwards (1968a), Frye and Adams (1959), and Lubin, Levitt, and Zuckerman (1962). The latter two studies found essentially no significant differences, but the study by Edwards actually found a number of nearly significant differences that tended to be conceptually contradictory of one another. Thus, on the EPPS, Edwards' volunteers for sleep and hypnosis research scored lower on autonomy ($p < .08$; effect size $= .66\sigma$) and on dominance ($p < .06$; effect size $= .69\sigma$) than did the nonvolunteers, results that are directionally consistent with those of Lubin et al., who had also employed student nurses as subjects in their survey research. In addition, Edwards' volunteer student nurses were rated by their psychiatric nursing instructors to be more conforming than the nonvolunteers. In apparent contradiction to these results, however, was the finding that on Carl Edwards' own Situation Preference Inventory, volunteers scored as less cooperative in their approach to interpersonal interaction when compared to nonvolunteers ($p < .06$; effect size $= .72\sigma$). It is the contradictory nature of Edwards' interesting findings, rather than their not having quite reached the .05 level of significance, that led us to list his study as one not showing a significant relationship between conformity and volunteering. We may note, too, that despite their inconsistent directionality, Edwards' obtained relationships were substantial in magnitude.

A similarly complex result was obtained in the study by Spiegel and Keith-Spiegel (1969). Male volunteers were found as more yea-saying on the Couch –Keniston Scale but also as more self-assertive on the Spiegel Personality Inventory than were male nonvolunteers, an apparently inconsistent set of results. For female subjects the results were exactly opposite. We should recall, however, that volunteering in this study was not for a behavioral research experience but for a program of companionship with psychiatric patients.

The as yet unmentioned studies of Table 2-13 were those by Foster (1961) and McConnell (1967). McConnell found essentially no relationship between volunteering and scores on (1) a sociometric measure of dependency or (2) a measure of dependency based on the Rotter Incomplete Sentence Blank. Furthermore, there was no relationship between the two measures of dependency. Finally, Foster found no relationship between volunteering for an experiment and conformity in an Asch-type situation.

To summarize the data bearing on the relationship between volunteering and conformity, we found most often that the relationship was not significant. However, there were too many studies finding a significant relationship to permit a conclusion that, in nature, there is no relationship. Furthermore, all five studies reporting significant relationships agreed in direction—less conforming subjects volunteered more.

In comparing those experiments in which a significant relationship was found with those in which no significant relationship was found, no single moderating variable is clearly implicated. Both types of outcomes have been found for male and female subjects, for a variety of incentives to volunteer, for a variety of types of task for which volunteering was solicited, and for a variety of measures of conformity, broadly defined. One clue does emerge from an analysis of the potential co-moderating effects of sex and type of research for which volunteering was requested. Based on the results of three studies, we might expect that when the task falls in the "clinical" domain and the subjects are females, greater volunteering may occur among the more, rather than less, conforming subjects. *Clinical* is here defined as involving research on hypnosis, sleep, or group counseling, and the studies providing these indications are those by Martin and Marcuse (1957), Edwards (1968a, 1968b), and Lubin, Levitt, and Zuckerman (1962). Even if further research were to bear out this fairly specific prediction, however, we would not expect the magnitude of the effect to be very large.

AUTHORITARIANISM

Volunteers have been compared to nonvolunteers on a variety of measures of authoritarianism, and overall the results suggest that volunteers tend to be less authoritarian than nonvolunteers. The most commonly used measure of authoritarianism has been the California F Scale; Table 2-14 shows the results of eight studies in which volunteers for behavioral research were compared to nonvolunteers on the F Scale. The entries for each study are the approximate effect sizes defined as the degree of authoritarianism of the volunteers subtracted from the degree of authoritarianism of the nonvolunteers, with the

Table 2-14.   Studies of the Relationship Between Volunteering for Behavioral Research and Authoritarianism (California F Scale)

	Effect Sizes (in σ Units)			
Author and Task	Male	Female	Combined[b]	Total
Horowitz and Gumenik (1970): experiment	—	—	—[c]	
MacDonald (1972a): experiment	—	—	+.16[a]	
MacDonald (1972b): experiment	—	—	+.29[a]	
Newman (1956): perception	+.52[a]	+.15	—	
Newman (1956): personality	+.03	+.31	—	
Poor (1967): questionnaire	+.26	+.22	—	
Poor (1967): social psychology	—	—	+.01	
Rosen (1951): personality	+.65[a]	+1.31[a]	—	
Median	.39	.26	.16	.26
Number of results	4	4	4	12
% significant	50	25	50	42
% positive signs	100	100	100	100

[a] $p < .05$.
[b] Separate analysis for males and females not possible.
[c] Effect size could not be computed; result not significant.

difference divided by the standard deviation of the sample's F Scale scores. An effect size with a positive sign, therefore, means that volunteers were less authoritarian than the nonvolunteers. Where it was possible to do so, effect sizes were calculated separately for males and females.

The most striking result of an inspection of Table 2-14 may be that all 11 effect sizes are positive in sign, a result that would occur only very rarely if there were no relationship between volunteering and authoritarianism ($p < .002$). In addition, 42% of the listed results showed significant relationships. We would expect to find only 5% obtaining such results if there were no relationship between volunteering and authoritarianism.

Neither sex of the sample nor the type of task for which volunteering was requested appears to be strongly related to the magnitude of the effect obtained. There may be a hint that type of task may interact with sex of sample in affecting the strength of relationship. Thus, in personality research, female subjects show a stronger relationship between volunteering and authoritarianism than do male subjects, while in perception research the opposite trend is found. There are not enough studies available, however, to permit any rigorous test of this indication. Before leaving Table 2-14, we may note that the grand median effect size is about a quarter of a standard deviation with a range from very nearly 0 to about 1 1/3 standard deviations.

AROUSAL-SEEKING

Schubert (1964) and Zuckerman, Schultz, and Hopkins (1967) have proposed that volunteers for behavioral research are likely to be more motivated than nonvolunteers to seek arousal, sensation, or input. Table 2-17 shows the results of studies investigating the relationship between volunteering and arousal-seeking. Although there are a good many studies showing no significant relationship, and even a few showing a significant (p < .10) reversal of the relationship, there is a large set of studies in support of the hypothesis. Furthermore, there are a number of studies showing effect sizes greater than a full standard deviation (Aderman, 1972; Zuckerman et al., 1967 I and 1967 II), and the median effect size for the studies showing volunteers to be more arousal-seeking was $.52\sigma$. For the three studies showing volunteers to be less arousal-seeking, the effect sizes were smaller (.23, .24, and .54).

In trying to understand the factors that might account for the obtained differences in outcome, we grouped the studies by the nature of the task for which volunteering had been solicited; Table 2-18 shows the results. Studies involving stress (e.g. electric shock, temperature extremes), sensory isolation, and hypnosis showed much larger effect sizes than did other types of research. The 11 results comprising these three types of studies included 8 (73%) with an effect size greater than a third of a standard deviation in the predicted direction of greater volunteering by subjects higher in arousal-seeking. The 14 results comprising the remaining types of studies included only 2 with effects that large (14%). Significance testing is of limited value in this type of situation, but should one want the results of a Kolmogorov–Smirnov test of the

Table 2-17. Studies of the Relationship Between Volunteering and Arousal-Seeking

Arousal-Seekers Volunteer Significantly More	No Significant Difference	Arousal-Seekers Volunteer Significantly Less
Aderman (1972)	MacDonald (1972a)	London et al. (1962)
Barker and Perlman (1972)	MacDonald (1972b)	Rosen (1951) II
Howe (1960)	Myers et al. (1966)	Rosnow et al. (1969)
Jaeger et al. (1973)	Ora (1966)	
Myers et al. (1967)	Poor (1967) I	
Riggs and Kaess (1955)	Poor (1967) II	
Schubert (1964)	Rosen (1951) I	
Schultz (1967b)	Waters and Kirk (1969) I	
Schultz (1967c)	Waters and Kirk (1969) II	
Siess (1973)	Waters and Kirk (1969) III	
Zuckerman et al. (1967) I		
Zuckerman et al. (1967) II		
Zuckerman et al. (1967) III		

Table 2-18.   Median Effect Sizes (in σ Units) Obtained in Seven Types of Studies

Type of Study	Effect Size	Number of Studies
Stress	+ .54	4
Sensory isolation	+ .54	5[a]
Hypnosis	+ .54	3[a]
Group research	+ .25	2
Questionnaire	+ .12	2
Personality—clinical	+ .12	4
General experiments	.00[b]	6

[a] One study is listed in both categories.
[b] Approximation only.

maximum difference of cumulative distributions, p would be found to be less than .02 ($\chi^2 = 8.42$, $df = 2$).

About half of the studies examining the relationship between volunteering and arousal-seeking were conducted with samples composed of both males and females, samples for which it was not possible to obtain separate estimates of effect sizes for the two sexes. The remaining studies were conducted with subjects of one sex only, or they could be analysed for each sex separately. Table 2-19 gives the median effect sizes for male, female, and mixed samples for studies involving stress (including sensory isolation) or hypnosis and for more general studies. For both types of studies, results based on male samples are quite similar to results based on female samples and the grand median effect sizes for males (.46) and females (.51) are very nearly the same. Interestingly, but inexplicably, those studies for which the data were not analyzable separately for males and females were the studies most likely to show no relationship between volunteering and arousal-seeking. Examination of the number of studies in each cell of Table 2-19 also shows an interesting relationship between type of study and whether data could be analysed separately for each sex. Of studies investigating stress or hypnosis, 77% studied males and/or females separately, while in the remaining, more general studies only 31% did so ($\chi^2 = 4.30$, $p < .05$, $\phi = .39$). This difference may be due to investigators of stress and hypnosis having more often found sex to be a variable moderating the outcomes of their research than has been the case for investigators of more standard research topics. Our own analysis of sex differences in volunteering suggests that although women generally volunteer more readily than men, they volunteer substantially less than men when the research for which they are being recruited involves stress. This finding, that men and women volunteers are differentially more or less representative depending on the type of research for which volunteering was solicited, further supports the practice of analyzing the results of research separately for male and female subjects.

Table 2-19.   Median Effect Sizes (in σ Units) by Type of Study and Sex of Subject[a]

Subject Sex	Stress and Hypnosis		Other Studies		Total	
	Effect	N	Effect	N	Effect	N
Males	.61	6	.24	2	.46	8
Females	.80	4	.33	3	.51	7
Mixed	.00	3	.00	11	.00	14
Total	.52	13	.00	16	.25	29

[a] Values given as .00 are approximations.

For the studies listed in Table 2-17, various definitions of arousal-seeking have been employed. A specially developed measure, the Sensation-Seeking Scale, was employed in seven of these studies (Schultz, 1967b; Waters and Kirk, 1969 I, II, III; Zuckerman, et al., 1967 I, II, III) with a median effect size of .54σ. Eight studies employed as their definition of arousal-seeking the use of alcohol, caffeine, or tobacco (MacDonald, 1972a, b; Myers et al., 1966; Ora, 1966; Poor, 1967, I, II; Rosnow et al., 1969; and Schubert, 1964) with a median effect size of approximately zero. We cannot conclude, however, that the measure of arousal-seeking employed determines whether there will be a significant relationship between volunteering and arousal-seeking. The reason is that the particular measure of arousal-seeking employed is highly correlated with the type of study conducted. Thus, 71% of the studies employing the Sensation-Seeking Scale were in our group of stress studies, while only 12% of the studies employing the use of chemicals were in our group of stress studies. For the studies employing these two measures of arousal-seeking, then, we cannot decide whether it is the measure employed or the type of task that accounts for the difference in magnitude of the effect of arousal-seeking on volunteering. It may well be both. Among the remaining studies, in which various measures of arousal seeking were employed, there was still a tendency for the stress studies to show a greater effect size (median = .46σ) than the remaining studies (median = .25σ). It appears, then, that while the use of the Sensation-Seeking Scale may lead to a greater relationship between volunteering and arousal-seeking, even when other measures are employed, studies of stress and hypnosis show a greater effect of arousal-seeking on volunteering than do more typical studies. Table 2-20 summarizes this state of affairs.

Other measures that have been employed to investigate the relationship between arousal-seeking and volunteering include ratings of tasks (Aderman, 1972), Jackson's Personality Research Form "Play" Scale (Barker and Perlman, 1972), Shockavoidance (Howe, 1960), the Omnibus Personality Inventory "Impulsive" Scale (Jaeger, Feinberg, Weissman, 1973), the Ma Scale of the MMPI (London, Cooper, and Johnson, 1962; Rosen, 1951, I, II), the

Table 2-20.   Median Effect Sizes (in σ Units) by Type of Study and Type of Measure[a]

Type of Measure	Stress and Hypnosis		Other Studies		Total	
	Effect	N	Effect	N	Effect	N
Sensation-Seeking Scale	.71	5	.00	2	.54	7
Chemical usage	.00	1	.00	7	.00	8
Other measures	.46	6	.25	5	.44	11
Total	.50	12	.00	14	.24	26

[a] Values given as .00 are approximations.

Thrill-Seeking Scale (Myers, Smith, and Murphy, 1967), the Guilford Cycloid Scale (Riggs and Kaess, 1955), the Cattell 16-PF index of adventurousness (Schultz, 1967c), and the Harmavoidance Scale of the Jackson Personality Research Form (Siess, 1973). This last study differed from the others in that subjects were asked to judge their preferences for various types of experiments rather than being asked directly to volunteer for behavioral research.

In summarizing the results of studies of the relationship between volunteering and arousal-seeking, we note first that overall, volunteers are more arousal-seeking than nonvolunteers, with a median effect size of about a quarter of a standard deviation. The type of study for which volunteering is requested, however, appears to act as a moderator variable such that studies of stress, sensory isolation, and hypnosis tend to show this relationship to a much greater degree than do more ordinary kinds of studies. It is, in fact, possible that for these ordinary kinds of studies, the true effect size may be only trivially greater than zero. There is also some evidence to suggest that the relationship between volunteering and arousal-seeking may be somewhat greater when the latter variable is defined in terms of scores on a particular instrument, the Sensation-Seeking Scale.

ANXIETY

Many investigators have addressed the question of whether volunteers differ from nonvolunteers in their level of anxiety. Table 2-21 gives the results of 35 such studies. Although most of the results were not significant statistically, there are far too many results that were significant to permit a conclusion that there is no relationship between volunteering and anxiety level. Unfortunately, however, from the point of view of simple interpretation there are nearly equal numbers of studies showing volunteers to be more anxious and less anxious than nonvolunteers.

Table 2-21.   Studies of the Relationship Between Volunteering and Anxiety

Volunteers Significantly More Anxious	No Significant Difference	Volunteers Significantly Less Anxious
Barefoot (1969) I	Barefoot (1969) III	Cohler et al. (1968)
Barefoot (1969) II	Barefoot (1969) IV	Martin and Marcuse
Heckhausen et al. (1970)	Barefoot (1969) V	(1958) V
Jaeger et al. (1973)	Barefoot (1969) VI	Myers et al. (1966)
Martin and Marcuse (1958) I	Carr and Whittenbaugh (1968)	Myers et al. (1967) I
Riggs and Kaess (1955)	Cope (1968)	Myers et al. (1967) II
Rosen (1951) I	Francis and Diespecker (1973)	Philip and McCulloch
Rosen (1951) II	Heilizer (1960)	(1970) II
Schubert (1964)	Himelstein (1956)	Scheier (1959)
	Hood and Back (1971)	
	Howe (1960)	
	Lubin et al. (1962a)	
	Martin and Marcuse (1958) II	
	Martin and Marcuse (1958) III	
	Martin and Marcuse (1958) IV	
	Philip and McCulloch (1970) I	
	Siegman (1956)	
	Zuckerman et al. (1967) I	
	Zuckerman et al. (1967) II	

Two variables, fairly well confounded with one another, may serve as moderators for the relationship between volunteering and anxiety: the nature of the sample of subjects and the nature of the task for which volunteers had been solicited. All of the studies finding volunteers to be significantly more anxious were based on college students who had been asked to volunteer for fairly standard behavioral research. Of the studies finding volunteers to be less anxious, on the other hand, only two (29%) employed college samples (Martin and Marcuse, 1958 V; Scheier, 1959) and only two employed relatively standard requests for research participation (Cohler et al. 1968; Scheier, 1959). Of the studies making less standard requests of noncollege samples, three studies solicited volunteers for sensory deprivation from a population of military servicemen (Myers et al., 1966; 1967 I, II), and one study solicited questionnaire responses from males who had attempted suicide some time earlier (Philip and McCulloch, 1970). These four studies suggest that when the tasks for which volunteering is solicited are likely to be perceived as stressful or when the subject populations have undergone severe stress in their fairly recent past, only those who are relatively less anxious will be likely to volunteer. A more anxious, more fearful person may simply be unwilling to expose himself to further anxiety-arousing situations. It is interesting to note, too, that all four of these studies employed male subjects, so that our very tentative interpretation may be restricted to male subjects.

The study by Martin and Marcuse (1958 V) also found less anxious males to volunteer more, this time for a study of hypnosis. The study by Cohler et al. (1968), however, employed female subjects and also found the volunteers to be less anxious than the nonvolunteers. These volunteers were actually second-level volunteers drawn from a sample of mothers all of whom had answered newspaper advertisements requesting volunteers willing to participate in research on parent–child relations. Because the second-level volunteers of this research were compared to first-level volunteers rather than to true nonvolunteers, the size of the effect obtained may be an underestimate of the true effect size. Nevertheless, the effect size was substantial ($.47\sigma$). The remaining study reporting volunteers to be significantly less anxious (Scheier, 1959) employed both male and female subjects who were asked to volunteer for a relatively unspecified study characterized as somewhat threatening.

To recapitulate our hypothesis or interpretation, it appears that when the task for which volunteering is requested is potentially stressful or threatening and/or when the subjects are drawn from the world beyond the academic and when there is some significant difference to be found, it will be the less anxious persons who will be more likely to volunteer. For these studies the median effect size was $.36\sigma$. When the task for which volunteering is solicited is fairly standard and/or when the subjects are college students and when there is some significant difference to be found, it will be the more anxious persons who will be more likely to volunteer. These subjects may be concerned over what the recruiter will think of them should they refuse to cooperate, or they may simply be the subjects who are willing to run both the very minor perceived risk of participating in an experiment and the very minor perceived risk of admitting that they experience some anxiety. For these studies, the median effect size was $.34\sigma$.

While we may have a reasonable hypothesis for differentiating studies reporting volunteers to be significantly more versus less anxious, we do not have good hypotheses differentiating studies reporting some significant effect from studies reporting no significant effect. Thus, eight studies reporting no significant difference in anxiety between volunteers and nonvolunteers employed college samples and fairly standard types of tasks, so that we might have expected volunteers to be more anxious. For these studies, however, the median effect size was essentially zero. Of the remaining studies, four were of hypnosis (Heilizer, 1960; Lubin et al., 1962a; Martin and Marcuse, 1958 II; Zuckerman et al., 1967 I), two of sex research (Martin and Marcuse, 1958 IV; Siegman, 1956), two of sensory deprivation (Francis and Diespecker, 1973; Zuckerman et al., 1967 II), two of neuropsychiatric patients (Carr and Whittenbaugh, 1968; Philip and McCulloch, 1970 I), and one of electric shock (Howe, 1960). For these studies we might have expected to find the volunteers to be less anxious than the nonvolunteers, but that was not the case. The median effect size again was essentially zero. Further analysis of the studies shown in Table 2-21 failed to turn up any general suggestive relationship between gender composition of the samples and the studies' outcome.

Investigators of the relationship between volunteering and anxiety have employed a wide variety of measures of anxiety. The most commonly used measures, however, have been a derivative or a subtest of the MMPI. Fourteen studies employed the Taylor Manifest Anxiety Scale and five employed either the Pt or D scales of the MMPI. There was a tendency for studies employing these measures more often to find no significant difference than was the case for the wide variety (11) of other measures employed. Thus, of studies employing the Taylor Scale or the Pt (or D) scales, only 32% reported a significant result, while for the remaining studies 62% reported a significant result. It must be noted, however, that the use of any given measure of anxiety was partially confounded with the type of experiment for which recruitment of volunteers had been undertaken.

Less relevant to the question of volunteering but quite relevant to the related question of who finds their way into the role of research subject is the study by Leipold and James (1962). Male and female subjects who failed to appear for a scheduled psychological experiment were compared with subjects who kept their appointments. Among the female subjects, those who appeared did not differ in anxiety on the Taylor Scale from those who did not appear. However, male subjects who failed to appear—the determined nonvolunteers —were significantly more anxious than those male subjects who appeared as scheduled, and the effect was strong ($.84\sigma$). These findings not only emphasize once again the potential importance of sex as a moderating variable in studies of volunteer characteristics but also that it is not enough simply to know who volunteers; even among those subjects who volunteer there are likely to be differences between those who actually show up and those who do not.

To summarize the results of studies of the relationship between volunteering and anxiety, we note first that most studies report no significant relationship; however, a far larger percentage (46%) than could be expected to occur if there were actually no relationship between volunteering and anxiety do show a significant relationship. Among the studies showing significant relationships, those employing college students as subjects and fairly standard types of tasks tend to find volunteers to be more anxious than nonvolunteers. Studies employing nonstudent samples and potentially stressful types of tasks, on the other hand, tend to find volunteers to be less anxious than nonvolunteers. In both kinds of studies the magnitudes of the effects obtained tend to be about one-third of a standard deviation.

PSYCHOPATHOLOGY

We now turn our attention to variables that have been related to global definitions of psychological adjustment or pathology. Some of the variables discussed earlier have also been related to global views of adjustment, but our discussion of them was intended to carry no special implications bearing on subjects' psychopathology. For example, when anxiety was the variable under discussion, it was not intended that more anxious subjects be regarded as more maladjusted. Indeed, within the normal range of anxiety scores found, the converse might be equally accurate.

Table 2-22 shows the results of 34 studies of the relationship between volunteering and psychopathology. Most of the studies (71%) have reported a significant relationship, with 15 studies (44%) finding volunteers to be more maladjusted and nine studies (26%) finding volunteers to be better adjusted. In trying to understand the factors operating to produce such contradictory, yet so frequently significant, results, special attention was given to (1) the nature of the task for which volunteering had been solicited, (2) the gender composition of the samples, and (3) the measures of psychopathology employed.

Table 2-23 shows the median effect sizes, in standard deviation units, obtained in eight types of studies. A positive effect size indicates that volunteers were found to be more poorly adjusted; a negative effect size indicates that volunteers were found to be less poorly adjusted. Volunteers for studies of (1)

Table 2-22.   Studies of the Relationship Between Volunteering and Psychopathology

Volunteers Significantly More Maladjusted	No Significant Difference	Volunteers Significantly Better Adjusted
Bell (1962)	Bennett and Hill (1964)	Carr and Whittenbaugh (1968)
Conroy and Morris (1968)	Dohrenwend and Dohrenwend (1968)	Kish and Hermann (1971)
Esecover et al. (1961)	Francis and Diespecker (1973)	Maslow (1942)
Lasagna and von Felsinger (1954)	Myers, et al (1966)	Maslow and Sakoda (1952)
London et al. (1962)	Philip and McCulloch (1970) II	Poor (1967) II
Lubin et al. (1962 a,b)	Poor (1967) I	Schultz (1967c)
Ora (1966)	Rosen (1951) II	Sheridan and Shack (1970)
Philip and McCulloch (1970) I	Siegman (1956)	Tiffany et al. (1970)
Pollin and Perlin (1958)	Tune (1968)	Wrightsman (1966)
Riggs and Kaess (1955)	Tune (1969)	
Rosen (1951) I		
Schubert (1964)		
Silverman (1964)		
Stein (1971)		
Valins (1967)		

Table 2-23. Median Effect Sizes (in σ Units) Obtained in Eight Types of Studies

Type of Study	Effect Size	Number of Studies
High temperature	+ .80	1
General experiments	+ .49	11
Drugs and hypnosis	+ .47	5
Sensory deprivation	.00 [a]	3
Field interviews	.00 [a]	1
Questionnaire	− .10	9
Sex behavior	− .39	3
Sensitivity training	− .61	1

[a] Approximation only.

the effects on performance of high temperatures, (2) general psychological research topics, and (3) the effects of drugs and hypnosis tended to show greater degrees of psychopathology than did nonvolunteers with a median effect size of about half a standard deviation (.49σ). There was essentially no difference between volunteers and nonvolunteers in degree of maladjustment when recruitment was for studies involving sensory deprivation, field interviews, or questionnaires. However, when recruitment was for studies of sex behavior or for exposure to sensitivity training, volunteers were found to be better adjusted than nonvolunteers with a median effect size of exactly half a standard deviation.

The pattern of results described permits no simple or obvious interpretation. The studies for which volunteers tend to be more maladjusted, however, may have in common that subjects will be exposed to unusual situations (heat, drugs, or hypnosis) or believe that they may be exposed to unusual situations (general experiments). Perhaps more maladjusted subjects feel that if they were to react inappropriately under such circumstances, it would not be because of their (perhaps vaguely suspected) psychopathology but because of the unusualness of the research situation; that is, when the situation is acutely unusual, subjects may feel that they cannot be held responsible for their own chronically unusual behavior. At the same time, volunteering would put these more maladjusted subjects into contact with someone probably perceived as an expert in adjustment who might be able to help the volunteer with his or her adjustment problems. In short, the more maladjusted volunteer may see an opportunity for personal help in a context wherein the risk of "looking too bad" is low. After all, if the volunteer were to behave strangely, it could be ascribed to the heat, the drugs, the hypnosis, or the strange situation of the psychological experiment.

In research on sexual behavior or in sensitivity training, however, the situation may be somewhat different. While the more maladjusted person might still be motivated to obtain psychological assistance, such assistance might not be available at such low cost. In the area of sex behavior, for example, he or she will have to tell the investigator things that the more maladjusted person is more likely to believe will make him or her look bad (either because of "too little" or "too much" or the "wrong kind" of sex activity). Furthermore, in this situation the subject cannot easily ascribe any "strangeness" of behavior to the strangeness of the situation. Similarly, in the sensitivity-training research, the more maladjusted subject may feel that his or her insensitivity may become abundantly clear in the group interaction and any inadequacy of behavior again cannot be easily attributed to the situation, since, the maladjusted subject may feel, all the other group members will be behaving perfectly adequately. Accordingly, sensitivity-training research and sex research may be situations the more maladjusted person will try to avoid.

We turn now to a consideration of the possible moderating effects of the gender composition of the samples listed in Table 2-22 on the results of those studies. Most (65%) of the results shown were based on combined samples of males and females. Six studies employed only male subjects and six employed only female subjects; overall, there were no differences in the results obtained. When we consider the type of study for which volunteering was solicited along with sex of sample, however, there are some indications that these variables may interact to serve as co-moderator variables. Three studies of sensory deprivation were conducted in which the samples were composed of either males or females. The two results based exclusively on male subjects found essentially no relationship between volunteering and psychopathology (effect size $\cong 0.0\sigma$; Francis and Diespecker, 1973; Myers, Murphy, Smith, and Goffard, 1966). The single study of sensory deprivation employing only female subjects, however, showed the volunteers to be psychologically more stable, as defined by the 16 PF measure, than the nonvolunteers with an effect size of .44σ (Schultz, 1967c).

In three of the questionnaire studies, the samples were composed exclusively of males and females. The single result based on female subjects showed essentially no relationship between volunteering and psychopathology (effect size $\cong 0.0\sigma$; Philip and McCulloch, 1970 II). The two studies based on male subjects both showed very large effects of psychopathology on volunteering, but the results were in opposite directions from one another. For their male subjects, Philip and McCulloch (1970I) found that former psychiatric patients who had more often attempted suicide were more likely to respond to their questionnaire, with an effect size of .80σ. For their male subjects, however, Kish and Hermann (1971) found that patients discharged from an alcoholism treatment program were far more likely to respond to a questionnaire if their condition had improved, and the effect size was very large (approximately 1.4σ units).

Rosen (1951) conducted his research on volunteering with both male and female subjects. Recruitment was for participation in a personality experiment, and psychopathology was defined by scores on the Paranoia Scale of the MMPI. Among male subjects, there was essentially no relationship between volunteering and psychopathology, with a very small trend for better adjusted males to volunteer more (effect size $= .09\sigma$). Among female subjects, however, those who volunteered scored as significantly more maladjusted, with an effect size of $.49\sigma$.

There were two studies of sex behavior that employed only female subjects (Maslow, 1942; Maslow and Sakoda, 1952), and in both it was found that women scoring higher in self-esteem were more willing to volunteer, with effect sizes of $.65\sigma$ and $.39\sigma$, respectively. In a study of sex behavior that employed a combined sample of males and females, however, Siegman (1956) found no relationship between volunteering and self-esteem.

There are not enough studies of male versus female samples who have been requested to volunteer for any specific type of research to permit any conclusion about the moderating effects of sex on the relationship between volunteering and psychopathology. There does appear to be sufficient evidence, however, to suggest the possibility that sex may indeed operate as a moderator variable but perhaps in different directions for different types of tasks for which recruiting was undertaken.

For the 34 results shown in Table 2-22, a total of 20 different definitions of psychopathology were employed. Table 2-24 shows these 20 measures, the median effect size obtained in studies employing each of them, and the number of studies in which each was employed. An effect size with a positive sign indicates that volunteers were found to be more maladjusted, while an effect size with a negative sign indicates that volunteers were found to be better adjusted. A cursory examination of Table 2-24 does not suggest that the type of measure employed was a major determinant of the outcomes obtained. Thus, Silverman's measure of self-esteem was employed in a study finding volunteers to score lower in self-esteem ($+ .60\sigma$), while Maslow's measure of self-esteem was employed in 2 studies finding volunteers to score higher in self-esteem ($- .52\sigma$). It appears unlikely that these reversed outcomes could be ascribed to a strong negative correlation between these 2 measures of self-esteem. More likely, it is the nature of the task for which volunteering was requested that serves as the moderator variable. In general, paper-and-pencil measures of adjustment appear to be well scrambled among the positive, negative, and zero-magnitude effect sizes.

A closer examination of Table 2-24, however, does suggest one hypothesis about possible moderating effects of the type of measure employed on the relationship between volunteering and adjustment. When the definition of adjustment was clinical rather than psychometric, the results were more likely

Table 2-24.   Median Effect Sizes (in σ Units) Obtained in Studies Employing Various Measures of Psychopathology

Measure	Effect Size	Number of Studies
Lykken Emotionality	+ .85	1
Silverman Self-Esteem	+ .60	1
Guilford–Zimmerman	+ .49	1
Guilford STDCR	+ .48	2
Prior Psychiatric-Hospitalization	+ .48	1
Psychiatric Evaluation	+ .46	4
Suicide Attempts	+ .40	2
California Psychological-Inventory	+ .24	1
Paranoia Scale (MMPI)	+ .22	5
Rosenberg Self-Esteem	+ .10	2
Eysenck Neuroticism	.0 [a]	1
Heron Neuroticism	.0 [a]	3
Shostrom Personal Orientation-Inventory	.00	2
Siegman Self-Esteem	.0 [a]	1
Middletown NP Index	.0 [a]	1
Self-Esteem, Self-Rated	− .10	1
Revised Social Responsibility-Scale	− .41	1
16 PF	− .44	1
Maslow Self-Esteem	− .52	2
Improvement of Alcoholism	− 1.40	1

[a] Approximation only.

to show volunteers to be less well adjusted than the nonvolunteers. These clinical definitions included prior psychiatric hospitalization, psychiatric evaluation, history of suicide attempts, and improvement of alcoholism. The studies employing these definitions were all conducted either in medical contexts or under medical auspices, so that the measures employed are confounded with a particular context. The median effect size of the eight studies employing clinical definitions of psychopathology was + .46σ. When research is conducted in a medical, and primarily a psychiatric, context, it appears especially plausible to think that more maladjusted persons volunteer more in the explicit or implicit hope of receiving assistance with their psychological problems. Among the better adjusted volunteers for these more medical studies, especially for studies testing drug effects (Esecover, Malitz, and Wilkens, 1961; Lasagna and von Felsinger, 1954; Pollin and Perlin, 1958), motives for volunteering were more likely to include payment, scientific curiosity, or group expectations (as in the case of medical students, for example) than was the case among the more poorly adjusted volunteers.

Two of the studies listed in Table 2-22 defined their nonvolunteers in terms of failing to appear for their appointments (Silverman, 1964; Valins, 1967). Normally such studies would not be included in listings of studies comparing volunteers with nonvolunteers. In these particular cases, however, the grouping appeared reasonable. In the study by Silverman, for example, all persons in a pool that was required to serve as subjects comprised the target population. Of 40 subjects asked to come for the experiment, 15 did not appear. Among these 15 there were a number that called to say that they could not attend at the specified hour. These subjects are not like our "true" pseudovolunteers who simply do not show up. Analysis of the data in this study grouped together as the nonvolunteers those who notified the investigator and those who did not. Those who did appear were somewhat more like volunteers than would normally be the case when research participation is a course requirement, because this requirement had not been enforced. In the study by Valins, both the "volunteers" and "nonvolunteers" (no-shows) had actually participated in an earlier phase of his research, so that they were second-level subjects, whereas we usually think of pseudovolunteers as never finding their way into the research situation.

In our summary of the studies of the relationship between volunteering and psychopathology we must first note the very high proportion (71%) of studies showing a significant relationship. No case could be made that volunteering and adjustment are not related; however, while there are many studies showing volunteers to be better adjusted than nonvolunteers (26% of the total studies), there are even more studies showing volunteers to be less well adjusted than nonvolunteers (44% of the total studies). Studies showing the latter result appear to have in common a potentially unusual situation (e.g., drugs, hypnosis, high temperature, or vaguely described experiments) in which any unusual behavior by the volunteer might more easily be attributed to the situation. Studies showing more maladjusted subjects to volunteer less appear to have in common a situation in which volunteers must be self-revealing and in which any unusual behavior by the volunteer cannot easily be attributed to the situation but may be attributed instead to the volunteer's psychopathology. Volunteers for studies that are conducted in medical contexts and that employ clinical rather than psychometric definitions of psychopathology (e.g., prior psychiatric hospitalization, psychiatric diagnosis, history of suicide attempts) appear to be particularly likely to be more maladjusted than nonvolunteers, especially when there are no external incentives to volunteer. More maladjusted persons may be more likely to volunteer for this type of research in particular because of implicit or explicit hopes of receiving some form of psychological assistance with their psychological problems.

INTELLIGENCE

Table 2-25.   Studies of the Relationship Between Volunteering and Intelligence

Volunteers Significantly More Intelligent	No Significant Difference	Volunteers Significantly Less Intelligent
Abeles, Iscoe, and Brown (1954–1955)	Bennett and Hill (1964)	Edwards (1968a)[a]
Brower (1948)	Diab and Prothro (1968)[a]	Matthysse (1966)
Conroy and Morris (1968)	Kaess and Long (1954)	
Cudrin (1969)	Mann (1959)	
Ebert (1973)	Martin and Marcuse (1958) III[a]	
Eckland (1965)	Martin and Marcuse (1958) IV[a]	
Edgerton, Britt, and Norman (1947)	Mulry and Dunbar (n.d.)	
Ellis, Endo, and Armer (1970)	Myers et al. (1966)[a]	
Frey (1973) I	Poor (1967) I	
Frey (1973) II	Poor (1967) II	
Martin and Marcuse (1958) I	Rosen (1951)[a]	
Martin and Marcuse (1958) II[a]	Spiegel and Keith-Spiegel (1969)[a]	
Neulinger and Stein (1971)	Toops (1926)	
Reuss (1943)	Tune (1969)	
Rothney and Mooren (1952)	Underwood et al. (1964)	
Thistlethwaite and Wheeler (1966)		
Tune (1968)		
Weigel et al. (1971)		
Wicker (1968b)		
Wolfgang (1967)		

[a] Somewhat more unusual experiments; see text for description.

A good deal of evidence has accumulated bearing on the relationship between volunteering and intelligence. Table 2-25 shows the results of 37 studies that have examined that relationship. Although there are a good many results (15) showing no relationship between volunteering and intelligence, there are even more (20) showing volunteers to be significantly more intelligent, while only 2 results show volunteers to be significantly ($p < .10$) less intelligent. The median effect size obtained was $.50\sigma$ for studies showing volunteers to be more intelligent and approximately zero for all the remaining studies.

A large percentage of the 37 studies shown in Table 2-25 employed mailed questionnaires (49%) and the results of these studies were compared to the remaining, more laboratory-oriented studies. The median effect size for all questionnaire studies was .29, while for the remaining studies it was .16; in both cases the median effect sizes were in the same direction, that showing volunteers to be more intelligent. The laboratory studies could be further subdivided into those that requested volunteers for more-or-less standard or unspecified experiments and those that requested volunteers for somewhat more unusual experiences, including hypnosis, sleep and hypnosis, sensory isolation, sex research, small-group and personality research, and participation in a program of companionship for psychiatric patients. The median effect size for the 10 more typical or unspecified types of studies was .40, while for the 8 more "unusual" types of studies the median effect size was approximately zero. The 8 studies comprising this latter set are marked with an asterisk in Table 2-25. There was 1 additional experiment that does not fall into either the set of more standard studies or the set of less standard studies. This additional study by Cudrin (1969) solicited volunteers for medical research among the inmates of a federal prison. Prisoners who volunteered to be exposed to malaria or to gonorrhea scored significantly higher than nonvolunteers on the Revised Beta Examination, with an effect size of .71σ.

The two most commonly employed measures or definitions of "intelligence" were IQ scores on a variety of standardized tests (e.g., ACE, Beta, Henmon–Nelson, Mill Hill Vocabulary, Raven's Matrices, SAT, Shipley Hartford) and school grades.

Studies employing neither of these two types of measures employed a wide variety of other measures (e.g., motor skills performance, graduation from college, science achievement, intellectual efficiency, paired associate learning scores, study habits, marginality of student status, and even college administrators' knowledge of the validity of tests they were employing at their college). Table 2-26 shows the median effect sizes obtained in studies employing each of three types of measures for questionnaire and nonquestionnaire studies. The median effect size of these six cells is about a quarter of a standard deviation, a value appreciably lowered by the results of nonquestionnaire studies employing IQ tests or school grades as their definitions of intelligence. A closer examination of these studies reveals, however, that the zero effect sizes are caused by those studies we have referred to as somewhat less routine. While, in general, brighter or better-performing people are more likely to volunteer for relatively standard behavioral research, it appears that when the task for which volunteering is requested becomes more unusual, variables other than intelligence become more effective in predicting volunteering.

The vast majority of studies listed in Table 2-25 (78%) employed both male and female subjects. The number of studies employing only male or female subjects was, therefore, too small to permit very stable inferences about the possible role of sex of sample as a variable moderating the relationship between volunteering and intelligence. The median effect size of the six studies employing only male subjects was .44σ, while the effect sizes of the two studies employing only female subjects were + .73σ (Neulinger and Stein, 1971) and − .65σ (Edwards, 1968a). The latter study, showing volunteers to rank lower in class standing, was conducted with student nurses who were asked to

Table 2-26. Median Effect Sizes (in σ Units) by Type of Study and Type of Measure[a]

Type of Measure	Questionnaire		Nonquestionnaire		Total	
	Effect	N	Effect	N	Effect	N
IQ tests	.24	7	.00[b]	9	.18	16
School grades	.29	7	.00[c]	5	.14	12
Other measures	.38	4	.41	5	.41	9
Total	.29	18	.16	19	.23	37

[a] Values given as .00 are approximations.
[b] Median effect size for the four more ordinary experiments = .34.
[c] Median effect size for the two more ordinary experiments = .20.

volunteer for sleep and hypnosis research. Although sex of sample and type of task may have combined to serve as co-moderator variables, there is simply not enough evidence available to permit such a conclusion with any confidence.

There is one more study relevant to the question of the relationship of intelligence to finding one's way into the role of subject for behavioral research. The study by Leipold and James (1962), because it was of pseudovolunteering, was not listed in Table 2-25. Those who kept their appointments with the investigator had earned higher grades in their psychology examinations than those who failed to appear, with an effect size of .34σ. The differences were significant for the females (effect size = .52σ) but not for the males (effect size = .10σ).

A summary of the results of studies of the relationship between volunteering and intelligence can be relatively simple. When there is a significant relationship reported, and very often there is, it is overwhelmingly likely to show volunteers to be more intelligent. However, there appears to be a class of studies in which no relationship is likely to be found. That is the class of studies requesting volunteers for somewhat more unusual psychological experiences such as hypnosis, sensory isolation, sex research, and small-group and personality research.

EDUCATION

Most of the work on the relationship between level of education achieved and probability of finding one's way into the investigator's data pool has been conducted in the area of survey research rather than in the area of laboratory research. That is not surprising, given that most laboratory studies employ

Table 2-27.   Studies Showing Respondents or Volunteers to Be Better Educated

Less Personal Contact (e.g., questionnaires)	More Personal Contact (e.g., interviews)
Barnette (1950a)	Benson, Booman, and Clark (1951)
Baur (1947–1948)	Cohler, Woolsey, Weiss, and Grunebaum
Donald (1960)	(1968)
Eckland (1965)	Dohrenwend and Dohrenwend (1968)
Franzen and Lazarsfeld (1945)	Gaudet and Wilson (1940)
Gannon, Nothern, and Carroll (1971)	Kirby and Davis (1972)
Katz and Cantril (1937)	Meier (1972)
Kivlin (1965)	Robins (1963)
Pace (1939)	Stein (1971)
Pan (1951)	Teele (1967)
Reuss (1943)	
Rothney and Mooren (1952)	
Suchman (1962)	
Suchman and McCandless (1940)	
Wallace (1954)	
Wallin (1949)	
Zimmer (1956)	

college students as subjects. These students, often drawn from a single freshman or sophomore introductory course, show only a very small degree of variance in their level of education, so that no marked correlation between education and volunteering (or any other variable) could reasonably be expected. In survey research, on the other hand, the target population is often intended to show considerable variation in level of education attained. Survey researchers have long suspected that better educated people are more likely to find their way into the final sample obtained. That suspicion is remarkably well supported by the data. Table 2-27 lists 26 studies investigating the relationship between responding or volunteering and level of education. Every one of these studies shows the better-educated person more likely to participate in behavioral research, and in only two studies were the results not significant (Cohler et al., 1968; Dohrenwend and Dohrenwend, 1968). Here, then, is one of the clearest relationships obtained between participation in behavioral research and any personal characteristic of the subject. For all the studies considered together, the median effect size was $.40\sigma$. However, there appeared to be some moderating effects of the degree of personal contact between investigator and respondent on the magnitude of the relationship. Thus, for the 17 studies involving little or no personal contact between questioner and respondent, the median effect size was $.58\sigma$. For the remaining 9 studies in which there was a greater degree of personal contact between questioner and respondent, the median effect size was only $.32\sigma$, a full quarter of a standard deviation lower.

Most of the studies of this latter group involved face-to-face contact between investigator and respondent, so that anonymity was not possible. The studies of the former group were essentially all questionnaire studies in which anonymity could often be offered and in which no personal pressure to cooperate could be brought to bear on the potential respondent. Under these circumstances, better-educated persons may better appreciate the scientific value of their cooperation, and/or better-educated persons may feel they will have more favorable things to say about themselves in their responses to the questionnaires.

Not all of the studies requiring more personal contact between investigator and respondent were of the typical field-interview variety. Thus, the study by Cohler et al. (1968) invited a group of mothers who had already participated in research to volunteer for additional research on parent–child relationships. The study by Meier (1972) was based on the "biggest public health experiment ever: the 1954 field trial of the Salk poliomyelitis vaccine." The study by Stein (1971) was of patients in a university outpatient clinic who were invited to participate in research on psychotherapy. Finally, the study by Teele (1967), while a not atypical field interview study, did not directly investigate volunteering for behavioral research. Instead, general participation in voluntary associations was correlated with education level. In all four of these studies, as in the remaining, somewhat more typical, survey research studies, better-educated persons volunteered more.

Most of the studies (69%) of Table 2-27 employed both male and female subjects. Comparison of the results of studies employing only male or female subjects showed no marked difference in median effect size obtained either for questionnaire-type studies (males $= .64\sigma$; females $= .53\sigma$) or for studies requiring more personal contact with the investigator (males $= .18\sigma$; females $= .14\sigma$).

A summary of the relationship between volunteering and education can be unusually unequivocal. Better-educated people are more likely to participate in behavioral (usually survey) research and especially so when personal contact between investigator and respondent is not required.

SOCIAL CLASS

Many definitions of social class are based at least in part on level of education attained or on other variables that tend to be correlated with level of education. It will come as no surprise, therefore, that social class is related to volunteering just as educational level was found to be. Table 2-28 shows, however, that the evidence in the case of social class is not quite so univocal as it was for education. Of the 46 studies listed, 32, or 70%, do show that those defined as higher in social class are significantly more likely to participate in behavioral research. However, there are also 9 studies (20%) that report no significant relationship and another 5 studies (11%) that report a relationship significantly in the opposite direction.

With so many studies investigating the relationship between volunteering and social class, it will be useful to have a stem-and-leaf plot of the magnitudes of the effects obtained. For 40 of the 46 studies of Table 2-28, an effect size

Table 2-28.   Studies of the Relationship Between Volunteering and Social Class

Volunteers Significantly Higher in Social Class	No Significant Difference	Volunteers Significantly Lower in Social Class
Adams (1953)	Cohler, et al. (1968)	Donald (1960)
Barnette (1950a, b)	Dohrenwend and Dohrenwend	Edwards (1968a)
Belson (1960)	(1968)	Martin et al. (1968) II
Britton and Britton (1951)	Ellis, Endo, and Armer (1970)	Reuss (1943)
Clark (1949)	McDonagh and Rosenblum	Rosen (1951) II
Crossley and Fink (1951)	(1965)	
Fischer and Winer (1969) I	Poor (1967) I	
Fischer and Winer (1969) II	Poor (1967) II	
Franzen and Lazarsfeld (1945)	Rosen (1951) I	
Hilgard and Payne (1944)	Tune (1969)	
Hill, Rubin, and Willard	Waters and Kirk (1969)	
(1973)		
Katz and Cantril (1937)		
King (1967)		
Kirby and Davis (1972) I		
Kirby and Davis (1972) II		
Kivlin (1965)		
Lawson (1949)		
MacDonald (1972b)		
Martin et al. (1968) I		
Mayer and Pratt (1966)		
Meier (1972)		
Pace (1939)		
Pucel, Nelson, and Wheeler		
(1971)		
Robins (1963)		
Rothney and Mooren (1952)		
Stein (1971)		
Suchman (1962)		
Teele (1967)		
Tune (1968)		
Wallace (1954)		
Wicker (1968b)		
Zimmer (1956)		

Table 2-29.   Stem-and-Leaf Plot of Effect Sizes (in σ Units) Obtained in Studies of the Relationship Between Volunteering and Social Class

Plot (N = 40)							Summary	
+ .8	7						Maximum	+ .87
+ .7	0	3	5				Quartile₃	+ .42
+ .6	2	3					Median	+ .28
+ .5	1	8					Quartile₁	.00
+ .4	0	0	0	3	3		Minimum	− 1.40
+ .3	0	4	6	6	8			
+ .2	1	4	4	7	8	9	$Q_3 - Q_1$	+ .42
+ .1	0	0	3	7			$\hat{\sigma}$	.32
.0	0	0	0	0	0		S	.44
− .1	2	4	6	8			Mean	+ .19
− .2								
− .3								
− .4	8							
−1.0	6							
−1.4	0							

in standard deviation units could be computed or estimated with reasonable accuracy. Table 2-29 shows the stem-and-leaf plot along with a summary.

The left-hand column of the plot lists the first digit, the "stem," of the effect sizes given in two digit proportions of a standard deviation. The digits to the right of the stem are the second digits, the "leaves," of the various results. Thus, the leaf 7 following the stem .8 means that one study obtained an effect size of .87σ. The leaves 0, 3, and 5, following the stem .7 mean that there were three studies with effect sizes between .70 and .79—namely, .70, .73, and .75. Effect sizes with positive signs prefixed indicate that volunteering was more likely for persons higher in social class, while effect sizes with negative signs prefixed indicate that volunteering was less likely for persons higher in social class.

The stem-and-leaf display and its summary to the right show a skew in the distribution such that there are a few very low negative effect sizes straggling away from the main bunching of the distribution. In our efforts to understand this skew, we round up our usual candidates for the role of moderator variables: the type of task for which volunteering was requested, the definition or measure of social class, and the sex of the sample employed.

Table 2-30 shows the median effect sizes obtained in 10 types of studies. The most typical, least stressful, least threatening, and least dangerous types of tasks appear to be concentrated in the center of the listing. Large positive effect sizes were obtained in studies of the effects of exposure to air pollution (Martin et al., 1968 I) and of the personal counseling process (Kirby and Davis, 1972

Table 2-30. Median Effect Sizes (in σ Units) Obtained in 10 Types of Studies

Type of Study	Effect Size	Number of Studies
Exposure to air pollution	+ .87	1
Counseling research	+ .63	3
Questionnaires in laboratory	+ .53	2
Mailed questionnaires	+ .29	19
Field interviews	+ .17	5
Psychological research	+ .14	4
Interviews in laboratory	+ .13	2
Personality research	− .24	2
Sleep and hypnosis research	− 1.06	1
Exposure to malaria	− 1.40	1

I, II; Stein, 1971). Very large negative effect sizes were obtained in studies of sleep and hypnosis (Edwards, 1968a) and of exposure to malaria (Martin et al., 1968 II.) These results are puzzling, and there are not enough studies in either of our extreme groups to permit any strong inferences. Perhaps subjects higher in social class have a feeling of noblesse oblige when the risks are not unduly great. Experimental exposure to air pollution may not be much worse than living in a typical industrial urban area, and participating in research on counseling may not involve any degree of threat greater than that surmounted in having decided to seek counseling in the first place.

When the risks appear to be greater, subjects higher in social class may prefer to leave them to those lower in social class. Malaria is not part of the typical industrial urban picture, and it is traditionally left to prisoners or to servicemen to volunteer for that type of risk. That, at least, is what Martin, Arnold, Zimmerman, and Richart (1968) found. Not one of their 28 professional persons volunteered to contract malaria, but 8% of their firemen and policemen volunteered, 27% of their maintenance personnel and welfare recipients volunteered, and 67% of their prisoners volunteered. The situation for sleep and hypnosis research is less clear. The danger is less obvious in the physical sense, but perhaps those higher in social class are concerned that they might reveal something personal about themselves in the course of such research. Loss of control is at least believed to be more likely under conditions of either sleep or hypnosis. Some support for this interpretation comes from the finding that those higher in social class are also less willing to volunteer for research in personality. There, too, there may be a perceived potential for loss of privacy, a loss that may be more costly for those higher in social class, who have had greater opportunity to experience it. We repeat our caution that these interpretations are highly speculative and are in any case based only on a handful of studies. The next handful may show us to be quite clearly in error.

Table 2-31. Median Effect Sizes (in σ Units) Obtained When Employing Nine Measures of Social Class

Type of Measure	Effect Size	Number of Studies
Listing in *Who's Who*	+ .62	1
Military rank	+ .40	1
Composite index	+ .39	6
Income	+ .36	5
Own occupation	+ .29	15
Father's occupation	+ .12	4
Home and Appliance ownership	+ .10	1
Father's education	+ .06	4
Father's income	.00	3

We turn now to a consideration of the possible moderating effects on the relationship between volunteering and social class of the particular definitions or measures of social class that have been employed. Table 2-31 shows the median effect sizes obtained when nine different measures of social class were employed. Here our interpretation of the results can be less complex. Of the four measures of social class showing the smallest effect sizes, three employed definitions based on the social class of the subject's father (occupation, education, and income) rather than on his or her own social class. Of the 40 studies for which effect sizes could be computed or estimated, 11 employed father's status as the measure of social class with a median effect size of approximately zero. For the remaining 29 studies, the median effect size was $+ .34\sigma$. Table 2.32 shows the median effect size for studies defining social class in terms of the subject's own status versus father's status, for studies employing male, female, and mixed samples. Examination of the right-hand column suggests a rather clear effect of sex of sample. Those studies employing only female subjects show a significant reversal of our general finding. Three of the 4 studies employing female subjects found higher-status females to volunteer significantly less than lower-status females. Because there are only 4 such studies, we cannot draw a firm conclusion about the matter, especially since sex of sample is partially confounded with the type of study for which participation had been solicited. Thus, the 2 studies showing the largest (negative) effect sizes were a study of sleep and hypnosis (Edwards, 1968a; effect size $= - 1.06\sigma$) and a study of personality (Rosen, 1951 II; effect size $= - .48$ σ). We cannot be sure, then, whether these significantly reversed results were due to the sex of the sample, the potentially more threatening nature of the task, or both.

In addition to the effects of sex of sample and definition of social class employed, Table 2-32 suggests an interaction of these two factors. The bottom

Table 2-32. Median Effect Sizes (in σ Units) by Sex of Sample and Definition of Social Class

Sample Sex	Own Class		Parental Class		Total	
	Effect	N	Effect	N	Effect	N
Male	+ .40	8	+ .38	2	+ .40	10
Mixed	+ .30	19	.00	7	+ .28	26
Female	− .15	2	− .77	2	− .33	4
Total	+ .34	29	.00	11	+ .28	40
	Approximate Residuals					
Male	− .15		+ .15		.00	
Mixed	.00		.00		.00	
Female	+ .15		− .15		.00	
Total	.00		.00		.00	

half of the table shows the residuals when these two effects have been removed. For studies employing male samples, social status and volunteering are relatively more positively correlated when social status is defined in terms of parental social class than when it is defined in terms of the subject's own social class. For studies employing female samples, social status and volunteering are relatively more negatively correlated when social status is defined in terms of parental social class than when it is defined in terms of the subject's own social class. For studies employing combined samples of males and females, the results are just what we expect from an examination of the column and row medians: volunteering is positively related to social class only when social class is defined in terms of the subject's own status rather than in terms of his parents' social class. Because the interaction described is so complex and because the number of studies in three of the four cells showing large residuals is so small (i.e., 2), it seems wisest to forego interpretation until further research establishes the reliability of the interaction.

A summary of the relationship between volunteering and social class that would be robust even to a good number of future contradictory results would state only that, in general, participation in behavioral research is more likely by those higher in social class when social class is defined by the volunteer's own status rather than by his parents' status. There are some additional, but much weaker, findings as well. Persons higher in social class may volunteer somewhat more than usual when the task is slightly risky in biological or psychological terms, but they may volunteer a good deal less than usual, or even less than lower-class subjects, when the task is quite risky in a biological or psychological sense. There may also be a tendency for females to show less of the positive relationship between social class and volunteering than males.

AGE

A good bit of evidence is available to help us assess the relationship between age and volunteering for behavioral research. Table 2-33 shows the results of 41 studies of this relationship, results that permit no simple overall conclusion. While there are a good many studies (44%) that show no significant relationship between volunteering and age, there are far too many studies showing volunteers to be significantly younger (34%) or older (22%) than could reasonably be expected to occur if there were really no relationship between these

Table 2-33.   Studies of the Relationship Between Volunteering and Age

Volunteers Significantly Younger	No Significant Difference	Volunteers Significantly Older
Abeles, Iscoe, and Brown (1954–1955)	Baur (1947–1948)	Crossley and Fink (1951)
Belson (1960)	Benson, Booman, and Clark (1951)	Gannon, Nothern, and Carrol (1971)
Dohrenwend and Dohrenwend (1968)	Diamant (1970) I	King (1967)
Donald (1960)	Diamant (1970) II	Kruglov and Davidson (1953)
Kaats and Davis (1971) I	Ebert (1973)	Mackenzie (1969)
Lowe and McCormick (1955)	Edwards (1968a)	Mayer and Pratt (1966)
Marmer (1967)	Gaudet and Wilson (1940)	Sirken, Pifer, and Brown (1960)
Myers et al. (1966)	Kaats and Davis (1971) II	Tune (1969)
Newman (1956) I	Kaess and Long (1954)	Zimmer (1956)
Newman (1956) II	Martin et al. (1968)	
Pan (1951)	Newman (1956) III	
Rosen (1951) I	Newman (1956) IV	
Wallin (1949) I	Philip and McCulloch (1970)	
Wallin (1949) II	Poor (1967) I	
	Poor (1967) II	
	Rosen (1951) II	
	Stein (1971)	
	Tune (1968)	

variables. Before considering the possible role as moderator variables of the sex of the samples employed or the types of studies for which volunteering was requested, a stem-and-leaf plot of the effect sizes obtained will give a useful overview. Table 2-34 presents such a plot along with its summary. Effect sizes with positive signs prefixed indicate that volunteering was more likely for younger persons, while effect sizes with negative signs prefixed indicate that volunteering was more likely for older persons. The distribution of effect sizes appears to be strongly centered at about zero and if we did not know that there were significantly more significant results than could be expected by chance ($\chi^2 = 92$, $df = 1$, p near zero) we might conclude that there was "on the

Table 2-34.   Stem-and-Leaf Plot of Effect Sizes (in σ Units) Obtained in Studies of the Relationship Between Volunteering and Age

Plot (N = 39)										Summary	
+.6	4									Maximum	+.64
+.5	1	4	4							Quartile₃	+.17
+.4	0	1	3							Median	.00
+.3	0									Quartile₁	−.14
+.2	0									Minimum	−.47
+.1	0	4	5	7	7						
+.0	3	3	5	7	7	8				$Q_3 - Q_1$	+.31
.0	0	0	0	0	0	0	0	0	0	$\hat{\sigma}$	.23
−.0										S	.26
−.1	4	6	8	9						Mean	+.07
−.2	1	2	7	9							
−.3	0										
−.4	7										

average" no relationship between age and volunteering. The challenge of this stem-and-leaf plot is to try to discover the variables that lead to significant positive versus significant negative relationships between age and volunteering.

A fine-grained analysis of the different types of studies for which volunteers had been solicited revealed no substantial differences in effect sizes obtained. Table 2-35 shows the median effect sizes obtained when types of studies are coarsely grouped into laboratory versus survey research studies, for each type of outcome. Although the number of studies in each cell is too small to warrant

Table 2-35.   Median Effect Sizes (in σ Units) by Type of Study and Type of Outcome[a]

	Laboratory		Survey		Total	
Type of Outcome	Effect	N	Effect	N	Effect	N
Volunteers younger	+ .43	6[b]	+ .24	8	+ .35	14
No difference	.00	10	.00	8	.00	18
Volunteers older	− .47	1	− .21	8[b]	− .24	9
Total	+ .08	17	.00	24	+ .03	41

[a] Values given as .00 are approximations.
[b] Effect size for one of these studies could not be determined.

any firm conclusions, there is a hint in the table that when a significant relationship is obtained between age and volunteering, the magnitude of the effect may be larger in either direction in laboratory studies (+ .43σ; − .47σ) than in survey research (+ .24σ; − .21σ). That is a surprising result, given that the laboratory studies were so often conducted with college students, who show relatively little age variance, compared to the respondents of the surveys, who frequently span half a century in their ages. On psychometric grounds alone, we would have expected volunteering to correlate less with age in any sample showing low age variance.

Table 2-35 also suggests that there may be a difference in the pattern of outcomes for laboratory versus survey research studies. Thus, among the surveys, 67% show a significant relationship between age and volunteering, while among the laboratory studies only 41% do so. Among the studies that show a significant relationship, we find a difference in the distribution of outcomes for the laboratory versus survey studies. Thus, among the surveys conducted, 50% of the significant outcomes show respondents to be younger, while among the laboratory studies conducted, 86% of the significant outcomes show volunteers to be younger. A slightly different way of summarizing the distribution of outcomes shown in Table 2-35 is to note that among the laboratory studies there is only a single result out of 17 (6%) showing volunteers to be significantly older than nonvolunteers, a result that could reasonably be attributed to chance. Among the surveys, however, there are 8 results out of 24 (33%) showing respondents to be older than nonrespondents, a result that cannot be reasonably attributed to chance.

An effort was made to detect any communalities among the nine studies that found respondents to be older than nonrespondents. This effort was not successful, but for five of the nine studies, it appeared that social status may have been confounded with age such that it may have been volunteers' higher status rather than age per se that led to their higher rates of research participation. Thus, in King's (1967) study, older clergymen were more likely than younger clergymen to reply to a brief questionnaire. King's older clergymen, however, tended to occupy higher positions in the status hierarchy of the church. Similarly, Zimmer's (1956) older Air Force men were more likely to respond to a mailed questionnaire, but these older men were also those of higher military rank. Sirken, Pifer, and Brown (1960) found older physicians more likely to respond to a questionnaire than younger physicians, and it may be that these older physicians were professionally and financially better established than the younger physicians. Mayer and Pratt (1966) surveyed people who had been involved in automobile accidents and found that younger drivers were less likely to respond than older drivers. In terms of insurance records, police records, and public opinion, younger drivers appear to have a lower status than older drivers in the domain of driving performance. Finally, in his experimental study of high school students, Mackenzie (1969) found older students to volunteer more. Perhaps within the high school subculture, the older student is ascribed higher status than the younger student. On the basis of these studies, then, it appears reasonable to propose that in some of the studies finding older persons to volunteer more for behavioral research, we may expect to find a positive relationship between age and social status, so that it may be status rather than age that is the effective determinant of volunteering behavior.

Of the 41 studies investigating the relationship between volunteering and age, 14 were based on samples of males, 8 were based on samples of females, and 19 were based on samples of males and females combined. Table 2-36 shows the distribution of results of studies employing each of these three types of samples. The distributions of results employing male subjects and combined samples are very similar to each other. However, the distribution of results of studies employing only female subjects appears to differ substantially from the other two distributions. Studies employing only female subjects were much more likely (62% of the time) to find volunteers significantly younger than were studies employing male subjects (29%) or combined samples (26%).

Table 2-36. Distribution of Research Outcomes by Sex of Sample

Sample Sex	Volunteers Younger ($N=14$),%	No Significant Difference ($N=18$),%	Volunteers Older ($N=9$),%	Sum
Male ($N = 14$)	29	43	29	100
Mixed ($N = 19$)	26	47	26	100
Female ($N = 8$)	62	38	0	100
Total ($N = 41$)	34	44	22	100

Earlier, we noted that survey research studies were much more likely than laboratory studies to find older persons more willing to participate in behavioral research. Analysis of type of study conducted as a function of sex composition of the sample employed suggests that these variables are not independent. Thus, among studies employing female subjects, 75% were laboratory studies, while among all remaining studies, only 33% were laboratory studies. Because the number of studies in each resulting cell is sometimes quite small, we cannot isolate clearly the effects on the relationship between age and volunteering of the sex composition of the sample from the type of study for which volunteering was solicited. Indications from such an analysis, however, suggest that both sex of sample and type of study may operate as variables moderating the relationship between age and volunteering.

In our summary of the studies investigating the relationship between age and participation in behavioral research, we can be very confident of only a very modest proposition: that far too often some significant relationship between age and volunteering was obtained. Considering only those studies finding a significant relationship, there was a tendency for more studies to find volunteers to be younger rather than older when compared to nonvolunteers.

This tendency appears to be due in large part to the results of laboratory studies, which much more often than survey results report volunteers to be younger rather than older and which also report larger magnitudes of this relationship. There was also a tendency for studies employing female samples to report that volunteers tend to be younger. Many of the studies reporting volunteers or respondents to be older have in common the fact that their older subjects are also higher in social status, broadly defined. For these studies, therefore, it may be subjects' higher status rather than their greater age that serves as the effective partial determinant of volunteering.

MARITAL STATUS

There is no great profusion of evidence bearing on the relationship between volunteering and marital status. As is so often the case in our survey of correlates of volunteering, however, there are far more studies showing a

Table 2-37. Studies of the Relationship Between Volunteering and Marital Status

	No Personal Contact	Personal Contact
More volunteering by married persons ($N = 4$)	Donald (1960) Gannon, Nothern, and Carroll (1971) Tiffany, Cowan, and Blinn (1970) Zimmer (1956)	
No difference ($N = 5$)	Baur (1947–1948) Ebert (1973)	Belson (1960) Crossley and Fink (1951) Edwards (1968a)
Less volunteering by married persons ($N = 2$)	Scott (1961)	Stein (1971)

significant relationship than could reasonably be expected if the true correlation between volunteering and marital status were essentially zero. Table 2-37 shows the results of 11 studies divided into those in which there was some versus no personal contact between the investigator and the subject. There were 4 studies showing married persons to volunteer significantly more, 5 studies showing no significant relationship between volunteering and marital status, and 2 studies showing married persons to volunteer significantly less than single persons. Most of the studies involving personal contact between the investigator and his subjects found no relationship between volunteering and marital status. However, most of the studies that did not require personal contact between investigator and subject showed married persons more likely to participate in behavioral research.

Five of the 11 studies of Table 2-37 employed both male and female subjects, 4 studies employed only female subjects, and 2 studies employed only male subjects. No very noteworthy differences in median effect sizes were obtained as a function of differences in sex composition of the samples employed. The trend, if one could be discerned at all, was for the studies employing male samples to show greater volunteering by married persons than studies employing either female or combined samples

Table 2-38.   Studies of the Relationship Between Volunteering and Religious Affiliation

Jews Volunteer Significantly More Than Non-Jews	Protestants Volunteer Significantly More than Catholics	No Significant Difference
Fischer and Winer (1969) I	Lawson (1949)	Dohrenwend & Dohrenwend (1968)
Matthysse (1966)	Suchman (1962)	Ebert (1973)
Stein (1971)	Wallin (1949)	Fischer and Winer (1969) II
Teele (1967) I		Hill, Rubin, and Willard (1973)
		MacDonald (1972a)
		Ora (1966)
		Poor (1967) I
		Poor (1967) II
		Rosen (1951)
		Teele (1967) II

In summary, then, there appears to be a significant, but not too predictable, relationship between volunteering and marital status. For studies requiring no personal contact between investigator and subject, however, subjects who are married are more likely to volunteer than are subjects who are single.

RELIGION

There are a number of studies that have examined the relationship between volunteering and affiliation with the Catholic, Jewish, and Protestant faiths. Table 2-38 shows that most of these studies have not reported significant differences but once again there are more significant results than would entitle us to conclude that there was essentially no relationship between volunteering and religious affiliation.

Of the 17 studies listed in Table 2-38, there were 12 that permitted a comparison of volunteering rates of Jewish versus Catholic and/or Protestant subjects. Nine of these 12 studies showed Jewish subjects volunteering more than non-Jewish subjects; 4 of these 9 studies found the differences to be significant statistically, while none of the 3 studies showing Jewish subjects to volunteer less found the differences to be significant statistically. These 3 studies did not appear to differ from the remaining 9 studies in the type of task for which volunteering had been solicited.

Actually, rates of volunteering could be computed for Jews in six studies, for Protestants in seven studies, and for Catholics in eight studies. The median rates of volunteering or responding were 63% for Jewish, 46% for Protestant, and 48% for Catholic respondents. Although the median rates of volunteering available for Catholic and Protestant respondents are very nearly the same, we should note that of eight studies permitting a comparison between volunteering rates of Protestant versus Catholic subjects, the three results that were

Table 2-39.   Studies of the Relationship Between Volunteering and Religious Interest

Volunteers Significantly More Interested in Religion	No Significant Difference	Volunteers Significantly Less Interested in Religion
Ebert (1973)	Edwards (1968a)	Rosen (1951)
MacDonald (1972a)	MacDonald (1972b)	
Matthysse (1966)	McDonagh and Rosenblum (1965)	
Wallin (1949)	Ora (1966)	
	Poor (1967) I	
	Poor (1967) II	

significant statistically all showed Protestant subjects to be more likely to volunteer than Catholic subjects. All three of these studies involved mailed questionnaires, while only one of the five studies showing no significant differences involved a mailed questionnaire. We can pose as an hypothesis, at least, the proposition that especially in mailed-questionnaire studies, Protestants are more likely to volunteer than Catholics.

There are a number of studies available that have investigated the relationship between volunteering and degree of interest in, and commitment to, religious activity. Table 2-39 shows the results of 11 such studies. Most of these studies show no significant relationship, but again there are more showing a significant relationship than we would expect if there were really no association between volunteering and degree of religious interest. Four out of 5 of the studies showing a significant relationship report greater volunteering by those who are more interested in, and more active in, religious activity. While 1 of these 5 studies shows a large effect size ($.75\sigma$), the median effect size is quite small ($+.17\sigma$).

Three of the four studies showing significantly greater volunteering by those more interested in religion are questionnaire studies, while only two of the remaining seven are questionnaire studies. This finding suggests the hypothesis that it is particularly in questionnaire studies that those who are more interested in religious matters are more likely to participate in behavioral research.

A number of different definitions of degree of religious interest and activity were employed in the studies listed in Table 2-39. Seven of these studies defined religious interest in terms of frequency of church attendance, while the remaining definitions were more attitudinal in nature. There appeared to be no relationship between the type of definition of religious interest employed and the nature of the relationship between religious interest and participation in behavioral research.

To summarize the relationship between volunteering and religious affiliation, it appears that Jews are somewhat more likely to volunteer than either Catholics or Protestants. In questionnaire studies, there is the further tendency for Protestants to be more likely to respond than Catholics. When we consider the relationship between volunteering for behavioral research and degree of religious interest and activity, it appears that, particularly in questionnaire studies, those who are more interested or active in religious matters are more likely to find their way into the data pool of the behavioral researcher.

SIZE OF TOWN OF ORIGIN

A modest number of studies provide evidence on the relationship between volunteering and size of town of the subject's origin. Table 2-40 shows that (1)

Table 2-40. Studies of the Relationship Between Volunteering and Size of Town of Origin

Persons From Smaller Towns Volunteer Significantly More	No Significant Difference
Ebert (1973)	Britton and Britton (1951) I
Franzen and Lazarsfeld (1945)	Britton and Britton (1951) II
Reuss (1943)	MacDonald (1972a)
Sirken, Pifer, and Brown (1960)	MacDonald (1972b) I
	MacDonald (1972b) II
	Rosen (1951)

4 studies have reported significantly greater volunteering by persons from smaller towns, (2) 6 studies have reported no significant relationship, and (3) no studies have reported significantly less volunteering by persons from smaller towns.

Of the 10 studies listed in Table 2-40, 6 employed questionnaires and 4 employed more typical laboratory tasks. Four of the 6 questionnaire studies reported higher rates of responding by those from smaller towns, while none of the 4 laboratory studies reported a significant difference in volunteering rates between those from smaller, rather than larger, towns. The effect of size of town of origin on volunteering, then, may be limited to questionnaire-type studies. It should be noted that the effect sizes obtained tended to be quite modest; the largest effect obtained was about $.40\sigma$ and the median effect size was only $.16\sigma$.

In summary, then, it appears that, at least for studies employing questionnaires, those persons coming from smaller towns are more likely to participate in behavioral research than are those persons coming from larger towns.

SUMMARY OF VOLUNTEER CHARACTERISTICS

Proceeding attribute by attribute, we have now considered a large number of studies investigating the question of how volunteer subjects differ from their more reluctant colleagues. Both the number of studies and the number of attributes is large, so that we are in urgent need of a summary. Table 2-41 provides such a summary. The first column lists the characteristic more often associated with the volunteer subject (except for the extraversion variable, which was equally as often associated significantly with volunteering as was introversion.) The second column lists the number of studies providing evidence on the relationship between volunteering and the characteristic in question. The minimum requirement for admission to our list of volunteer characteristics was that there be at least three statistically significant results, in either direction, bearing on the relationship between any characteristic and volunteering.

The third column of Table 2-41 lists the percentage of the total number of relevant results that reported a significant relationship between volunteering and the listed characteristic. The range of percentages runs from 25% to 100%, indicating that for all the characteristics listed, there were more significant results than would be expected if there were actually no relationship between the characteristic listed and volunteering. Although this column indicates that all the listed characteristics are too often associated with volunteering, it does not provide evidence on the direction of the relationship. Thus, in

Table 2-41.   Summary of Studies of Volunteer Characteristics

Volunteer Characteristic	Number of Studies	% of Total Studies Found Significant	% of Total Studies Significantly Favoring Conclusion	% of Significant Studies Favoring Conclusion
A. Female	63	44	35	79
B. Firstborn	40	25	18	70
C. Sociable	19	68	63	92
D. Extraverted	8	50	25	50
E. Self-disclosing	3	100	100	100
F. Altruistic	4	100	100	100
G. Achievement motivated	9	67	44	67
H. Approval motivated	19	58	58	100
I. Nonconforming	17	29	29	100
J. Nonauthoritarian	34	44	35	80
K. Unconventional	20	75	55	73
L. Arousal-seeking	26	62	50	81
M. Anxious	35	46	26	56
N. Maladjusted	34	71	44	62
O. Intelligent	37	59	54	91
P. Educated	26	92	92	100
Q. Higher social class	46	80	70	86
R. Young	41	56	34	61
S. Married	11	55	36	67
T_1. Jewish > Protestant or Protestant > Catholic	17	41	41	100
T_2. Interested in religion	11	45	36	80
U. From smaller town	10	40	40	100
Median	20	57	42	80

the first row, the characteristic listed is "female" and the third column shows that 44% of the 63 relevant studies found some significant relationship between being female and volunteering. Some of these relationships were positive, however, while others were negative. It is the fourth column that gives the percentage of all relevant studies that showed volunteers to be more likely to show the characteristic listed in the first column. Thus, in the first row, the fourth column shows that 35% of the 63 relevant studies found females to be significantly more likely than males to volunteer for research participation. The range of percentages listed in the fourth column runs from 18% to 100%, indicating that for all the characteristics listed, there were more significant results than would be expected if volunteers were not actually more likely to be characterized by the attribute listed in the first column of Table 2-41.

Even this fourth column, however, does not give sufficient information, since it is possible that there was an equally large percentage of the total number of relevant studies that yielded results significant in the opposite direction. That is exactly what occurred in the fourth row listing "extraverted" as the volunteer characteristic. Of the eight relevant studies 50% showed a significant relationship between volunteering and extraversion (column 3) and 25% showed that extraverts were significantly more likely to volunteer than introverts (column 4). The difference between column 3 and column 4, however, shows that an equal number of studies (25%) showed a significantly opposite effect. As a convenient way of showing the net evidence for a specific relationship between volunteering and any characteristic, column five was added. This final column lists the percentage of all significant results that favor the conclusion that volunteers are more often characterized by the attribute listed in the first column. The range of percentages listed runs from 50% to 100%. This range indicates that for some characteristics all significant results favor the conclusion implied by the first column, while for others the evidence is equally strong for the conclusion implied by the first column and for the opposite of that conclusion. This latter situation occurred only once and that was in the case of the attribute we have already discussed, extraversion.

Table 2-41 lists the characteristics of volunteers in the order in which we originally discussed them. Table 2-42 lists the characteristics by the degree to which we can be confident that they are indeed associated with volunteering. Four groups of characteristics are discriminable, and within each of these groups the characteristics are listed in approximately descending order of the

Table 2-42.   Volunteer Characteristics Grouped by Degree of Confidence of Conclusion

I. Maximum Confidence	III. Some Confidence
1. Educated	12. From smaller town
2. Higher social class	13. Interested in religion
3. Intelligent	14. Altruistic
4. Approval-motivated	15. Self-disclosing
5. Sociable	16. Maladjusted
	17. Young
II. Considerable Confidence	IV. Minimum Confidence
6. Arousal-seeking	18. Achievement-motivated
7. Unconventional	19. Married
8. Female	20. Firstborn
9. Nonauthoritarian	21. Anxious
10. Jewish > Protestant or Protestant > Catholic	22. Extraverted
11. Nonconforming	

degree of confidence that we can have in the relationship between volunteering and the listed characteristic. The definition of degree of confidence involved an arbitrary, complex multiple cutoff procedure in which a conclusion was felt to be more warranted when (1), it was based on a larger number of studies, (2) a larger percentage of the total number of relevant studies significantly favored the conclusion, and (3) a larger percentage of just those studies showing a significant relationship favored the conclusion drawn. These three criteria are based on the second, fourth, and fifth columns of Table 2-41. The minimum values of each of these three criteria required for admission to each of the four groups of characteristics (as shown in Table 2-42) are shown in Table 2-43.

Table 2-43. Cut-off Requirements for Each Degree of Confidence

Degree of Confidence	Number of Studies	% of Total Studies	% of Significant Studies	Mean of Last Two Columns
Maximum	19	54	86	70
Considerable	17	29	73	51
Some	3	29	61	45
Minimum	3	18	50	34

To qualify for "maximum confidence," a relationship had to be based on a large number of studies, of which a majority significantly favored the conclusion and of which the vast majority of just the significant outcomes favored the conclusion drawn. To qualify for "considerable confidence," a large number of studies was also required, but the fraction of total studies significantly supporting the conclusion drawn was permitted to drop somewhat below one-third. The percentage of significant results that favored the conclusion, however, was still required to be large (73%). The major difference between the categories of "considerable" and "some" confidence was in the number of studies available on which to base a conclusion, although some characteristics that often had been investigated were placed into the "some" category when the fraction of significant studies favoring the conclusion fell to below two-thirds. The final category of "minimum confidence" was comprised of characteristics that did not so clearly favor one direction of relationship over the other and of characteristics that had not been sufficiently often investigated to permit a stable conclusion. To put the basis for the grouping shown in Tables 2-42 and 2-43 in a slightly different way, we can say that degree of confidence of a conclusion is based on the degree to which future studies reporting no significant relationships, or even relationships significantly in the opposite direction, would be unlikely to alter the overall conclusion drawn. Thus, for example, when 24 of 26 studies show volunteers to be significantly better educated than nonvolunteers, it would take a good many studies showing no significant relationship and even a fair number of studies showing a significantly opposite relationship before we would decide that volunteers were not, on the whole, better educated than nonvolunteers.

So far in our summary of characteristics associated with volunteering, we have counted all relevant studies, paying no attention to the type of task for which volunteering had been requested nor to the sex of the sample of subjects nor to the particular operational definition of the characteristic employed in each study. Yet each of these variables has been found to affect the relationship between volunteering and some of the characteristics investigated. On the one hand, then, our summary so far has been robust in the sense that conclusions drawn with good levels of confidence transcend the effects of these moderator variables. On the other hand, our summary has not been as precise as it might have been had we taken into account the effects of our several moderator variables. Hence, we conclude with a listing of the conclusions that seem warranted by the evidence, taking into account the effects of various moderator variables. The order of our listing follows that shown in Table 2-42, beginning with the conclusions warranting maximum confidence and ending with the conclusions warranting minimum confidence. Within each of the four groups, the conclusions are also ranked in approximate order of the degree of confidence we can have in each.

Conclusions Warranting Maximum Confidence

1. Volunteers tend to be better educated than nonvolunteers, especially when personal contact between investigator and respondent is not required.
2. Volunteers tend to have higher social-class status than nonvolunteers, especially when social class is defined by respondents' own status rather than by parental status.
3. Volunteers tend to be more intelligent than nonvolunteers when volunteering is for research in general, but not when volunteering is for somewhat less typical types of research such as hypnosis, sensory isolation, sex research, and small-group and personality research.
4. Volunteers tend to be higher in need for social approval than nonvolunteers.
5. Volunteers tend to be more sociable than nonvolunteers.

Conclusions Warranting Considerable Confidence

6. Volunteers tend to be more arousal-seeking than nonvolunteers, especially when volunteering is for studies of stress, sensory isolation, and hypnosis.

7. Volunteers tend to be more unconventional than nonvolunteers, especially when volunteering is for studies of sex behavior.

8. Females are more likely than males to volunteer for research in general, but less likely than males to volunteer for physically and emotionally stressful research (e.g., electric shock, high temperature, sensory deprivation, interviews about sex behavior.)

9. Volunteers tend to be less authoritarian than nonvolunteers.

10. Jews are more likely to volunteer than Protestants, and Protestants are more likely to volunteer than Catholics.

11. Volunteers tend to be less conforming than nonvolunteers when volunteering is for research in general, but not when subjects are female and the task is relatively "clinical" (e.g., hypnosis, sleep, or counseling research.)

Conclusions Warranting Some Confidence

12. Volunteers tend to be from smaller towns than nonvolunteers, especially when volunteering is for questionnaire studies.

13. Volunteers tend to be more interested in religion than nonvolunteers, especially when volunteering is for questionnaire studies.

14. Volunteers tend to be more altruistic than nonvolunteers.

15. Volunteers tend to be more self-disclosing than nonvolunteers.

16. Volunteers tend to be more maladjusted than nonvolunteers especially when volunteering is for potentially unusual situations (e.g., drugs, hypnosis, high temperature, or vaguely described experiments) or for medical research employing clinical, rather than psychometric, definitions of psychopathology.

17. Volunteers tend to be younger than nonvolunteers, especially when volunteering is for laboratory research and especially if they are female.

Conclusions Warranting Minimum Confidence

18. Volunteers tend to be higher in need for achievement than nonvolunteers, especially among American samples.

19. Volunteers are more likely to be married than nonvolunteers, especially when volunteering is for studies requiring no personal contact between investigator and respondent.

20. Firstborns are more likely than laterborns to volunteer, especially when recruitment is personal and when the research requires group interaction and a low level of stress.

21. Volunteers tend to be more anxious than nonvolunteers, especially when volunteering is for standard, nonstressful tasks and especially if they are college students.

22.   Volunteers tend to be more extraverted than nonvolunteers when interaction with others is required by the nature of the research.

CHAPTER 3

Situational Determinants of Volunteering

In the last chapter we examined the evidence bearing on the relationship between volunteering and a variety of more-or-less stable personal characteristics of those given an opportunity to participate in behavioral research. In the present chapter we shall examine the evidence bearing on the relationship between volunteering and a variety of more-or-less situational variables. As was the case in our discussion of the more stable characteristics of volunteers, our inventory of situational determinants was developed inductively rather than deductively. The question we put to the archives of social science was, What are the variables that tend to increase or decrease the rates of volunteering obtained?

The answer to our question has implications for both the theory and practice of the behavioral sciences. If we can learn more about the situational determinants of volunteering, we will also have learned more about the social psychology of social influence processes. If we can learn more about the situational determinants of volunteering, we will also be in a better position to reduce the bias in our samples that derives from volunteers' being systematically different from nonvolunteers in a variety of characteristics.

MATERIAL INCENTIVES

Considering the frequency with which money is employed as an incentive to volunteer, there are remarkably few studies that have examined experimentally the effectiveness of money as an incentive. The results of those studies that have investigated the issue are somewhat surprising in the modesty of the relationships that have been obtained between payment and volunteering. Thus, Mackenzie (1969) found high school students to be significantly more likely to volunteer when offered payment, but the magnitude of the relationship was not very large ($\phi \cong .3$). When college students were employed, MacDonald (1972a) found no effect of offered payment on rates of volunteering. In his study, however, the offer of payment interacted with sex of subject such that payment increased females' volunteering from 61% to 73%, while it decreased males' volunteering from 56% to 48% ($p \cong .10$).

In a mail survey of attitudes toward retail stores, Hancock (1940) employed-three experimental conditions: (1) questionnaire only, (2) questionnaire with a promise of 25 cents to be sent on receipt of the completed questionnaire, and (3) questionnaire with 25 cents enclosed. Only 10% of the questionnaires were returned in usable form by those who received only the questionnaire. The addition of the promise of a future "reimbursement" for cooperation increased the usable return rate to 18%, while the addition of the "payment in advance" increased the return rate to 47%! An enormous reduction of potential bias, then, was effected by a fairly modest financial incentive that probably served to obligate the respondent to the survey organization. This technique of payment in advance may be seen as more a psychological than an economic technique in enlisting the assistance of the potential volunteer. Later we shall describe additional evidence bearing on the relationship between volunteering and experimentally aroused guilt.

In the studies described so far, the actual amounts of money offered were quite small, ranging from 25 cents to $1.50 In a study by Levitt Lubin and Zuckerman (1962), however, the financial incentive was more substantial—$35.00 for from three to six hours of hypnosis research. The subjects were a group of student nurses who had not volunteered for research in hypnosis. Of the nonvolunteers, half were exposed to a lecture on hypnosis and half were offered the $35. Somewhat surprisingly, there was essentially no difference in volunteering rates associated with the different additional "motivaters" employed.

A similar procedure of trying to convert nonvolunteers to volunteers was exployed by Bass, Dunteman, Frye, Vidulich, and Wambach (1963; Bass, 1967). Three target groups of subjects were established by employing Bass's Orientation Inventory: (1) task-oriented, (2) interaction-oriented, and (3) self-oriented persons. When no pay had been offered, task-oriented subjects tended to volunteer most. Nonvolunteers were then offered pay ($1.50) for participation and this did increase the total number of subjects now willing to participate. The interesting results, however, were the differential effects of adding a financial incentive on the three groups of nonvolunteers. The self-oriented subjects were most influenced by the offer of pay (57% volunteering), followed by the task-oriented subjects (44%) and trailed by the interaction-oriented subjects (36%). Some people are predictably more likely than others to be greatly affected by an offer of payment for service as a research participant.

Table 3-1, based upon data provided by Bass, summarizes the results of the research. The subtable A gives the proportion of each type of subject to volunteer under conditions of pay and no pay as well as the proportion who never volunteered. Subtable B gives the proportions in each cell after having corrected for the differences in the row margins. The purpose of this procedure is to highlight cell effects uninfluenced by the frequently arbitrary differences in the margin totals (Mosteller, 1968). The procedure is to divide each cell entry by its row total to equalize the row margins and then to divide the new cell values by the column total to equalize those, and so on, until further iteration produces no change in the cell values. Subtable C expresses the values above as residuals from the expected values so as to highlight the more extreme deviates. The first row shows that under conditions of no pay, the task-oriented subjects volunteer too often, while the self-oriented subjects volunteer too rarely. The second row shows that self-oriented subjects volunteer too often for pay, while both other groups of subjects volunteer too rarely for pay. The third row shows that interaction-oriented subjects too often fail to volunteer at all, while the other two groups do not fail to volunteer "often enough." The research by Bass's group, although very instructive, did not actually

Table 3-1. **Proportion of Subjects Volunteering for Three Types of Subjects (After data provided by Bass, 1967)**

	Type of Subject			
	Task-Oriented	Interaction-Oriented	Self-Oriented	Sum
A. Basic data				
Volunteered. no pay	.71	.62	.57	1.90
Volunteered: pay	.13	.14	.25	0.52
Never volunteered	.16	.24	.18	0.58
Sum	1.00[a]	1.00[a]	1.00[a]	3.00
B. Standardized margins				
Volunteered: no pay	.41	.32	.27	1.00
Volunteered: pay	.28	.27	.45	1.00
Never volunteered	.31	.41	.28	1.00
Sum	1.00	1.00	1.00	3.00
C. Residuals (from .333)				
Volunteered: no pay	+.08	−.01	−.06	
Volunteered: pay	−.05	−.06	+.11	
Never volunteered	−.03	+.08	−.05	

[a]$N = 42$ for each group.

involve an experimental manipulation of financial incentive, since all the non-volunteers were offered pay after it was learned that they had not volunteered. This research, then, constituted an important contribution to the literature on volunteering, following an individual difference approach to the problem. Another study to employ such an approach was that by Howe (1960). He found that volunteers showed a much greater need for cash than did the nonvolunteers (effect size = 1.10σ, $p < .001$);Howe had offered payment of $3.00 for participation. In this study, need for cash was determined after the volunteering occurred, so it is possible that the incentive was viewed as more important by those who had already committed themselves to participate, by way of justifying their committment to themselves and perhaps to the investigator.

Another approach to the study of the role of financial incentives in volunteering has been to ask subjects to state their reason for having volunteered. Jackson and Pollard (1966) found that only 21% of their subjects listed payment ($1.25) as a reason for volunteering, while 50% listed curiosity as a reason. Interestingly, only 7% listed being of help to science as a reason for volunteering, and 80% of those who did not volunteer gave as their reason that they had no time available. In their study of prisoners volunteering for research on malaria, Martin, Arnold, Zimmerman, and Richart (1968) found about half to report that payment was the major reason for their participation, while the other half reported altruistic motives as their major reason for participation. Another motive that may operate with prisoners who volunteer for research is the implicit hope that a parole board might take into favorable account the prisoner's participation in research. That such hopes are implicit rather than explicit stems from the typical structuring of such research for the prisoner in terms that make clear that volunteering will in no way affect the prisoner's term of time to be served. Nevertheless, parole boards are likely to know that a prisoner participated in research, and they are likely to view this with increasing favor as a function of the degree of jeopardy into which they feel the prisoner has placed himself. Similar results to those reported by Martin et al. (1968) have been obtained by Nottingham (1972) in his study of attitudes and information-seeking behavior. Payment was the primary reason given for subjects' participation by 45%, while another 34% gave altruistic motives as their primary reason for participation.

There are some suggestions in the psychiatric literature that the use of financial incentives might change the nature of the volunteer sample in the direction of greater psychiatric stability. Esecover, Malitz, and Wilkens (1961), in their research on hallucinogens, found that the more well adjusted volunteers were motivated more by payment than were the less well adjusted volunteers. Other motivations operating to get the better-adjusted subjects into the volunteer sample included scientific curiosity or normative expectations that volunteering would occur, as in samples of medical students. Such findings tend to be consistent with those of Pollin and Perlin (1958).

In our discussion so far, we have examined the relationship between volunteering and financial incentives. There is some fascinating preliminary evidence to suggest that whether volunteers were paid or not may be a significant determinant of the direction and magnitude of the effects of the experimental conditions to which the paid and unpaid volunteers are assigned at random. Thus, Weitz (1968) employed paid and unpaid college student volunteers and paid and unpaid nonvolunteers in a study of the effects on subjects' responses of biased intonation patterns in experimenters' reading of experimental instructions. She reported that unpaid volunteers were significantly more influenced to respond in the direction of the experimenter's biased vocal emphasis than were the other three groups ($p < .02$). In a similar study conducted with high school students, Mackenzie (1969) found that the results depended on which of two investigators was in charge of the study. For one of the investigators, it was the paid nonvolunteers who were most influenced to respond in the direction of the biased intonation pattern found in the tape-recorded instructions. For the other investigator, it was the paid volunteer subjects who were most influenced, while the paid nonvolunteers were least influenced. Taken together, these studies suggest that volunteer status and level of financial incentive can jointly interact with the effects of the investigator's independent variable. There are not yet enough studies available, however, to permit any conclusion about the particular moderating effects that volunteering and incentive level are likely to have on the operation of any particular independent variable.

So far in our discussion of material incentives the particular incentives have been financial. There are other studies that have investigated the effects on volunteering of material incentives that were more in the nature of small gifts and courtesies. Thus, Pucel, Nelson, and Wheeler (1971) in their survey of 1128 graduates of post–high-school vocational–technical schools in the Minneapolis area, enclosed various numbers and combinations of small incentives with their mailed questionnaires. These incentives included small pencils, packets of instant coffee, use of green paper, and a preliminary letter telling of the subsequent arrival of the questionnaire. When respondents were grouped on the basis of the number of incentives employed (0, 1, 2, and 3), a monotonic relationship ($p < .01$) emerged between response rates and number of incentives received (43%, 51%, 55%, and 63%). In this study, females tended to volunteer more than males overall but appeared to be somewhat less affected by the employment of incentives than were the males. Thus, adding a third incentive increased the volunteering rate of females by only 4 percentage points, while it increased the volunteering rate of males by 17 percentage points. Enclosing a stamped, self-addressed envelope with mailed questionnaires also appears to increase the response rate appreciably (Dillman, 1972). Feriss (1951), for example, found that such an enclosure increased the response rate from 26% to 62%, while Price (1950) found that stamped return envelopes increased the response rate over unstamped return envelopes by 11% (from 17% to 26%). The generally lower response rate obtained by Price was probably caused by respondents' having to pay $6.00 in membership fees to join a national organization.

A frequently employed incentive to volunteering is the offering of extra academic credit. On intuitive grounds this might appear to be a powerful incentive indeed, but there is surprisingly little experimental evidence to tell us just how effective extra credit might be in increasing rates of volunteering. This question is just one more that MacDonald (1972a) has helped to answer in his important research. While 58% of his subjects volunteered when no incentive was offered and 57% volunteered for modest pay, 79% volunteered when extra academic credit was offered. MacDonald's research dealt with a positive academic incentive. The research by Blake, Berkowitz, Bellamy, and Mouton (1956), on the other hand, dealt with negative academic incentives. They found that more subjects volunteered when their reward was getting to miss a lecture, and a great many more volunteered when their reward was getting to miss an examination.

We have already raised the possibility that one incentive for participation in behavioral research might be the volunteer's perception that expert assistance with personal problems might be a side benefit. The evidence for this hypothesis is suggestive and intuitively appealing, but it is far from conclusive. When the research takes on a medical cast, however, there is more direct evidence available. In his longitudinal study of the normative aging of veterans, for example, Rose (1965) found volunteers to give as one reason for their participation the likelihood of prevention of serious illness by their obtaining regular tests and checkups.

Because the evidence is still in somewhat preliminary form, we cannot be overly confident in our summary of the relationship between volunteering and the material incentives offered to the potential volunteer. Financial incentives do appear to increase rates of volunteering but not dramatically so, at least not for the small amounts of money that are customarily offered. Small gifts and courtesies may be somewhat more effective in raising rates of volunteering than somewhat larger amounts of cash, particularly if they are given before the potential volunteer has decided whether or not to volunteer and if they are outright gifts, not contingent on the subject's decision. Thus, the symbolic value of a small gift may far outweigh its cash value. A small gift may obligate the recipient to participate and may further impress the recipient with the seriousness of the giver's purpose. Both these variables, the subject's sense of obligation and the seriousness of the recruiter's intent, will be discussed in more detail later in this chapter. There is additional evidence to suggest that the effect of material incentives on volunteering may be moderated by stable personal characteristics of the potential volunteer. Finally, volunteering and level of incentive offered, appear to moderate the effects of independent variables such that research results may be less replicable when levels of incentive and volunteering status are altered in subsequent replications.

AVERSIVE TASKS

Not surprising is the finding that when potential subjects fear that they may be physically stressed, they are less likely to volunteer. Subjects threatened with electric shocks were less willing to volunteer for subsequent studies involving the use of shock (Staples and Walters, 1961). More surprising perhaps is the finding that an increase in the expectation of pain does not lead concomitantly to much of an increase in avoidance of participation. In one study, for example, 78% of college students volunteered to receive very weak electric shocks, while almost that many (67%) volunteered to receive moderate-to-strong shocks (Howe, 1960). The difference between these volunteering rates was of only borderline significance ($p < .15$). The motives to serve science and to trust in the wisdom and authority of the experimenter (Orne, 1969) and to be favorably evaluated by the experimenter (Rosenberg, 1969) must be strong indeed to have so many people willing to tolerate so much, for so little tangible reward. But perhaps in Howe's (1960) experiment the situation was complicated by the fact that there was more tangible reward than usual. The rates of volunteering that he obtained may have been elevated by a $3.00 incentive that he offered in return for participation.

Eisenman (1965) also recruited subjects for research involving electric shock. He found that volunteering rates under conditions of strong shock were affected by subjects' birth order. Firstborns were nearly unanimous in their refusal to submit to strong shock. When the task involved an isolation experience, Suedfeld (1969) reported, firstborns were likely to volunteer less than laterborns if the recruiting procedure made the isolation experience appear frightening. Some evidence in support of this hypothesis was put forward by Dohrenwend, Feldstein, Plosky, and Schmeidler (1967). These workers found sensory deprivation to be more aversive to firstborns than to laterborns ($p = .05$, one-tail), suggesting that firstborn volunteers must have been quite eager to serve as subjects to be willing to undergo so much anxiety. Dohrenwend's group also suggested that because subjects may volunteer in order to affiliate with the investigator, volunteers might be especially prone to the biasing effects of the experimenter's expectations.

When volunteering is requested for research with a medical cast, the results are similar to what we would expect in the case of behavioral research. The more severe the perceived risk or stress to which the volunteer is to be exposed, the less likely he is to volunteer. Thus, in the research by Martin et al. (1968) people volunteered more for exposure to risks perceived as less serious: 79% volunteered to be exposed to air pollution, 47% to be exposed to the common cold, 38% to be exposed to new drugs, and 32% to be exposed to malaria. While all subgroups studied showed the same monotonic decrease, the slopes were quite different from group to group, with prisoners showing the most gentle slope and professional persons showing the steepest slope (93% for air pollution down to 0% for malaria). Earlier we saw that recruitment conditions might interact with independent variables of a psychological nature. We should note here that recruitment conditions may also interact with independent variables of a biological nature. Thus, Brehm, Back, and Bogdonoff (1964) found that those who volunteered to fast with only a low level of incentive not only reported themselves as less hungry but actually showed less physiological evidence of hunger.

Although a number of investigators have discussed the incidence and consequences of subjects' fears in the psychological experiment (e.g., Gustav, 1962; Haas, 1970) there is little evidence available to tell us exactly what type of study inspires how much fear in what type of subject. Such information would be very useful in helping us to estimate the selection biases likely to operate in different kinds of research. A somewhat related line of inquiry has been undertaken, however, by Sullivan and Deiker (1973), who asked subjects to indicate the type of experiments for which they would theoretically be likely to volunteer. When the research called for alteration of subjects' level of self-esteem, 80% said they would volunteer; when the research called for experimental pain, 52% said they would volunteer; but when the research called for the experimental induction of unethical behavior, only 39% said they would volunteer.

In summary, there does appear to be a tendency for subjects to volunteer less for more painful, stressful, or dangerous tasks when the pain, stress, or danger are either psychological or biological. There are further indications that personal characteristics of the subject and the level of incentive offered may act as variables moderating the relationship between volunteering and the aversiveness of the task.

GUILT, HAPPINESS, AND COMPETENCE

There is increasing evidence to suggest that the feeling states experienced by subjects at the time of their recruitment can significantly affect their probability of volunteering for behavioral research. The evidence, while not overwhelming in number of studies conducted, is unusually unequivocal in terms of drawing causal inference, based as it is on direct experimental manipulations of subjects' subjective experience.

Freedman, Wallington, and Bless (1967) conducted three experiments investigating the effects of induced guilt on volunteering. In their first study, half their male high school subjects were induced to lie to the investigator. These subjects had been told by a confederate about the experimental task, the Remote Associates Test, but reported to the investigator that they had not heard about the task. Subsequently, 65% of those who had been induced to lie volunteered, compared to only 35% of those who had not been induced to lie ($p < .05$). In their second study, they arranged to have some of their college student subjects knock over a stack of 1000 note cards that had been prepared for a doctoral dissertation. Of these presumably guilt-ridden subjects, 75% agreed to volunteer compared to 38% of subjects who had not knocked over the note cards ($p < .02$). Somewhat surprisingly, the effects of guilt were much less pronounced when volunteering was to assist the person who had been harmed by the subjects' "clumsiness" than when volunteering was to assist another and unharmed person. Volunteering rates were 60% versus 50% for the guilty versus nonguilty subjects asked to help the harmed person, but they were 90% versus 25% for the guilty versus nonguilty subjects asked to help a nonharmed person. In their third study, an altered replication of their second study, recruiting was always on behalf of the harmed person, but for half the subjects there would be contact with that person and for half the subjects there would be no contact. Overall, the presumably guilty subjects volunteered significantly ($p = .02$) more (56%) than the nonguilty subjects (26%). The effects of guilt were much less pronounced when volunteering required contact with the harmed person (41% versus 35%) than when volunteering did not require contact with the harmed person (73% versus 18%). Although the difference between these differences was not significant in either the second or third studies described, taken together they are very suggestive of the hypothesis that while guilt may increase volunteering, it is more likely to do so when personal contact with the victim can be avoided. Apparently subjects want to atone for their guilt while avoiding the awkwardness of personal contact with their unintended victim.

In their research on the relationship between guilt and volunteering, Wallace and Sadalla (1966) divided their 39 subjects into three groups. In two of these groups, subjects were led to believe that they had ruined a piece of laboratory equipment, but in one group this damage was "detected" by the experimenter and in the other it remained undetected. The third group did not "ruin" the equipment. Of the 13 subjects in each group, only 2 of those who had not ruined the equipment volunteered to participate in a subsequent stress experiment, 5 volunteered from the undetected group, and 9 volunteered from the detected group ($p < .05$). Apparently private guilt may increase volunteering but public guilt may increase it even more.

In his study of the relationship between guilt and volunteering, Silverman (1967) employed much younger subjects: sixth-grade boys and girls from a primarily lower-middle-class background. Children were exposed to the temptation to cheat and then given an opportunity to volunteer for further experiments lasting from one minute to one hour. In every case, volunteering meant sacrificing time from the children's recess. Surprisingly, children who cheated were slightly less likely to volunteer for further research. The difference in results between this study and those summarized earlier might have been the result of the difference in ages or social class of the subjects involved or of the fact that in the earlier studies the subjects' transgressions appeared to harm someone while the cheating of the children in the Silverman study may have been more in the nature of a "victimless crime."

Earlier, in our discussion of material incentives to volunteering, we reported that the enclosure of 25 cents with a questionnaire raised the response rate from 10% to 47% (Hancock, 1940). This dramatic difference in response rates can be interpreted as possibly caused by the operation of guilt. If we assume that very few people would trouble themselves sufficiently to return the 25 cents, then we would have a great many people in possession of money they had done nothing to earn. That might have resulted in guilt feelings for many of the recipients, guilt feelings that might have been reduced by their answering the questionnaire accompanying the unsolicited cash.

Other feeling states than guilt have been employed as independent variables in the study of situational determinants of volunteering. Aderman (1972) found that subjects who had been made to feel elated were considerably more likely to volunteer for research (52%) than subjects who had been made to feel relatively depressed (31%). Holmes and Appelbaum (1970) assigned their subjects to positive, negative, or control experiences and subsequently asked them to volunteer for additional hours of research participation. Subjects who had been exposed to positive experience in the subject role volunteered for significantly more research time (2.0 hours) than did the subjects of the control group (0.7 hours) while those who had been exposed to negative experience in the subject role volunteered slightly more (0.9 hours) than the control group subjects.

In their research, Kazdin and Bryan (1971) examined the relationship between volunteering and subjects' feelings of competence. Subjects made to feel more competent volunteered to donate blood dramatically more (54%) than did the comparison group subjects (21%). A replication of this research found similar results when one research assistant was employed, but obtained no such effect when a different research assistant was employed. Such interactions of experimental manipulations with the person of the data collector are, unfortunately, not particularly rare in the behavioral sciences (Rosenthal, 1966, 1969).

To summarize now the indications bearing on the relationship between volunteering and feeling states, we can be somewhat confident that under certain conditions, subjects feeling guilty are more likely to volunteer for behavioral research. This relationship may be stronger when contact with the subject's unintended victim can be avoided and when the cause of the subject's guilt is public rather than private. In addition, the relationship may not hold for lower-middle-class children who feel they have not harmed another person by their transgression. There is also some evidence to suggest that subjects made to "feel good" or to feel competent are more likely to volunteer for research participation.

NORMATIVE EXPECTATIONS

Volunteering for behavioral research appears to become more likely the more it is viewed as the normative, expected, proper thing to do. One suggestive indication of this hypothesis comes from the experience of psychology departments that, even when they do not require research participation from their students, create a climate of normative expectations that results in reasonably successful recruitment of volunteers for behavioral research (Fraser and Zimbardo, n.d.; Jung, 1969).

A more specific theoretical position has been set out, and a more explicit empirical investigation has been undertaken, by Schofield (1972). In her research, subjects were asked to read and evaluate a number of sex education pamphlets as part of an investigation of their effectiveness. In the normative expectation condition, subjects were led to believe that almost all other subjects had volunteered to read a large number of these pamphlets. Subjects in this condition volunteered to read an average of 18 pamphlets, compared to the subjects of the control condition, who volunteered to read an average of only 14 pamphlets.

In his research, Rubin (1969, 1973b) employed four groups of young couples. Half the couples were rated as being more strongly in love than the remaining couples. Half the couples in each of these two groups were asked to interact with their fellow couple member, and half were asked to interact with an opposite sexed member of a different couple. Subjects from all four groups were then asked to volunteer for a couples T-group experience over a weekend. Three times more couples who were both strongly in love and who had interacted with their fellow couple member volunteered (39%) than did couples who were either less strongly in love (13%) or who were strongly in love but had interacted with a member of a different couple (14%). This higher rate of volunteering may have been brought about by those couples' (i.e., those who were strongly in love and who had been asked to interact with each other) feeling that they were the type whose patterns of interaction during the T-group experience would be of greater interest to scientists studying the behavior of couples in love. Since all the couples in this research program had agreed to help in the scientific task of learning more about couples, those who had been studied as couples and who were strongly in love may have felt most keenly the pressure of normative expectations to participate in the T-group experience.

A relatively extreme case of the effect of normative expectations on volunteering has been documented by Ross, Trumbull, Rubinstein, and Rasmussen (1966). They reported a study in which 34 Naval Reserve officers had volunteered to participate in a two-week seminar on problems of fallout shelters. When the officers arrived for their seminar, they were simply put into a fallout shelter for a five-day experiment. Although the officers were permitted to withdraw from the experiment, the pressure of normative expectations was so great that not one of the men asked to be excused. Normative expectations have also been employed widely in academic contexts. Thus, medical students, medical residents, clinical-psychology interns, and similar groups of advanced students have often been employed in research in which their refusal to "volunteer" would have been regarded as a fairly marked violation of normative expectations (e.g., Esecover, Malitz, and Wilkens, 1961)

There are other studies also suggesting that when other persons are seen by the potential volunteer as likely to consent, the probability increases that the potential volunteer will also consent to participate (Bennet, 1955; Rosenbaum, 1956; Rosenbaum and Blake, 1955). Interestingly, it appears that once the volunteer has consented, he may find it undesirable to be denied an opportunity actually to perform the expected task. Volunteers who were given the choice of performing a task that was either more pleasant but less expected or less pleasant but more expected tended relatively more often to choose the latter (Aronson, Carlsmith, and Darley, 1963).

In summary of the relationship between volunteering and normative expectations, it does seem warranted to suggest as a strong hypothesis that persons are more likely to volunteer for behavioral research when volunteering is viewed as the normative, expected, appropriate thing to do.

PUBLIC VERSUS PRIVATE COMMITMENT

The evidence is equivocal about the relationship between volunteering and whether the commitment to volunteer is made in public or in private. As we might expect, when normative expectations are in support of volunteering, a public commitment to volunteer may result in higher rates of volunteering.

Thus, in Schofield's (1972) experiment, when subjects believed that others would see their written commitment to evaluate sex-education pamphlets, subjects agreed to evaluate 20 pamphlets, compared to only 12 when subjects believed others would not see their written commitment. Consistent with this result was that of Mayer and Pratt (1966), who surveyed persons involved in automobile accidents. Their high rate of returns (about 75%) may have been caused by the respondents' knowledge that their indentities as persons involved in accidents was a matter of public record and that a failure to respond would be known and regarded as a transgression of a normative expectation.

When incentives to volunteer are not very strong, there is evidence to suggest that subjects may volunteer more when volunteering is more private (Blake, Berkowitz, Bellamy, and Mouton, 1956), unless almost everyone else in the group also seems willing to volunteer publicly (Schachter and Hall, 1952). Bennett (1955), however, found no relationship between volunteering and the public versus private modes of registering willingness to participate.

Schachter and Hall (1952) have performed a double service for students of the volunteer problem. They not only examined conditions under which volunteering was more likely to occur but also the likelihoods that subjects recruited under various conditions would actually show up for the experiment to which they had verbally committed their time. The results were not heartening. Apparently it is just those conditions that increase the likelihood of a subject's volunteering that increase the likelihood that he will not show up when he is supposed to. This should serve further to emphasize that it is not enough to learn who will volunteer and under what circumstances. We will also need to learn more about which people show up, as our science is based largely on the behavior of those who do. In the case of personality tests there is evidence from Levitt, Lubin, and Brady (1962) to suggest that pseudovolunteers are psychologically more like nonvolunteers than they are like true volunteers. However, Jaeger, Feinberg, and Weissman (1973) found that pseudovolunteers were psychologically more like volunteers than nonvolunteers.

It is difficult to summarize with confidence the relationship between volunteering and public versus private commitment. If there is a trend in the research evidence, perhaps it is that public commitment conditions increase volunteering when volunteering is normatively expected but decrease volunteering when nonvolunteering is normatively expected.

PRIOR ACQUAINTANCESHIP

There is some evidence that an increase in the potential respondent's degree of acquaintanceship with the recruiter may lead to an increase in volunteering (Norman, 1948; Wallin, 1949). When high school graduates were surveyed, those who responded promptly were likely to have been part of an experimental counseling program in high school that provided them with additional personal attention (Rothney and Mooren, 1952). These students presumably were better acquainted with, and felt closer to, the sponsors of the survey than did the students who had not received the additional personal attention. In his survey of 79 universities known to employ psychological tests, Toops (1926) found those respondents who knew him better personally to return their replies more promptly. Similarly, Kelley (1929) found in his survey of his Stanford University colleagues that replies were more likely to be received from those with whom he was better acquainted. Increases in the acquaintanceship with the investigator may reduce volunteer bias, but there is a possibility that one bias may be traded in for others. Investigators who are better acquainted with their subjects may obtain data from them that is different from data obtained by investigators less well known to their subjects (Rosenthal, 1966). We may need to learn which biases we are better able to assess, which biases we are better able to control, and with which biases we are more willing to live.

Related to the variable of acquaintanceship with the recruiter are the variables of recruiter friendliness or "personalness." Hendrick, Borden, Giesen, Murray, and Seyfried (1972), for example, found that for their seven-page questionnaire higher return rates were obtained when their cover message was more flattering to the respondent as long as the cover message did not also try to be too flattering of the researchers themselves. This effect of flattery, incidentally, did not occur when only a one-page questionnaire was employed. MacDonald (1969) has suggested that the personalness of the recruitment procedure may interact with the birth order of the subject such that firstborns may be more likely to volunteer than laterborns only when recruitment is more personalized.

When attempts to personalize the relationship between recruiter and potential respondent have been relatively superficial, there has usually been no marked effect on volunteering. Thus, the use of respondents' names as a technique of personalization has been judged ineffective by both Clausen and Ford (1947) and by Bergen and Kloot (1968–1969). The latter investigators, however, found an interesting interaction between using respondents' names and the respondents' sex. Among female subjects, using names increased the volunteering rate from 56% to 76%, while using names decreased the volunteering rate from 76% to 71% among male subjects. Although these interaction effects were substantial in magnitude, they could not be shown to be significant, because of the small size of the sample. In his research, Dillman (1972) compared the effects of using metered mail versus postage stamps on the return rates of questionnaires. The assumption was that postage stamps were more personal than postage meters, but no difference in return rates was found.

A summary of the relationship between volunteering and degree of prior acquaintanceship with the recruiter suggests that when subjects actually know the recruiter, they are more likely to agree to participate in the recruiter's research. When subjects are not personally acquainted with the recruiter, the addition of a more personal touch to the recruiting procedure may, under certain conditions that are not yet well understood, also increase the rate of volunteering.

RECRUITER CHARACTERISTICS

Although there is considerable evidence bearing on the unintended effects on research results of a variety of experimenter characteristics (Rosenthal, 1966; 1969), there is no comparably systematic body of data bearing on the effects on volunteering of various personal characteristics of the recruiter. Nevertheless, there are at least suggestive indications that such effects may occur. There are studies, for example, suggesting directly and indirectly that volunteering may be more likely as the status or prestige of the recruiter is increased (Epstein, Suedfeld, and Silverstein, 1973; Mitchell, 1939; Norman, 1948; Poor, 1967; Straits, Wuebben, and Majka, 1972).

A number of investigators have examined the effect on volunteering of the sex of the recruiter. Ferree, Smith, and Miller (1973) found that female recruiters were significantly more successful in soliciting volunteers than were male recruiters. Similarly, Weiss (1968) found that subjects who had been in experiments conducted by female experimenters were significantly more likely to volunteer for further research than were subjects who had been in experiments conducted by male experimenters. Also consistent with these findings were the results reported by Rubin (1973a;in press). He found that female recruiters obtained a volunteer rate of 74%, compared to the rate of 58% obtained by male recruiters ($p < .001$). Rubin also found a tendency for the sex of the recruiter to make a greater difference for female than for male subjects. In addition, for male subjects, the type of task for which volunteering was solicited interacted with the sex of the recruiter. When recruitment was for a study of handwriting analysis, there was no effect of the sex of the recruiter. However, when recruitment was for a study of how people describe themselves, female recruiters obtained a volunteering rate of 67%, while male recruiters obtained a rate of only 45% ($p < .01$). Rubin suggested that this difference might be caused by American men's difficulty in communicating intimately with other men.

A very large study of the interaction of sex of the recruiter and sex of the subject was conducted by Tacon (1965). He employed five male and five female recruiters to solicit volunteering from 980 male and female subjects. When recruiters were of the same sex as the subject, there were significantly more refusals to participate and significantly fewer subjects who actually appeared for the scheduled experiment than when the recruiters were of the opposite sex. These results, although significant ($p < .05$), were quite modest in magnitude. Finally, in an experiment by Olsen (1968), the effects of sex of recruiter were found to interact with the type of task, at least for male subjects. When recruitment was for an experiment in learning, male subjects volunteered more for a female recruiter. When recruitment was for an experiment in personality, male subjects volunteered more for a male recruiter.

There are several other experiments that have investigated individual differences between recruiters in their success at obtaining volunteers. Mackenzie (1969) employed two graduate student recruiters to solicit volunteering among high school students and found that the two recruiters differed significantly in the rates of volunteering obtained. Hood and Back (1971) also found different recruiters to obtain different rates of volunteering but only when the subjects were female. Kazdin and Bryan (1971) also found individual differences in volunteering rates obtained by two recruiters but only in interaction with the level of perceived competence that had been experimentally induced in subjects. Finally, Schopler and Bateson (1965) found that the level of the recruiter's dependency on the subject interacted with the sex of the subject in producing different rates of volunteering. When the recruiter was in great need of help, females volunteered more than when he was less dependent (40% versus 25%). When the recruiter was in great need of help, however, males volunteered less than when he was less dependent (50% versus 71%).

Our summary of the relationship between volunteering and recruiter characteristics must be quite tentative. Although there are a good many studies showing significant individual differences among recruiters in their obtained volunteering rates, there are not enough studies relating obtained volunteering rates to specific recruiter characteristics to permit any firm conclusions. There are some indications, however, that recruiters higher in status or prestige are more likely to obtain higher rates of volunteering. There are also indications that female recruiters may be more successful than male recruiters in obtaining agreement to volunteer. This relationship may be modified, however, by such variables as the sex of the subject and the type of task for which volunteering was solicited.

TASK IMPORTANCE

There is a fair amount of evidence to suggest that volunteering rates are likely to increase when the task for which volunteering is requested is seen as important. There are several ways in which greater task importance can be communicated to the potential volunteer including intensity or urgency of recruitment requests, high status or prestige of the recruiter, and offers of large material incentives. We have already examined the evidence suggesting the latter two variables may serve to increase volunteering rates. Indeed, it appears difficult at times to distinguish between the variables of task importance and material incentives. Thus, we noted earlier that a $35 incentive to volunteer increased the volunteering rate in the research by Levitt, Lubin, and Zuckerman (1962). We cannot distinguish, however, the effects of the magnitude of this generous incentive from the communication to the subjects that this research must be important indeed to warrant so large an expenditure of money on the part of the investigators.

Undergraduate students are generally well aware of the importance to advanced graduate students of the progress of their doctoral dissertation, and Rosenbaum (1956) found substantially greater volunteering for an experiment in which a doctoral dissertation hung in the balance than for an experiment in which a more desultory request was made. Weiss (1968) found that subjects who had been in an experimental condition of higher importance also volunteered more for subsequent research than did subjects in an experimental condition of lower importance. In his research, Wolf (1967) found a modest (but not significant) increase in volunteering when the instructor of the course in which recruitment took place gave his strong endorsement of the research. In the comparison group condition, the instructor was absent, but the fact that recruitment occurred with his knowledge and approval probably meant that the instructor endorsed the research implicitly. This implicit level of endorsement may have decreased the magnitude of the effect of task importance from the effect size that might have been obtained in a comparison of groups receiving strong instructor endorsement versus true instructor neutrality. This experiment by Wolf also illustrates the difficulty of distinguishing sometimes between the variables of task importance and normative expectations. An instructor's strong endorsement bespeaks both his view of the task as important and his explicit expectation that students should volunteer.

Task importance has also been found to interact with sex of subject and with the ingratiation tactics of the recruiter. Thus, Hendrick et al. (1972) found that increasing the perception of the recruiters' seriousness of purpose increased volunteering except when the recruitment message simultaneously flattered the respondent. Schopler and Bateson (1965) found that recruiters in more urgent need of volunteers obtained more volunteering from female subjects but less volunteering from male subjects than did recruiters in less urgent need of volunteers.

Based on his assessment of the literature, Dillman (1972) employed certified mail as a method of increasing the rate of return of his mailed questionnaires, although he did not employ the use of certified mail as an independent variable.

That was done, however, by Sirken, Pifer, and Brown (1960) in their survey of physicians on the topic of death statistics. They found certified mail follow-ups to be 80% effective, compared to the effectiveness of 60% of regular mail. In their survey of the next of kin of the deceased, these workers also found certified mail to be more effective than regular mail. In his follow-up of Fisk University graduates, Phillips (1951) found special delivery letters to be 64% effective, compared to the effectiveness of 26% of ordinary first-class mail. Similar effectiveness of special delivery letters was demonstrated by Clausen and Ford (1947). The use of certified and special delivery letters would appear to be an effective means of emphasizing to potential respondents the importance of the survey at hand and the seriousness of purpose of the researchers. Earlier, in our discussion of small courtesies offered to potential respondents, we noted that the employment of stamped, self-addressed envelopes tended to increase the rate of response (Ferriss, 1951; Price, 1950). One explanation of this result is in terms of the increased convenience to the respondent, but a plausible alternative explanation is in terms of the increased perception of the importance of the survey and the increased urgency of the request to participate.

In summary, there does appear to be a positive relationship between volunteering and level of perceived task importance. The evidence in support of this summary comes not only from studies directly manipulating task importance. Those studies that have varied the status or prestige of the recruiter, or the level of material incentive offered, have also provided evidence, although of a more indirect kind, that adds to the tenability of our tentative conclusion.

SUBJECT INTEREST

More-General Interests

There is a large body of data to suggest that subjects who are more interested in behavioral research, or more interested in and involved with the particular topic under investigation, will be more likely to volunteer. The better to test this and related hypotheses, Adair (1970) developed the Psychology Research Survey, which permits an assessment of the subject's favorableness to psychology. He found that volunteers for behavioral research scored significantly higher in favorableness to psychology than nonvolunteers ($p < .05$, effect size $= .37\sigma$). The differences obtained were somewhat larger when volunteering was requested with no offer of pay and substantially larger than when volunteering was requested for nutritional, rather than behavioral research. Such results add appreciably to the discriminant validation of Adair's measure of favorableness toward psychology.

Even when working with a population of coerced volunteers, Adair's measure of favorableness to psychology was able to discriminate between more- and less-eager participants. Adair found that those subjects who signed up earlier for their required research participation scored significantly higher than did those who signed up later. This study was replicated twice, and the results of one of these replications were significant in the predicted direction, although the results of the other, while also in the predicted direction, did not reach significance. Not only do subjects more favorable to psychology appear to volunteer more, but there are indications as well that once in the experiment they may be more willing to comply with the task-orienting cues of the experiment ($p < .02$; $r = .28$; Adair and Fenton, 1971).

In their research, Kennedy and Cormier (1971) administered their own measures of favorableness to behavioral research and to participating in an experiment, to paid and unpaid volunteers and to subjects who had been required to serve. For both measures, both paid and unpaid volunteers were found to be significantly more favorable in attitude than the subjects who had not volunteered, with effect sizes ranging from $.66\sigma$ to $.35\sigma$. All three groups of subjects were employed in a verbal conditioning experiment that showed greatest conditioning on the part of the unpaid volunteers. This result, although not significant (effect size $= .27\sigma$), is very much in line with the result obtained by Adair and Fenton (1971).

Twenty years before these last two studies were conducted, Rosen (1951) investigated the relationship between volunteering and attitudes toward psychology. Results showed that volunteers found psychology to be significantly more rewarding and enjoyable than nonvolunteers, and they were more favorably disposed toward psychological experiments (median correlation $= .17$). In his more recent research, Ora (1966) found volunteers to be significantly more interested in psychology than were nonvolunteers ($r = .25$).

Employing their own measures of favorableness to scientific research, psychological research, participating as a subject, and the department's policy about research participation, Wicker and Pomazal (1970) investigated the relationship between these attitudes and volunteering for research participation. Results showed no relationship between general attitudes toward scientific or psychological research and volunteering but did show a significant positive relationship ($p < .01$) between volunteering and favorableness toward serving as a subject ($r = .17$) and toward the department's policy on research participation ($r = .19$). Research by Meyers (1972) also showed that volunteers were more favorable to the conduct of experimentation than were nonvolunteers, although this result was not significant statistically, because of the very small sample sizes involved (for $p = .05$, and an effect size of $.50\sigma$, power was only 28%).

In the studies described so far, the investigators examined explicitly the hypothesis that volunteering was more likely by those subjects with attitudes favorable to behavioral research. There are additional studies, however, in which the assessment of attitudes was less direct. Thus, it seems reasonable to suppose that college students majoring in psychology would be more interested in, and more favorably disposed toward, the field than nonmajors. Jackson and Pollard (1966) found in their study of sensory deprivation that twice as many psychology majors volunteered than did other majors. Similarly, Black, Schumpert, and Welch (1972) found far greater commitment to the experimental task on the part of their volunteers (more advanced students) than on the part of their "nonvolunteers" (less advanced students), who were actually a combined group of volunteers and nonvolunteers. Despite the tendency for contrasts between groups of volunteers and of mixed volunteers and nonvolunteers to be diminished by the fact of overlapping memberships, these investigators found the effects on task commitment to be very large (1.56σ). The substantive results of the experiment, incidentally, were greatly affected by volunteer status. Intermittent knowledge of results led to much greater resistance to extinction in perceptual–motor performance than did constant knowledge of results for volunteers (effect size $= 1.41\sigma$) than it did for nonvolunteers (0.56σ).

In their research, Mulry and Dunbar (n.d.) compared subjects participating earlier in the term with those participating later. Perhaps we can view the earlier participants as the more eager volunteers. Results showed that these more eager volunteers spent significantly more time on each of their questionnaire items than did the more reluctant participants. Presumably, the greater amount of time spent per item reflected the greater seriousness of purpose of the more eager volunteers. An interesting additional finding of this study was the very strong tendency ($p < .001$) for the participants believed to be more eager, to arrive earlier for their experimental appointment (eta $= .40$). Additional evidence for the assumption that the early participants were more interested in, and more favorably inclined toward, psychology comes from the finding that although early and later participants did not differ in general ability (SAT scores), the early participants earned significantly higher psychology course grades than did the later participants ($p < .025$; effect size $= .40\sigma$). The greater interest and involvement of volunteers as compared to nonvolunteers is also suggested in the work of Green (1963). He found that when subjects were interrupted during the performance of their task, volunteers recalled more of the interrupted tasks than did nonvolunteers. Presumably the volunteers' greater involvement and interest facilitated their recall of the tasks that they were not able to complete.

More-Specific Interests

In the studies considered so far, investigators have examined the relationship between volunteering and somewhat general attitudes toward behavioral research. We consider now the research relating volunteering to more-specific attitudes toward particular areas of inquiry. We consider first the area of hypnosis. Boucher and Hilgard (1962) and Zamansky and Brightbill (1965) found that subjects holding more-favorable attitudes toward hypnosis were more likely to volunteer for hypnosis research, although Levitt, Lubin, and Zuckerman (1959) found results in the opposite direction but not significantly so. Particularly threatening to the validity of inferences drawn from studies employing volunteer subjects are the results of several studies showing that volunteers may be more susceptible to hypnosis than nonvolunteers (Bentler and Roberts, 1963; Boucher and Hilgard, 1962; Coe, 1964; Shor and Orne, 1963; Brightbill and Zamansky, 1963; Zamansky and Brightbill, 1965). In a number of these studies, the effect sizes were substantial; as large as $.75\sigma$ in the research of Shor and Orne (see also Hilgard, 1965).

The literature of survey research also suggests greater willingness to participate by those more favorable toward, or more interested in, the topic under investigation. Persons more interested in radio and television were found to be more likely to answer questions about their listening and viewing habits (Belson, 1960; Suchman and McCandless, 1940). When Stanton (1939) inquired about teachers' use of radio in the classroom he found that those who owned radios were more likely to respond. Reid (1942) replicated Stanton's research twice but with a sample of school principals rather than teachers. In one of his studies he found no difference in the use of radio in the classroom between those responding earlier to his questionnaire and those more leisurely in their response. In his other study, however, Reid found that earlier responders owned more radios and used them significantly more than did later responders. In a related result, Rollins (1940) found in a survey on the use of commercial airlines that early responders were more than twice as likely as later responders to have flown.

Consistent results have also been obtained in studies of sex behavior, religion, and public policy. Diamant (1970), Kaats and Davis (1971), and Siegman (1956) all found volunteers to be sexually more experienced and/or sexually more permissive than nonvolunteers. These results were not only significant statistically but in some cases very large in magnitude. Thus, Siegman found that 92% of his volunteers advocated sexual freedom for women, while only 42% of his nonvolunteers did so. Matthysse (1966) wrote follow-up letters to research subjects who had been exposed to proreligious communications. He found respondents to be those who regarded religious matters as relatively more important. Benson (1946) obtained data suggesting that in studies of public policy, respondents may be overrepresented by individuals with strong feelings against the proposed policy—a kind of political protest vote. In their research, Edgerton, Britt, and Norman (1947), Franzen and Lazarsfeld (1945), Gaudet and Wilson (1940), Mitchell (1939), and Scott (1961) all concluded that responders to surveys tended to be more interested in the topic under study than the nonresponders.

The vast majority of studies of the relationship between volunteering and interest on the part of the potential respondent are correlational rather than experimental. Few investigators have experimentally varied respondents' degree of interest or involvement, but Greenberg's (1956) rare exception showed that such investigations may prove valuable. His approach was to employ argumentative role-playing to increase respondents' ego-involvement. These respondents then went on to provide the investigator with more information, fewer stereotyped answers, more thoughtful answers, and fewer "don't knows."

Organizational and Interpersonal Bonds

Another body of literature supports the hypothesis that volunteering is a positive function of subjects' degree of interest and involvement in the content of the research. In this body of literature, the subject's interest is defined in terms of his level of activity in, and affiliation with, formal organizations or his level of commitment and favorableness to interpersonal relationships that are the subject of the investigation. Table 3-2 summarizes the results of these studies, which are grouped into four sets on the basis of the definition of interest or involvement. In the first set of seven studies, interest was defined by the subject's level of activity in such local organizations as colleges, unions, and churches and in such national organizations as the League of Women Voters. In six of the seven studies, subjects who volunteered were more active in their relevant organization, such activity ordinarily being part of the information requested by the sponsors of the research. The one exception to this general trend was obtained by Lawson (1949), who investigated the topic of gambling in England. He found that bookmakers, who presumably were vitally interested in gambling, responded substantially less often (9%) than did any other group contacted (up to 48%). That result, of course, runs counter to our hypothesis, but there are other results in the Lawson study that do support our hypothesis. Thus, among three groups of clergymen, ordered on the degree to which their positions were strongly against gambling, most returns were obtained from clergymen whose position was most strongly against gambling (44%) and fewest returns were obtained from clergymen least opposed to gambling (13%). Clergymen who held intermediate positions against gambling showed an intermediate rate of response (26%). As a possible example of

Table 3-2. Studies of the Relationship Between Volunteering and Subjects' Interest as Defined by Organizational and Interpersonal Bonds

Organizational Bonds

Level of activity:	*Degree of affiliation:*
Donald (1960)	Britton and Britton (1951)
Laming (1967)	Kish and Barnes (1973)
Larson and Catton (1959)	Lehman (1963)
Lawson (1949)[a]	Wallace (1954)
Phillips (1951)	
Schwirian and Blaine (1966)	
Wicker (1968a)	

Interpersonal Bonds

Favorableness to treatment:	*Commitment to partner:*
Carr and Whittenbaugh (1968)	Hill, Rubin, and Willard (1973)
Kaess and Long (1954)[b]	Kirby & Davis (1972)
Kish and Herman (1971)	Rubin (1969, pp. 197–198)
	Locke (1954)

[a] Results in opposite direction.
[b] No difference obtained.

professional courtesy stands the additional finding that of all groups contacted, psychologists showed the highest response rate (48%).

In the second set of four studies of Table 3-2, interest was defined by the subject's degree of affiliation with the organization about which questions were asked and/or which directly sponsored the research (e.g., college attended by one's children, YMCA, and *Time* magazine). The results of all four studies were consistent with the interest hypothesis.

In the third set of three studies of Table 3-2, interest was defined by the subject's favorableness to treatment procedures as measured by his continuation in, or benefit from, his treatment. Two of the three studies were in support of the interest hypothesis. In the fourth set of four studies, all involving research on couples, interest was defined by subjects' degree of commitment to their partners; all four studies were in support of the interest hypothesis.

Of the 18 studies listed in Table 3-2, 16 were in support of the interest hypothesis (usually at the .05 level), 1 showed no relationship between interest and volunteering, and 1 showed a result in the opposite direction. Even this last study, however, yielded some additional results that were in support of the interest hypothesis. For most of the studies listed, the volunteering rates for the more- and less-interested subjects were available. The median volunteering rate for the more interested persons was 57%, compared to the median rate for the less-interested persons of only 28%. In terms of magnitude of effect, then, the interest or involvement of the subject appears to be one of the most powerful determinants of volunteering.

Survey research literature is rich with suggestions for dealing with potential sources of volunteer bias. One practical suggestion offered by Clausen and Ford (1947) follows directly from the work on respondent interest and involvement. It was discovered that a higher rate of response was obtained if, instead of one topic, a number of topics were surveyed in the same study. People seem to be more willing to answer a lot of questions if at least some of the questions are on a topic of interest to them. Another, more standard technique is the follow-up letter or follow-up telephone call to remind the subject to respond to the questionnaire. However, if the follow-up is perceived by the subject as a bothersome intrusion, then, if he responds at all, his response may reflect an intended or unintended distortion of his actual beliefs. The person who has been reminded several times to fill out the same questionnaire may not approach the task in the same way as he would if he had been asked only once, although Eckland (1965) has shown that high levels of prodding need not necessarily lead to the production of data that are factually inaccurate.

Finally, there is another extensive body of literature that bears directly and indirectly on the relationship between volunteering and subjects' level of interest in the topic under investigation. That is the literature (examined in Chapter 2) showing very clearly that better-educated persons are more likely to volunteer for participation in behavioral research. In some of the studies the questionnaires dealt specifically with the respondents' level of education, so that the assumption appears warranted that a more educated person would be more interested in a survey involving educational experience. In other studies, questionnaires did not deal specifically with respondents' level of education but with a wide variety of matters. The assumption we must make in these cases to bring them to bear on the interest hypothesis is that better educated persons are generally more interested in a wider variety of topics than are less well educated persons. That assumption does not appear to be farfetched, however. A similar line of reasoning also brings to bear on the interest hypothesis the additional and related bodies of literature showing more intelligent persons and those scoring higher on social-class variables to be more likely to volunteer for behavioral research.

In summarizing the results of the research on the relationship between volunteering and subjects' level of interest in the topic under investigation, we can be unusually brief and unusually unequivocal. Not only do interested subjects volunteer more than uninterested subjects, but the size of the effect appears to be substantial.

EXPECTATION OF FAVORABLE EVALUATION

In this section we shall examine the evidence suggesting that subjects are more likely to volunteer when they have reason to believe that they will be evaluated favorably by the investigator. When a subject is invited to volunteer, he is asked to make a commitment of his time for the serious purposes of the investigator. The responses subjects will be asked to make during the course of their participation in the research will make the investigator wiser about the subject without making the subject wiser about the investigator. Within the context of the psychological experiment, Riecken (1962) has referred to this as the "one-sided distribution of information." On the basis of this uneven distribution of information the subject or respondent is likely to feel an uneven distribution of legitimate negative evaluation.

From the subject's point of view, the investigator may judge him to be maladjusted, stupid, unemployed, lower class, or in possession of any one of a number of other negative characteristics. The possibility of being judged as any one of these might be sufficient to prevent someone from volunteering for either surveys or experiments. The subject, of course, can, and often does, negatively evaluate the data-collector. He can call the investigator, his task, or his questionnaire inept, stupid, banal, and irrelevant but hardly with any great feeling of confidence as regards the accuracy of this evaluation. After all, the data-collector has a plan for the use of his data, and the subject or respondent usually does not know this plan, although he is aware that a plan exists. He is, therefore, in a poor position to evaluate the data-collector's performance, and he is likely to know it.

Although few would deny the importance of other motivations of the subject in behavioral research, there is wide agreement among investigators that one of the important motives of the research subject is to "look good." Riecken has suggested that one major aim of the research subject is to "put his best foot forward." Rosenberg (1965, 1969) has shown the importance to an understanding of the social psychology of behavioral research of the concept of "evaluation apprehension." Other investigators have further increased our understanding of this concept, broadly defined, through both their empirical efforts and their theoretical analyses (e.g., Adair, 1973; Argyris, 1968; Belt and Perryman, 1970; Kennedy and Cormier, 1971; Sigall, Aronson, and Van Hoose, 1970; Silverman and Shulman, 1970; Weber and Cook, 1972). While the bulk of the work in this area is of recent vintage, sophisticated theoretical attention was accorded this and related motives of the research subject by Saul Rosenzweig (1933) before many of the above investigators were born.

If research participants are indeed so concerned with what the investigator will think of them, we would expect them to volunteer more when their expectation is greater that they are likely to be evaluated favorably by the investigator. The evidence suggests strongly that such is indeed the case. Table 3-3 lists 19 studies showing greater volunteering when subjects are in a position to say more favorable things about themselves (or their children). The studies

Table 3-3.   Studies of the Relationship Between Volunteering and Favorableness of Self-Reports About Achievement and Adjustment

Achievement	Adjustment
Barnette (1950a, b)	Anastasiow (1964)
Baur (1947–1948)	Ball (1930)
Bradt (1955)	Loney (1972)
Cope (1968)	Milmoe (1973)
Eckland (1965) I	Speer and Zold (1971)
Eckland (1965) II	
Edgerton, Britt, and Norman (1947)	
Gannon, Nothern and Carroll (1971)	
Jones, Conrad, and Horn (1928)	
Kelley (1929)	
Kirchner and Mousley (1963)	
Rothney and Mooren (1952)	
Shuttleworth (1940)	
Toops (1926)	

listed in the first column are those in which the favorable self-reports were about occupational or educational achievement. Those listed in the second column are those in which the favorable self-reports were about psychiatric or gender-related adjustment. Although not all the studies listed in Table 3-3 showed the differences to be significant statistically, all the studies showed greater volunteering by those who had more favorable things to say about themselves in terms of achievement or adjustment. Not only are the results remarkably consistent in direction, but they also suggest that the effect sizes may be quite substantial. For eight of the studies, the volunteering rates of those with more versus less favorable things to say about themselves were available. The median rates were 84% and 49%, respectively.

    Further support for the hypothesis under examination comes from three studies that could not be easily subsumed under the headings of Table 3-3. Mayer and Pratt (1966), in their survey of persons involved in automobile accidents, found higher response rates by those who had been passengers, rather than drivers, of automobiles involved in accidents. Presumably passengers could not be considered to be at fault, and nothing they reported could serve to implicate them, an advantage not shared by those who had been driving when the accident occurred. Wicker (1968a), in his survey of church members, found those more likely to respond who could report more favorably on their attendance at church. Finally, in what was perhaps the only investigation that specifically varied the independent variable of probability of favorable evaluation, Olsen (1968) found significantly greater volunteering when subjects were more likely to be favorably evaluated (36%) than when they were less likely to be favorably evaluated (15%).

Olsen's study is especially important because in so many of the other studies summarized it is not possible clearly to differentiate the variable of expectation of favorable evaluation from the variables of subject interest, intelligence, education, and social class. Subjects may be more interested in things in which they have done well, and we are usually in no position to say whether it is their interest or their having done well that prompts them to respond by participating in our research. Better-educated, more-intelligent subjects and those classified as higher in social class are by common cultural definition in a position to say "better" things about themselves than those less well educated, less intelligent, or those classified as lower in social class. The very clear results showing higher rates of volunteering by those more interested in the research area, by those who are better educated or more intelligent, and by those classified as higher in social class may, in a sense, provide additional support for the hypothesis that volunteering rates increase with the increased expectation of favorable evaluation.

Our summary of the relationship between volunteering and expectation of favorable evaluation can be brief and unequivocal. Increased expectation of favorable evaluation by the investigator not only increases the probability of volunteering but it appears to increase that probability to a substantial degree.

SUMMARY OF SITUATIONAL DETERMINANTS OF VOLUNTEERING

In this chapter we have examined the evidence bearing on the relationship between volunteering and a variety of more-or-less situational variables. The evidence has not always been as plentiful or as direct as it was in the case of the relationship between volunteering and more-or-less stable characteristics of the potential participant in behavioral research. Nevertheless, there appears to be sufficient evidence to permit a summary of the present stage of our knowledge.

Table 3-4 lists the situational determinants of volunteering by the degree of confidence we can have that each is indeed associated with volunteering. Four groups of determinants are discriminable, and within each group the determinants are listed in approximately descending order of the degree of confidence we can have in the relationship between volunteering and the listed determinant. The definition of degree of confidence was based both on the number of studies relevant to the relationship under consideration and on the proportion of the relevant studies whose results supported a directional hypothesis. To qualify for "maximum confidence" a relationship had to be based on at least 20 studies, and at least 6 out of 7 studies had to be in support of the relationship. To qualify for "considerable confidence" a relationship had to be based

Table 3-4.   Situational Determinants of Volunteering Grouped by Degree of Confidence of Conclusion

Maximum confidence:
 1. Subject interest
 2. Expectation of favorable evaluation
Considerable confidence:
 3. Task importance
 4. Guilt, happiness, and competence
 5. Material incentives
Some confidence:
 6. Recruiter characteristics
 7. Aversive tasks
 8. Normative expectations
Minimum confidence:
 9. Prior acquaintanceship
10. Public versus private commitment

on at least 10 studies, and at least two-thirds had to be in support of the relationship. To qualify for "some confidence" a relationship had to be based either on 3 studies all of which were in support of the relationship or on 9 studies most of which were in support of the relationship with none showing a significant reversal of the relationship. Relationships not meeting these minimum standards are listed under the heading of "little confidence." We conclude our summary with a listing of the conclusions that seem warranted by the evidence, taking into account the effects of various moderator variables where these are suggested by the data. The order of our listing follows that shown in Table 3-4, beginning with the conclusions warranting maximum confidence and ending with the conclusions warranting minimum confidence. Within each of the four groups, the conclusions are also ranked in approximate order of the degree of confidence we can have in each.

Conclusions Warranting Maximum Confidence

1.   Persons more interested in the topic under investigation are more likely to volunteer.
2.   Persons with expectations of being more favorably evaluated by the investigator are more likely to volunteer.

Conclusions Warranting Considerable Confidence

3.   Persons perceiving the investigation as more important are more likely to volunteer.

4. Persons' feeling states at the time of the request for volunteers are likely to affect the probability of volunteering. Persons feeling guilty are more likely to volunteer, especially when contact with the unintended victim can be avoided and when the source of guilt is known to others. Persons made to "feel good" or to feel competent are also more likely to volunteer.

5. Persons offered greater material incentives are more likely to volunteer, especially if the incentives are offered as gifts in advance and without being contingent on the subject's decision to volunteer. Stable personal characteristics of the potential volunteer may moderate the relationship between volunteering and material incentives.

Conclusions Warranting Some Confidence

6. Personal characteristics of the recruiter are likely to affect the subject's probability of volunteering. Recruiters higher in status or prestige are likely to obtain higher rates of volunteering, as are female recruiters. This latter relationship is especially modifiable by the sex of the subject and the nature of the research.

7. Persons are less likely to volunteer for tasks that are more aversive in the sense of their being painful, stressful, or dangerous biologically or psychologically. Personal characteristics of the subject and level of incentive offered may moderate the relationship between volunteering and task aversiveness.

8. Persons are more likely to volunteer when volunteering is viewed as the normative, expected, appropriate thing to do.

Conclusions Warranting Minimum Confidence

9. Persons are more likely to volunteer when they are personally acquainted with the recruiter. The addition of a "personal touch" may also increase volunteering.

10. Conditions of public commitment may increase rates of volunteering when volunteering is normatively expected, but they may decrease rates of volunteering when nonvolunteering is normatively expected.

SUGGESTIONS FOR THE REDUCTION OF VOLUNTEER BIAS

Our review of the literature bearing on situational determinants of volunteering suggests fairly directly a number of steps that may prove to be useful in reducing the magnitude of volunteer bias. A list of recommendations, offered in a tentative spirit and subject to further empirical test, follows:

1. Make the appeal for volunteers as interesting as possible, keeping in mind the nature of the target population.

2. Make the appeal for volunteers as nonthreatening as possible so that potential volunteers will not be "put off" by unwarranted fears of unfavorable evaluation.

3. Explicitly state the theoretical and practical importance of the research for which volunteering is requested.

4. Explicitly state in what way the target population is particularly relevant to the research being conducted and the responsibility of potential volunteers to participate in research that has potential for benefiting others.

5. When possible, potential volunteers should be offered not only pay for participation but small courtesy gifts simply for taking time to consider whether they will want to participate.

6. Have the request for volunteering made by a person of status as high as possible and preferably by a woman.

7. When possible, avoid research tasks that may be psychologically or biologically stressful.

8. When possible, communicate the normative nature of the volunteering response.

9. After a target population has been defined, an effort should be made to have someone known to that population make the appeal for volunteers. The request for volunteers itself may be more successful if a personalized appeal is made.

10. In situations where volunteering is regarded by the target population as normative, conditions of public commitment to volunteer may be more successful; where nonvolunteering is regarded as normative, conditions of private commitment may be more successful.

A hasty reading of these recommendations gives the impression that they are designed only to increase rates of volunteering and thus to decrease volunteer bias. A more careful reading reveals that the recommendations may have other beneficial effects as well. They should make us more careful and thoughtful not only in how we make our appeals for volunteers but in our planning of the research itself. Our relations with our potential subjects may become somewhat more reciprocal and more human, and our procedures may become more humane. Finally, if we are to tell our subjects as much as possible about the significance of our research as though they were another granting agency, which in fact they are, granting us time instead of money, then we will have to give up trivial research.

CHAPTER 4

Implications For The Interpretation Of Research Findings

We concentrate now on the implications of the preceding discussions for the validity of inferred causal relationships in behavioral research and their generalizability beyond the particular circumstances in which they were demonstrated. Cook and Campbell (1974) have drawn a useful distinction between several threats to the tenability of inferred relationships in behavioral experimentation, and their typology encompasses this difference. The good experiment, they have observed, clearly establishes the temporal antecedence of the causal relationship; is strong enough to demonstrate that cause and effect covary; rules out alternative explanations and confounding variables; and is sufficiently representative to assure the robustness of the causal relationship. In our earlier discussions we examined studies that focused on voluntarism as a dependent variable, from which we could postulate some likely personality and demographic differences between willing and unwilling subjects as well as situational determinants of volunteering. Now we treat volunteer status as an independent variable and explore how such differences can in fact make a difference in the interpretation of research findings. We begin, however, with a consideration of the dilemma prompted by recent ethical concerns in psychology and their ramifications for the control of sampling errors in general.

AN ETHICAL DILEMMA

What is called *error* in behavioral experimentation will depend on the purposes of the research (Winer, 1968). Error may be an independent variable and the main object of study in one case, a randomly occurring source of imprecision in another, and a systematic source of bias in a third. Speculating on the life cycle of inquiries into the nature of nonrandom errors like volunteer bias,

McGuire (1969a) described three stages he named *ignorance, coping,* and *exploitation.* Initially, researchers seem unaware of the variable producing systematic error and may deny its existence. Once it becomes certain that the variable exists, means of coping with it are sought and attention focuses on techniques for reducing its contaminating influence. In the third stage, the variable is seen as a significant independent factor in its own right and not just an unintentional contaminant to be eliminated: "Hence, the variable which began by misleading the experimenter and then, as its existence became recognized, proceeded to terrorize and divert him from his main interest, ends up by provoking him to new empirical research and theoretical elaboration" (McGuire, 1969a, pp. 15–16).

If this cycle has accelerated in the case of the volunteer variable, it may be the result of the sense of urgency attached to ethical concerns that have been voiced with increasing frequency of late. At the root of those concerns is a question about the personal responsibilities of scientists for assuring the moral acceptability of their research. Beecher (1970) and Kelman (1965, 1967, 1968, 1972), among others, have examined the issue in depth as it applies to medical and psychological experimentation, and the ramifications of certain proposed ethical guidelines for research with human subjects have been articulated in symposia as well as in the journals (c.f. Sasson and Nelson, 1969). Lately, some of that discussion has shifted from a concern over ethical precautions to the conviction that there must be legal guarantees made that research subjects (including informed volunteers) be assured of compensation and financial protection against mental and physical risks (Havighurst, 1972; Katz, 1972).

Impetus was lent to this important issue in 1954 as a result of Edgar Vinacke's comments in the *American Psychologist.* Vinacke questioned the ethicality of "dissimulation" experiments, studies where "the psychologist conceals the true purpose and conditions of the experiment, or positively misinforms the subjects, or exposes them to painful, embarrassing, or worse, experiences, without the subjects' knowledge of what is going on" (p. 155). While recognizing the methodological desirability of naïvety in subjects, Vinacke asked whether it was not time to consider the ethical bounds of experimental deceptions:

> So far as I can tell, no one is particularly concerned about this. . . . In fact, one can note an element of facetiousness. It has reached the point where a man who reads a paper at the APA convention is almost embarrassed when he adds, with a laugh, that the subjects were given the "usual" post-session explanations. . . . What is at stake? Do subjects really feel happy about their experiences in some of these emotionally stressful experimental situations, even after a standardized attempt to reassure them? What possible effects can there be on their attitudes toward psychologists, leaving out entirely any other consequences? Beyond this, what sort of reputation does a laboratory which relies heavily on deceit have in the university and community where it operates?

What, in short, is the proper balance between the interest of science and the thoughtful treatment of the persons who, innocently, supply the data? . . . Perhaps it is going too far to propose that an APA committee be appointed to look into the ethical precautions to be observed in human experimentation, but it is a possibility.

The zeitgeist may not have been propitious for such an inquiry in 1954, but the time was certainly ripe a decade and a half later when a committee of psychologists was formed by the American Psychological Association (APA) to draft a set of ethical guidelines for research with human subjects (Cook, Kimble, Hicks, McGuire, Schoggen, and Smith, 1971, 1972). The final version, comprised of the following ten principles adopted by the APA Council, was published in January 1973, in the APA journal *American Psychologist:*

1. In planning a study the investigator has the personal responsibility to make a careful evaluation of its ethical acceptability, taking into account these Principles for research with human beings. To the extent that this appraisal, weighing scientific and humane values, suggests a deviation from any Principle, the investigator incurs an increasingly serious obligation to seek ethical advice and to observe more stringent safeguards to protect the rights of the human research participant.

2. Responsibility for the establishment and maintenance of acceptable ethical practice in research always remains with the individual investigator. The investigator is also responsible for the ethical treatment of research participants by collaborators, assistants, students and employees, all of whom, however, incur parallel obligations.

3. Ethical practice requires the investigator to inform the participant of all features of the research that reasonably might be expected to influence willingness to participate, and to explain all other aspects of the research about which the participant inquires. Failure to make full disclosure increases the investigator's responsibility to maintain confidentiality, and to protect the welfare and dignity of the research participant.

4. Openness and honesty are essential characteristics of the relationship between investigator and research participant. When the methodological requirements of a study necessitate concealment or deception, the investigator is required to ensure the participant's understanding of the reasons for this action and to restore the quality of the relationship with the investigator.

5. Ethical research practice requires the investigator to respect the individual's freedom to decline to participate in research or to discontinue participation at any time. The obligation to protect this freedom requires special vigilance when the investigator is in a position of power over the participant. The decision to limit this freedom increases the investigator's responsibility to protect the participant's dignity and welfare.

6. Ethically acceptable research begins with the establishment of a clear and fair agreement between the investigator and the research participant that clarifies the

responsibilities of each. The investigator has the obligation to honor all promises and commitments included in that agreement.

7.The ethical investigator protects participants from physical and mental discomfort, harm and danger. If the risk of such consequences exists, the investigator is required to inform the participant of that fact, to secure consent before proceeding, and to take all possible measures to minimize distress. A research procedure may not be used if it is likely to cause serious and lasting harm to participants.

8.After the data are collected, ethical practice requires the investigator to provide the participant with a full clarification of the nature of the study and to remove any misconceptions that may have arisen. Where scientific or humane values justify delaying or withholding information, the investigator acquires a special responsibility to assure that there are no damaging consequences for the participant.

9.Where research procedures may result in undesirable consequences for the participant, the investigator has the responsibility to detect and remove or correct these consequences, including, where relevant, long-term aftereffects.

10.Information obtained about the research participants during the course of an investigation is confidential. When the possibility exists that others may obtain access to such information, ethical research practice requires that this possibility, together with the plans for protecting confidentiality, be explained to the participants as a part of the procedure for obtaining informed consent.

Of particular interest from a methodological standpoint are those four principles (3 through 6) advocating informed, volitional consent. Apart from questions about (1) the merits, real or apparent, of such recommendations (Baumrind, 1964, 1971, 1972; Beckman and Bishop, 1970; Gergen, 1973; Kerlinger, 1972; May, 1972; Seeman, 1969), (2) whether or not they could be legislated and the legislation effectively enforced (Alumbaugh, 1972; Pellegrini, 1972; Smith, 1973), and (3) who should be delegated the role of ethical ombudsman (Adams, 1973), there is also scientific interest in whether compliance with the letter of the law could accidentally introduce an element of error that might jeopardize the tenability of inferred causal relationships. To reveal to a subject the exact substance of the research in which he is participating might distort his reaction and thus ultimately limit the applicability of the findings.

A study by Resnick and Schwartz (1973) is empirically illustrative of the nature of the problem. The experiment centered on a simple, widely used verbal-conditioning task developed by Taffel (1955) as a method for repeating the operant conditioning effects demonstrated by Greenspoon (1951) and Ball (1952) in a more controlled fashion. All the subjects in Resnick and Schwartz' study were volunteers half of whom had been forewarned as to the exact nature of the Taffel procedure following provisional APA guidelines, and the rest of whom had not. The subject and the experimenter were seated at opposite sides of a table, and the experimenter passed a series of 3-by-5-inch cards to the subject one at a time. Printed on each card was a different verb and six pronouns (I, WE, YOU, THEY, SHE, HE); the subject was told to construct a sentence containing the verb and any of the six pronouns. On the first 20 (operant) trials the experimenter remained silent. On the following 80 trials he reinforced the subject with verbal approval ("Good" or "Mmm-hmmm" or "Okay") every time a sentence began with I or WE. The difference in results between the two groups is shown in Fig. 4.1. The uninformed subjects conditioned as had been expected, but those who had been fully informed along APA standards showed a reversal in the conditioning rate. (Every set of differences between groups was significant beyond the .01 level for blocks 1–4, and the groups were not different at the operant level; a significant trend over trials was reported for both the informed and uninformed groups.) One plausible explanation for the difference was that subjects in the informed group may have become suspicious about the "real" demands of the study when its purpose was spelled out for them so blatantly, and feeling their freedom of response restricted by that awareness, their frustrations may have led them to respond counter to the experimenter's expressed intent. Does ethically forewarning subjects trigger paranoid ideation in otherwise trusting individuals? Resnick and Schwartz mentioned that several subjects in the informed group said they felt they were involved in an elaborate double-reverse manipulation; none of the uninformed subjects expressed this belief. One wonders how different our current laws of verbal learning might be if all the earlier studies in this

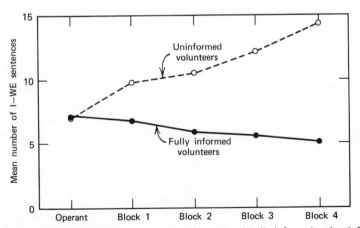

Fig. 4-1. Mean number of I–WE sentences constructed by ethically informed and uninformed subjects (after Resnick and Schwartz, 1973).

area had been carried out under the conditions of informed consent that Resnick and Schwartz inferred from the APA ethical code.

These research findings emphasize the complexity of the ethical dilemma. Fully informed voluntarism, at the same time that it may satisfactorily cope with one ethical concern, could be contraindicated for another. Pity the poor experimenter confronted with a conflict of values in which he must weigh the social ethic against the scientific ethic and decide which violation would constitute the greater immorality. Should the current social temper of the times persist, an already complicated issue may become increasingly more complex in the future. Given whatever strengths are added to the civil libertarian movement in psychology by a society also properly concerned with individual rights, could this unprecedented soul-searching ultimately lead to a behavioral science whose data were drawn from an elite subject corps of informed volunteers? Kelman (1972, p. 1006) has talked about a "subjects' union" and a "bill of rights" for research subjects, and Argyris (1968) mentioned that enterprising students at two universities have also started thinking in this direction with the notion of organizing a group along the lines of Manpower, but which, instead of secretaries, would offer informed volunteers to interested experimenters:

> They believe that they can get students to cooperate because they would promise them more money, better de-briefing, and more interest on the part of the researchers (e.g., more complete feedback). When this experience was reported to some psychologists their response was similar to the reactions of business men who have just been told for the first time that their employees were considering the creation of a union. There was some nervous laughter, a comment indicating surprise, then another comment to the effect that every organization has some troublemakers, and finally a prediction that such an activity would never succeed because "the students are too disjointed to unite" (p. 189).

However, perhaps we need not end on an overly pessimistic note. Is it possible that some of these fears by psychologists could be a projection of their own stringent ethical views? So the results of a study by Sullivan and Deiker (1973) would suggest. These investigators compared the questionnaire responses of a sample of American psychologists with those of undergraduate students at Louisiana State University and Wheaton College to assess their perceptions of ethical issues in human research. The respondents were each presented with a hypothetical experiment from among a group of experiments characteristically varying in stress, physical pain, or the threat to a subject's self-esteem, and the questions to the respondents focused on ethical issues. For example, the students were asked if they would have volunteered for the experiment had they known its exact nature; they were also asked whether the deception involved seemed to them unethical. The psychologists were also questioned on the propriety of using deception, and they had to say whether subjects showing up for the experiment would have volunteered otherwise. Surprising certainly to most psychologists at least, the students' answers revealed a high percentage of volunteering even after aversive aspects of the studies became known. And, in general, there was a discernible difference in the reported perceptions of the professionals and the students that showed the psychologists as having the more stringent ethical views. If ever a decision need be made about who should regulate what happens in our experiments, one favoring the professional psychologist should produce the more conservative watchdogs according to these data. (Both groups, incidentally, most often identified as unethical the offering of course grades as a pressure to get more students to participate as research subjects.)

THE THREAT TO ROBUSTNESS

We began this book by reiterating McNemar's familiar assessment of psychology as "the science of the behavior of sophomores" and emphasized his concern, voiced more than a quarter of a century ago, that college students were being used so exclusively by research psychologists as to seriously restrict the robustness of experimental findings in psychological research. In light of the idea of unionizing research subjects and organizing informed volunteers for interested experimenters, McNemar's observation may now seem too conservative an assessment. A science of informed and organized volunteer sophomores may be on the horizon. It will be recalled from Chapter 1 that, as McNemar ascertained, a very large chunk of the research on normal adults may be restricted to the reactions of college undergraduates (see Table 1-1). Since no one can be certain of all the significant ways in which college students as research subjects may differ from the rest of the population, one can only speculate on the dangers of conveniently tapping the most accessible universe (Higbee and Wells, 1972; White and Duker, 1971). Smart warned:

Such students are probably at the peak of their learning and intellectual abilities and this could mean that many findings in learning, especially verbal learning, could be special to the college student with limited applicability to other groups. Some might argue that only the speed of learning would be different in the college population, and that the general principles of learning would be the same in any group. However, the college student is selected for verbal learning ability and we have little evidence that this is a trivial consideration. We have little indication that the public school graduate or high school drop-out learns according to the same principles, because the question has never been investigated (1966, pp. 119–120).

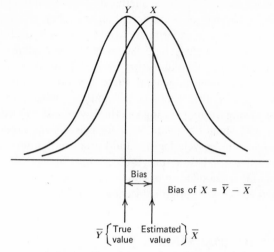

Fig. 4-2. The curve symbolized as Y represents a theoretical normal distribution of IQs in the general population, and the curve labeled X represents a theoretical normal distribution of IQs among volunteers. To the extent that the mean of X is different from the mean of Y, the resultant bias constitutes a threat to the generalizability of the data.

The threat to generalizability from using volunteer subjects can be seen as a specific case of sampling bias. To the extent that a pool of volunteers was different from the population at large, the resulting positive or negative bias could lead to an overestimate or underestimate of population parameters. See, for example, Fig. 4.2, which depicts roughly the positive bias that might result from using other than random sampling to estimate IQ parameters. We noted that volunteers scored higher on intelligence tests than nonvolunteers. If one relies entirely on volunteer subjects to standardize norms for an IQ test, it follows that the estimated population mean could be artificially inflated by this procedure. Merely increasing the size of the sample would not reduce such bias, although improving the representativeness of sampling procedures certainly should (Kish, 1965).

Another illustration of this type of sampling bias was described by Maslow and Sakoda (1952), who hypothesized that Kinsey's survey research findings on human sexual behavior were distorted by the interviewees' volunteer status. For example, Diamant (1970) has shown that estimates of premarital sexual behavior can be inflated when only volunteer subjects are interviewed. He found college-age male volunteers more apt to report having experienced sexual intercourse than male nonvolunteers and also to be significantly more permissive than the nonvolunteers in their attitudes about sex. Similar results were reported by Kaats and Davis (1971) and by Siegman (1956). Kinsey and his associates conducted a series of intensive interviews of about 8,000 American men and 12,000 American women in order to uncover the predominant sexual customs in the United States (Kinsey, Pomeroy, and Martin, 1948; Kinsey, Pomeroy, Martin and Gebhard, 1953). Their fascinating findings became a source of intense discussion and controversy when the question of sampling representativeness was raised by critics (Cochran, Mosteller, and Tukey, 1953; Dollard, 1953; Hyman and Sheatsley, 1954). Might Kinsey's interviewees, by virtue of their willingness to cooperate in the research, have shared other characteristics that distinguished them from the rest of the population and thereby restricted the generality of the data? Maslow and Sakoda explored this idea empirically in a study they designed with Kinsey. It was arranged for Kinsey to set up an office near the Brooklyn College campus and for Maslow to make an appeal for volunteers in his psychology classes. This made it possible to compare the volunteers and nonvolunteers and see how they differed in ways that could affect the generalizability of Kinsey's data. Earlier, Maslow (1942) had discovered that people who are high in self-esteem often have relatively unconventional sexual attitudes and behavior, and he and Sakoda now observed that students who volunteered for the Kinsey interview tended to be higher in self-esteem than nonvolunteers. Based on this correlational evidence, Maslow and Sakoda concluded that there may have been an overestimation of population means in Kinsey's original data because his subjects had all been willing participants.

Of course, it is also possible to conceive of situations where population means were underestimated because volunteer subjects were used. Since volunteers are generally less authoritarian than nonvolunteers, standardizing a test that correlated positively with authoritarianism on volunteer subjects should yield underestimates of the true population mean. The important point is that insofar as any of the variables discussed in Chapter 2 (see again Tables 2-41 and 2-42) may be conceived as a threat, directly or indirectly, to generalizability when the subjects are willing participants, there might automatically result estimates of population parameters that were seriously in error. In the same way, we might expect that routinely sampling just volunteer subjects in behavioral research should jeopardize the robustness of any research conclusions if the subjects' educational background, social class, intelligence, need for social approval, sociability, and so on, could be indicted as pertinent differentiating characteristics related to the estimation of parametric values for the research problem in question. In studies involving any sort of stress, the subjects' sex, arousal-seeking inclinations, and anxiety could be crucial differentiating characteristics affecting the estimation of parameters. In clinical research, nonconformity may be suspect; in medical research, the subjects' psychological adjustment; in laboratory behavioral experimentation, their age; and so on.

MOTIVATIONAL DIFFERENCES AND REPRESENTATIVENESS

There is another side to this problem, which has to do with the naturalistic motivations of human beings. Some scaling research to be discussed in the next chapter suggests that nonvolunteer types of subjects may amplify the distinction between work and nonwork activities and judge research participation as a work-oriented experience. This may help to account for why such subjects are ordinarily so unenthusiastic about participating in psychology experiments when they are unpaid captives, and it might suggest that nonvolunteers would also be less cooperative in real-life work situations where they were forced to participate without personal financial benefits. From this slightly different perspective, volunteer status might be seen as merely another organismic variable, like all the other myriad variables that affect human behavior. Indeed, insofar as volunteer status as an organismic variable was related to the dependent variable of an investigation, the study of voluntarism could be the raison d'être for the research (cf. Sommer, 1968; Sarason and Smith, 1971). Illustrative of this point was an experiment by Horowitz (1969) on the effects of fear-arousal on attitude change.

A fear-appeal is a persuasive communication that arouses emotional tensions by threatening the recipient in some way and then providing a conclusion reassuring him of relief should he change his attitude in the recommended direction. It is a technique commonly used by political propagandists. For example, in the 1972 American presidential campaign, which saw Richard M. Nixon running against George McGovern, one anti-McGovern television spot showed a hand sweeping away toy soldiers and miniature ships and planes while a voice announced, "The McGovern defense plan—he would cut the Marines by one-third; he would cut Air Force personnel by one-third and interceptor planes by one-half; he'd cut Navy personnel by one-fourth, the Navy fleet by half and carriers from 16 to 6." The announcer then recalled a statement about McGovern made by Sen. Hubert H. Humphrey during the presidential primaries, when the two Democrats were fiercely competing for their party's nomination, "It isn't just cutting into the fat, it isn't just cutting into manpower, it's cutting into the very security of this country." Finally, the spot shifted to President Nixon aboard a Navy ship, visiting troops in Vietnam. With "Hail to the Chief" playing in the background, the message concluded, "President Nixon doesn't believe we should play games with our national security; he believes in a strong America to negotiate for peace from strength; that's why we need him now more than ever." An earlier application of essentially the same political stratagem was a Democratic-sponsored TV spot in the 1964 presidential campaign that showed a little girl plucking petals from a daisy while a voice was heard gloomily counting down to zero. As the last petal disappeared, the screen was filled with a frightening atomic explosion and

President Lyndon Johnson's voice was heard saying, "These are the stakes . . . to make a world in which all of God's children can live, or go into the dark . . . we must either love each other, or we must die." The message concluded with the announcer urging viewers to vote for Johnson: "The stakes are too high for you to stay home." In both cases, the idea was to evoke a feeling of anxiety by associating the opponent's view—Sen. George McGovern or Sen. Barry Goldwater—with some highly threatening event whose probability of occurrence would purportedly increase were he elected to the presidency. Emotional relief was provided by the reassuring recommendation at the end, that voting for the incumbent president was the surest way to avoid disaster.

In communications research, a question of long standing has been the effect of inducing emotional tensions by persuasion on attitude change pursuant to the fear-arousing message (cf. Rosnow and Robinson, 1967, p. 147ff.). Is attitude change directly or inversely proportional to the amount of anxiety aroused by a fear-appeal? What would be the effect of a persuasive communication inducing greater (or lesser) emotional tension? Would compliance be greater if the threat to personal security were more strongly emphasized? Most present-day research on these questions grew out of an experiment by Janis and Feshbach (1953) using three different intensities of fear in a communication on dental hygiene. Their results showed that while all three forms were equally effective in teaching factual content, the greatest compliance was to the position advocated in the least threatening communication. Presumably, communications that elicit a great deal of fear or anxiety may provoke a defensive reaction that interferes with acceptance of the message; hence, the greater the threat, the less attitude change in the recommended direction. While several studies have supported the Janis–Feshbach relationship (DeWolfe and Governale, 1964; Haefner, 1956; Janis and Terwilliger, 1962; Kegeles, 1963; Nunnally and Bobren, 1959), others have suggested the opposite relationship: the more fear, the more attitude compliance (Berkowitz and Cottingham, 1960; Insko, Arkoff, and Insko, 1965; Niles, 1964; Leventhal, Singer, and Jones, 1965; Leventhal and Niles, 1964), and there have been various alternative proposals for adjudicating this difference in outcomes (Janis, 1967; Leventhal, 1970; McGuire, 1966, 1968a,b, 1969b).

In examining this literature closely, Horowitz (1969) noticed that experiments that used volunteers tended to produce the positive relationship between fear-arousal and attitude change, whereas experiments using captive subjects tended toward the inverse relationship. Reasoning that volunteers and nonvolunteers may be differentially disposed to felt emotional–persuasive demands, Horowitz then studied the difference in persuasability of willing and unwilling subjects by randomly assigning them to two groups, in one of which there was a high level of fear aroused and in the other of which there was a low level of fear aroused. (There was manother aspect to the experiment; it dealt with the number of exposures to the materials, but it is not relevant to the present discussion.) The high-fear group read pamphlets on the abuse and effects of drugs and watched two Public Health Service films on the hazards of LSD and other hallucinogens and the dangerous effects of amphetamines and barbiturates. The low-fear group did not see the films; they read pamphlets on the hazards of drug abuse, but the vivid verbal descriptions of death and disability were omitted. To measure the subjects' attitude changes, they were all administered a postexperimental questionnaire asking them to respond anonymously to 10-point scales corresponding to recommendations contained in the persuasive appeals. Also, to provide a check on the different levels of emotional arousal presumed to be operating in the two groups, the subjects responded to another scale ranging from "It did not affect me at all" to "It made me greatly concerned and upset."

The check on the manipulation of fear-arousal revealed that the treatments were successful ($p < .01$) and that the volunteers were significantly more affected by the arousal manipulations than were the nonvolunteers (effect size $= .74\sigma$). More important, though, the attitude-change data clearly indicated that voluntarism was a crucial organismic variable for assessing the generality of the fear-arousal relationship. Volunteers exhibited greater attitude compliance than nonvolunteers ($p < .01$, effect size $= 1.01\sigma$), and as shown in Fig. 4.3, the predicted positive relationship between fear-arousal and influenceabil-

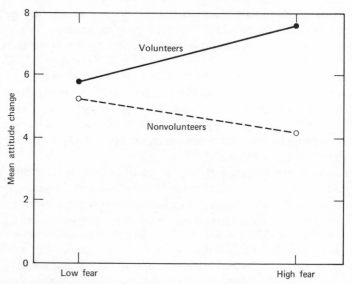

Fig. 4-3. Mean attitude changes of volunteers and nonvolunteers in response to low and high fear-appeals. The higher the attitude-change score, the more congruent was the postexperimental attitude with the position advocated in the fear-appeals (after Horowitz, 1969).

ity was obtained for volunteers (effect size $= .91\sigma$) and the expected inverse relationship for nonvolunteers (effect size $= .47\sigma; p < .01$). The illuminating methodological contribution of this study is its empirical emphasis on the fact that the validity of behavorial data must always be interpreted within the operating motivational context (cf. Adair, 1971; Oakes, 1972).

THE THREAT TO THE VALIDITY OF INFERRED CAUSALITY

Voluntarism as an organismic variable complicates interpretation of the generalizability of research data; the threat it poses to the validity of inferred causal relationships is no less serious. For example, if volunteer status correlated with the dependent variable of a study, the reduction in individual variation of subjects on the criterion variable owing to the increased homogeneity of the experimental and control groups could result in nonrejection of the null hypothesis when it was actually false. Suppose we wanted to assess the validity of a new educational procedure that was purported to make people less rigid in their thinking. A simple way of testing this hypothesis would be to compare volunteers who were randomly assigned to a control group with others who were assigned to an experimental group that was administered the new procedure. However, people who are low in authoritarianism (as volunteers apparently are) may also be less rigid in their thinking (Adorno, Frenkel-Brunswik, Levinson, and Sanford, 1950), and it therefore follows that our control subjects could already be unusually low on the dependent variable. The effect in this case, which would be to minimize the true difference between the experimental and control groups, would increase the likelihood of a type-II error.

It is also possible to imagine volunteer situations in which one was led to make the opposite type of error. Suppose someone wanted to find out how persuasive a propaganda appeal was before using it in the field. Again, a simple procedure would be to expose volunteers to the appeal and compare their reactions with a control group of unexposed subjects. If the magnitude of opinion changes in the exposed group significantly exceeded changes occurring in the control, one would probably conclude that the propaganda was an effective persuasive device. However, we noted before that volunteers tend to be higher in the need for approval than nonvolunteers, and people who score high in approval-need apparently are more readily influenced than low-scorers (Buckhout, 1965; Crowne and Marlowe, 1964). Hence, it follows that the volunteers who were exposed to the propaganda could have overreacted to it and that the comparison of their change scores with those in the control group may have exaggerated the true impact of the propaganda. There is a more subtle side to the problem of the validity of research conclusions that these *Gedanken* experiments allude to only very indirectly; it concerns errors systematically occurring in behavorial research because of its social nature.

Demand Characteristics

The results of experimental research can be attributed to controlled and uncontrolled sources. Controlled sources are conditions that are experimentally imposed or manipulated; uncontrolled sources are conditions left untreated and conceptualized as random errors when their own antecedents cannot be specified and as artifacts, or systematic errors—the two terms are interchangeable—when their antecedents are known (McGuire, 1969a; Rosnow, 1971). Complexities of human behavior that can be traced to the social nature of the behavioral research process can be seen as a set of artifacts to be isolated, measured, considered, and sometimes reduced or eliminated. Such complexities stem from the fact that subjects are usually aware that they are being studied and that their role is to be played out in interaction with another human being, the investigator.

An early discussion of the general threat to validity resulting from this special role relationship was Rosenzweig's 1933 paper in *Psychological Review* on the psychology of the experimental situation. In this perceptive account, Rosenzweig considered several ways in which psychological experimentation had more inherent complexities than research in the natural sciences, complexities resulting from the fact that "one is obliged to study psychological phenomena in an intact conscious organism that is part and parcel of a social environment" (p. 337). For instance, one peculiarity of psychological experimentation is that the "thing" being studied, the research subject, has motives, and they may propel him in directions that could threaten the validity of research conclusions. When self-report measures are used, as is typically the case in attitude research, there could be a disruptive interaction of the subject's observational set and the experience he was reporting about. "It is the interdependence of the experimentally imposed conditions and the contribution of the individual personality which must, in the last analysis, serve as the basis for interpreting experimental results," Rosenzweig (1952, p. 344) advised in a subsequent paper on the artifact problem.

Several of Rosenzweig's ideas have appeared in the important research and writings of other, more contemporary "artifactologists" (cf. Silverman and Shulman, 1970). Some of the most impressive research in this area is that of Martin Orne (1969, 1970) on the biasing effects of subjects' compliance with the demand characteristics of the experimental situation. Orne's contention is that a principal motive in this situation is cooperation and that research subjects, and perhaps volunteers especially, play out their experimental roles guided by an altruistic wish to help science and human welfare in general. The term *demand characteristic,* which derived from Kurt Lewin's (1929) concept of *Aufforderungscharakter* (Orne, 1970), refers to the totality of task-orienting cues that govern subjects' hypotheses about role expectations. According to this view, a person who agrees to be a subject in an experiment also implicitly agrees to cooperate with a wide range of actions without questioning their purpose or duration, and almost any request should automatically be justified by the fact that it was "part of an experiment" (Orne, 1962a, p. 777). To illustrate, Orne (1970) explored the idea that subjects in experimental hypnosis will behave in whatever ways they think are characteristic of hypnotized individuals. To test this hypothesis, he concocted a novel characteristic of hypnotic behavior—"catalepsy of the dominant hand." This experimental demand was then demonstrated to a large college class in a lecture on hypnosis using three "volunteers" who had been previously hypnotized and given a posthypnotic suggestion that the next time they entered hypnosis they would exhibit a waxen flexibility of their dominant hand. In another class, the same lecture on hypnosis was given except that there was no mention of catalepsy. One month later, students from both classes were invited to participate as research subjects in an experiment. When they came to the laboratory and were hypnotized by the experimenter, catalepsy of the dominant hand was exhibited by almost all the subjects who had attended the lecture, suggesting that catalepsy was characteristic of the hypnotized state. None of the subjects who had attended the control lecture showed this phenomenon.

Other research has shown similar effects of compliance with demand characteristics. Silverman (1968) randomly assigned undergraduates to four groups that read a 250-word argument in favor of using closed-circuit television tapes to give lectures to large classes. He found that the students showed more persuasibility when they were told that they were subjects in an experiment than if this demand was not explicitly conveyed to them and that they complied more when they had to sign their opinions than when they were tested anonymously. Page (1968) manipulated demand characteristics in a figure –ground perception experiment and found that subjects, particularly those having some elementary knowledge of psychology, were apt to respond in the ways they thought the experimenter anticipated they should behave. Other studies have probed the contaminating influence of demand characteristics in such varied contexts as prisoners' dilemma games (Alexander and Weil, 1969), attitude change (Kauffmann, 1971; Page, 1970; Rosnow, 1968; Sherman, 1967; Silverman and Shulman, 1969), verbal operant conditioning (Adair, 1970; Levy, 1967; Page, 1972, White and Schumsky, 1972) and classical conditioning (Page, 1969; Page and Lumia, 1968), the autokinetic effect (Alexander, Zucker, and Brody, 1970; Bruehl and Solar, 1970), hypnosis and sensory deprivation (Coe, 1966; Jackson and Kelley, 1962; Orne, 1959, 1969; Orne and Scheibe, 1964; Raffetto, 1968), perceptual defense (Sarbin and Chun, 1964), psychophysics (Juhasz and Sarbin, 1966), taking tests (Kroger, 1967), comparative psychotherapeutic evaluations (McReynolds and Tori, 1972), autonomic activity (Gustafson and Orne, 1965; Orne, 1969), and small-group research on leadership and conformity (Allen, 1966; Bragg, 1966; Geller and Endler, 1973; Glinski, Glinksi, and Slatin, 1970; Leik, 1965). This collection of studies emphasizes the ubiquitous threat to the tenability of research conclusions stemming from the peculiar role relationship between subject and experimenter in behavioral research.

The Role of Research Subject

The conception of research subjects' performances as role behaviors is an idea that originated in the sociological contention that human performance is affected by the social prescriptions and behavior of others. The theory of role, which sprang from the dramaturgical analogy, argues that social behavior can be conceived as a response to demands associated with specific propriety norms and that individual variations in performance can be expressed within the framework created by these factors (Thomas and Biddle, 1966); that is, people occupy different positions—the position of experimenter or research subject, for example—and situational regularities in their behavior are a function, in part, of the prescribed covert norms and overt demands associated with such positions and of certain mediating factors (for example, their original willingness to accept the position) that could make them more-or-less compliant with role expectations (cf. Alexander and Knight, 1971; Biddle and Thomas, 1966; Jackson, 1972; Sarbin and Allen, 1968).

If we may proceed on the assumption that within the context of our Western culture the transitional role of research subject in a psychology experiment is now well understood by most normal adults who find their way into our experiments (cf. Epstein, Suedfeld, and Silverstein, 1973) and that the stereotypic role expectation associated with this position is that of an alert and cooperative individual (or the "good subject"), then it is possible to recast these ideas in a social-influence mold and provide a simple model to depict the role behavior of research subjects in response to demand characteristics. Some recently gathered evidence for this assumption also implies that the good-subject stereotype may be well ingrained. With the assistance of Susan Anthony and Marianne Jaeger, the question, "How do you think the typical human subject is expected to behave in a psychology experiment?" was directed to 374 experimentally naïve Pennsylvania high school boys and girls, who responded by circling any characteristics they wished from a list of positive and negative ones (Aiken and Rosnow, 1973). There was a high degree of similarity in the male and female rankings ($\rho = .90$, $p < .0001$), and the collective results (which were alluded to in Chapter 2 in connection with the differentiating characteristics of self-disclosure and altruism) are summarized in Table 4-1. Although it was revealed that none of the students had ever participated as a subject in a psychology study or could recall ever having been asked to do so, the image of this role projected in their minds was congruent with the assumption above. "Cooperative" and "alert" were the most frequently circled characteristics, and the only others noted by the majority of students—"observant," "good-tempered," "frank," "helpful," "trustful," "logical"—also reinforce the good-subject stereotype.

Of course, not all subjects will automatically conform to this role expectation, just as not all human beings will consistently conform to societal norms (Latané and Darley, 1970; Macaulay & Berkowitz, 1970), although recalcitrant subjects may be relatively rare in our experimental studies. If one imagines a continuum representing the range of compliance to what we presume is the prescribed behavior usually associated with the role of research subject, it would be the intensely eager and cooperative subject who anchors the compliance end of the continuum (cf. Rosnow, 1970) and the recalcitrant type who anchors the counter-compliance end. Neither type is probably all that common, however; most of our volunteers and even our coerced research subjects in psychology probably fall somewhere around the middle or between the middle and the compliance end.

One way of conceptualizing these role enactments was to view the reaction to demand characteristics as the dependent variable in a social-influence paradigm where the predominant sources of artifact operate via a few main interv-

TABLE 4-1. Characteristics Ranked According to the Percentage of Students Who Circled Them in Response to the Question, "How do you think the typical human subject is expected to behave in a psychology experiment?" Percentages Are Given in Parentheses (After Aiken and Rosnow, 1973).

1. (78) cooperative	20. (16) sophisticated	39. (9) self-possessed
2. (72) alert	(16) idealistic	(9) wholesome
3. (60) observant	22. (15) outspoken	41. (8) amusing
4. (57) good-tempered	(15) wordy	42. (7) eccentric
(57) frank	24. (14) argumentative	(7) irrational
6. (56) helpful	(14) daring	44. (6) egotistical
7. (52) logical	(14) impressionable	(6) shy
(52) trustful	27. (13) jumpy	(6) boastful
9. (43) efficient	(13) excited	47. (5) painstaking
10. (42) agreeable	(13) crafty	(5) careless
11. (41) conscientious	30. (12) gracious	(5) unsocial
12. (39) useful	(12) grateful	50. (4) daydreamer
13. (38) curious	(12) untiring	51. (3) prudent
14. (34) confident	33. (11) nonconforming	(3) childish
15. (30) good	(11) moody	(3) impolite
(30) loyal	(11) excitable	(3) petty
17. (24) punctual	(11) disturbed	55. (2) disrespectful
18. (19) inoffensive	(11) irritable	(2) impractical
(19) critical	38. (10) touchy	(2) wasteful

ening variables, and there is a detailed discussion of this artifact-influence model in Chapter 6. For present purposes, it will suffice to say that voluntarism as an artifact-independent variable is presumed to operate on the motivational mediator in the chain, the subject's acquiescent, counteracquiescent, or nonacquiescent response-set pursuant to demand characteristics.

Volunteer Status and the Motivation Mediator

There are alternative possibilities as to how experimental performances could be affected by this action. For example, it might be thought that volunteers and nonvolunteers would be differentially responsive to task- and ego-orienting cues. This hypothesis was first elaborated by Green (1963), who sought to clarify some of the conditions that promote and inhibit the psychological phenomenon in which people tend to recall a larger proportion of interrupted than completed tasks (cf. Zeigarnik, 1927). Green wondered if volunteers, because they would be curious about, and interested in, the experimental task, might therefore be strongly disposed to comply with task-orienting cues. Captive nonvolunteers, on the other hand, might be more oriented to ego cues in order to paint a good picture of themselves, for Green reasoned that it could have been those subjects' concerns about being unfavorably evaluated that led them to reject the volunteering solicitation in the first place and that being drafted into an experiment could intensify their ego needs and bolster ego responsiveness. Given that willing and unwilling subjects may indeed be motivationally different in their concerns with task- and ego-orienting cues, does it follow then that volunteers and nonvolunteers would be differentially responsive to demand characteristics? In an experimental situation where demand characteristics were operating in conflict with ego-orienting cues, would volunteers' and nonvolunteers' contrasting motivations guide their experimental performances in ways that could threaten the tenability of research conclusions? For example, say that they perceived cooperative behavior as likely to result in an unfavorable assessment of their intellectual capacities. How would this cognition affect the experimental behaviors of volunteers and nonvolunteers? Would they react differently to the motivational dilemma, volunteers perhaps being the demand responsive subjects and nonvolunteers, the ego-responsive subjects? Silverman (1965) has also discussed this possibility, and Vidmar and Hackman (1971) raised it again recently in discovering that their volunteer subjects in a small-group interaction study produced longer written products than did a replication group of conscripted subjects. The volunteers also complained more about not having sufficient time to work on the experimental tasks—findings that are certainly suggestive of a stronger task-oriented set.

An alternative hypothesis can be derived with reference to the concept of approval-need. We posited that volunteers have a relatively high approval-need, and it has been shown that high-need-for-approval subjects have a high affiliation-need (Crowne and Marlowe, 1964). One means of satisfying the affiliation need could be found in volunteering for certain kinds of research participation, although once committed to participating, the volunteer's approval motivation might emerge as the prepotent determiner of his experimental behavior. Crowne and Marlowe drew a parallel between what is sometimes an unusually favorable self-image that some subjects project and the characters in Eugene O'Neill's play *The Great God Brown*. It is especially those subjects who have a high need for social approval who fit this image. The characters in O'Neill's play wear masks to conceal their identities from each other, just as volunteers may hide aspects of their true personality, projecting instead a more uniformly favorable image that seems likely to gain them the social approval they desire. To the extent that their experimental behavior was uncharacteristic of their naturalistic behavior, a threat to the tenability of any conclusions drawn from the experimental data would be posed. Such subjects could be initially different from the rest of the population because of their high approval-need, and this need could contribute further to invalidation by motivating them to respond to demand characteristics in ways that could distort their reactions to the experimental treatment.

There is other work that also tentatively links voluntarism to the motivation mediator. In a study of the effects of signaled noncontingent rewards on human operant behavior, Remington and Strongman (1972) administered contingent or random presentations of a conditioning stimulus and an unconditioned stimulus to college volunteers, while the subjects worked on a time-related baseline schedule of reinforcement. In contrast to earlier studies in which operant acceleration was obtained on differential reinforcement of low rates schedules (DRL) and a suppression on variable interval schedules (VI), their subjects on DRL showed no effect, while those on VI showed a response facilitation—which the authors tentatively interpreted as the result of a volunteer species-by-schedule interaction. Brower (1948) compared the performances of volunteers and captive subjects in a visual–motor skills experiment where the task was to traverse a brass-plate apparatus with a stylus under three conditions: (1) when the subjects could directly observe their own performance, (2) when they could only observe their performance through a mirror, and (3) when blindfolded. The volunteers consistently made fewer errors than the captive subjects (although differences in mean error rates were significant at the .05 level only in conditions 2 and 3), results that, together with earlier findings, Brower thought indicative of the influence of motivational differences connected with the recruitment procedures. In a similar vein, a study by Cox and Sipprelle (1971) also has argued for the link between voluntarism and experimental motivation. Unable to replicate a finding by Ascough and Sipprelle (1968) demonstrating operant control of heart rate without the subjects' (verbalized) awareness of the stimulus–response contingency, Cox and Sipprelle set about to discover the reason for their failure. Wondering if it could have been because of differences in motivation between the two subject pools —Ascough and Sipprelle having used undergraduates who volunteered for the experiment, and the replication failure being based on the responses of coerced subjects—Cox and Sipprelle experimented with using a small monetary incentive to elicit responding from their unwilling subjects. Each time there was a verbal reinforcement, the subject was awarded a penny. Examining some of the collective findings from the two studies, which are shown in Fig. 4.4, statistically similar rates of autonomic conditioning were obtained among verbally reinforced volunteers and a small group of nonvolunteers who were both verbally and monetarily reinforced, and these comparable rates were significantly different from those obtained among verbally conditioned nonvolunteers and a noncontingent control group. Interpreting the combined results as evidence that an acquired reinforcer can compensate for an initial lack of motivation, the investigators' conclusions, which were stated in the context of their failure to replicate the earlier findings, conveyed the notion that the

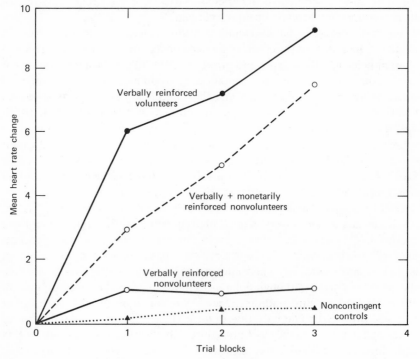

Fig. 4-4. Combined accelerate and decelerate heart rate changes (after Cox and Sipprelle, 1971).

replication failure was seen somehow as less "internally" valid than results with the experimentally motivated subjects; that is, they implied that the results might jeopardize the validity of inferred causality, as opposed to the generalizability of the presumed relationship.

Finally, Black, Schumpert, and Welch (1972) compared voluntary and nonvoluntary subjects in a perceptual–motor skills experiment with a slight twist. The subjects had to track a target circle on a pursuit rotor, and they were assigned to groups with a predetermined level of feedback for their performance. Thus, one group of subjects got 100% feedback; another, 50%; a third, no feedback; and a fourth group, complete feedback but only after the initial set of trials. The novel aspect to the study was that the subjects were told that they could drop out whenever they began to feel bored. As one might anticipate from the preceding studies, the volunteers showed considerably more staying power than did the nonvolunteers; and the more feedback the subjects got, the more persistent did the volunteers become.

Although these studies tentatively link voluntarism with the motivation mediator, it should be recognized that the results could just as easily be interpreted in the context of external as internal validity, to draw upon Campbell's (1957) familiar distinction that external validity refers to sampling representativeness and internal validity to the plausible existence of a causal relationship. The discussion now shifts to findings that are more directly indicative of the influence of this artifact-independent variable on the validity of inferred cause-and-effect relationships in behavioral research.

CHAPTER 5

Empirical Research on Voluntarism as an Artifact-Independent Variable

So far, with the exception of the study by Horowitz (Chapter 4), our discussion of the threat from subjects' volunteer status to the validity of inferred causality has been speculative. Conjectures were derived mainly from a knowledge of characteristics that distinguished willing from unwilling subjects, from which it was possible to hypothesize different types of error outcomes. In this chapter, we summarize the main results of a series of studies that experimentally probed the subtle influence of this artifact in psychological experimentation. We begin with three exploratory studies that were designed to determine whether volunteer status actually had any marked influence on experimental outcomes and to identify possible circumstances in which this biasing effect could be reduced. We then describe an experiment that demonstrated the sort of type-I–type-II confounding postulated earlier and next a study that linked voluntarism as an artifact-independent variable more definitely with the motivation mediator. We then turn to the question posed earlier concerning whether willing and unwilling subjects are differentially responsive to task- and ego-orienting cues, and finally we examine the role expectations of voluntary and nonvoluntary subjects.

Before proceeding to a discussion of this program of research, it may be useful to reemphasize an important idea about the nature of the volunteer construct that is apparently a source of confusion for some psychologists. A recent criticism of this research by Kruglanski (1973) has argued that because there are many reasons why a person might or might not volunteer to participate in behavioral research, volunteer status is, therefore, a nonunitary construct and, hence, "of little possible interest." That is a troublesome chain of logic, however, as it would make much of psychology, perhaps most of it, "of little interest." Patients who commit suicide, for example, do so for many different reasons; yet it is quite useful to characterize certain behaviors as

142

suicidal. Suicide prevention centers have been established throughout the United States to conduct research and provide services for this class of persons who do what they do for many different reasons. People score high or low on the California F Scale, the Taylor Manifest Anxiety Scale, the MMPI scales, CPI scales, and various tests of ability, interest, and achievement, all for a variety of reasons, including many situational determinants. It would be a mistake to conclude that persons cannot usefully be grouped on the basis of their test scores, their suicidal status, or their willingness to participate in behavioral research, because their scores or their status may have multiple determinants.

However, perhaps the basic difficulty in grasping this idea lies in the confusion between constructs and measures thought to be related to constructs. One does not, of course, compute the reliability of constructs but of measures. And, as noted earlier, when the measure of volunteering is simply stating one's willingness to participate, the reliabilities for volunteering range from .67 to .97—values that compare very favorably with the reliabilities of virtually any type of psychological test. When reliability is defined in terms of volunteering for sequentially different types of tasks, significant reliabilities are again obtained (Barefoot, 1969; Laming, 1967; Rosen, 1951; Wallace, 1954; median correlation $= .42$, every $p < .05$). The magnitudes of correlation are comparable to those found between subtests of standard tests of achievement and intelligence (cf. Rosnow and Rosenthal, 1974). Our point is that the exclusion from psychological theory of constructs that are not "unitary" might not be prudent, since this implies the abandonment of such constructs as intelligence, which have been studied profitably for decades employing orthogonal factor structures (i.e., nonunitary elements).

Although there were minor variations in procedure, a similar overall design was used in all the following studies. Since college undergraduates are apparently the most frequently used research subjects in social and experimental psychology (Higbee and Wells, 1972; Schultz, 1969; Smart, 1966), the subjects were culled from sections of introductory courses in behavioral science. They were identified as willing or unwilling subjects by their having been asked to volunteer for a psychology experiment. By comparing the names of the students who signed up for the experiment with the class roster, we could label subjects as volunteers and nonvolunteers (although in some cases the nonvolunteer groups may have contained a few absentee volunteers). In order to establish whether there were any differences in experimental outcome or in ratings of role expectations between willing and unwilling subjects, the reactions to an entirely different experimental treatment in which they all participated, or their responses to a questionnaire, were then subdivided according to the subjects' volunteer status. There was, of course, a potential danger in this procedure of comparing *verbal* volunteers and nonvolunteers, since not everyone who signs up for an experiment will show up for his appointment. Cope and Kunce (1971) discovered differences in some linguistic behaviors between early shows and later shows, some of the latter being subjects who missed an earlier appointment and had to be rescheduled. Indeed, to the extent that verbal voluntarism could be confounded by this pseudovolunteering artifact, observed differences might be overestimates or underestimates of true differences between willing and unwilling subjects. While the collective data on the problem are equivocal, as discussed in Chapter 2, still they suggest that inferred experimental differences between true volunteers and nonvolunteers would probably be underestimated by this verbal voluntarism comparison (e.g., Conroy and Morris, 1968; Jaeger, Feinberg, and Weissman, 1972; Levitt, Lubin, and Brady, 1962).

EXPLORATORY RESEARCH

Study 1

The first study explored whether volunteer status could have a biasing effect on experimental outcomes that might jeopardize the validity of inferred causal relationships, as it was not firmly established yet that this artifact variable was of more than passing theoretical concern. The possibility was investigated in a traditional attitude-change experiment in which we sought to determine whether volunteers responded any differently to a persuasive communication than nonvolunteers (Rosnow and Rosenthal, 1966).

The subjects were 42 undergraduate women, 20 of whom had been identified as volunteers by their affirmative response to a request for psychological research subjects. Initially, they were all administered a lengthy opinion survey in which were embedded four 7-point items about American college fraternities. One week later, the subject pool was randomly divided into three groups. Two of these groups heard and read a pro- or antifraternity argument and the third group served as a noncommunication control. At the conclusion of the treatment, attitudes toward social fraternities were again measured and each subject was asked to guess the purpose of the study. (The subjects' perceptions were generally in agreement about the experimenter's persuasive intent, although not a single subject mentioned the voluntarism solicitation or said anything that might imply that she drew a connection between the attitude manipulation and the recruitment procedure.)

Table 5-1 gives the mean attitude changes of volunteers and nonvolunteers in the three treatment groups. Overall, the direction of change was toward whichever side was advocated ($p < .005$), although volunteers changed more than nonvolunteers if the communication was antifraternity (effect size = .72

Table 5-1. Mean Attitude Changes of Volunteers and Nonvolunteers. (After Rosnow and Rosenthal, 1966)[a]

	Profraternity Argument	Antifraternity Argument	Control Group
Volunteers	+1.7	−3.5[b]	+0.4
Nonvolunteers	+2.5[b]	−1.2	−0.9
Mean changes	+2.1[b]	−2.4[c]	−0.3

[a] Positive scores reflect profraternity attitude gains and negative scores, antifraternity gains. Means differed from their respective control group mean at the indicated p level.
[b] $p < .05$.
[c] $p < .10$.

σ) and less so if the communication was profraternity (effect size $= .26\sigma$). The interaction p was less than .05, the magnitude of this effect being 1.7σ units, or about twice the size of what Cohen (1969) would call large.

A simple explanation for the reversal would have been that voluntarism correlated with initial attitude scores. Recalling the discussion in Chapter 2, if volunteers are more sociable than nonvolunteers, perhaps volunteers also are more favorably disposed in their attitudes toward social fraternities. Because the volunteers in this study could have been far to the positive side of the attitude scale, there may have been little room for them to move much further in the profraternity direction; maybe the antifraternity side was the only open direction in which their attitudes could sway. On the other hand, if volunteers initially leaned more in the antifraternity direction than nonvolunteers, this too could account for the reversal as the volunteers might then have been more receptive to the antifraternity arguments than those that were counter to their original attitudes. In either case, an attitude difference between volunteers and nonvolunteers on the pretest questionnaire would automatically raise doubts about the methodological significance of a treatment $\times$ volunteer status interaction. In fact, however, the data provided no basis of support for either generalization; a comparison of the pretest scores revealed only a negligible difference between the volunteers and nonvolunteers, neither group's original attitudes deviating very far from the middle of the scale.

Another tentative explanation for the reversal was that the volunteers, possibly because of their higher approval-need, were more strongly motivated than the nonvolunteers to confirm what they thought to be the experimenter's hypothesis. If volunteers are more accommodating to demand characteristics than nonvolunteers and if the subjects perceived the (faculty) communicator as being antifraternity, this could explain why the volunteers were so much more responsive to the negative communication. We found some circumstan-

Table 5-2.   Rank–Order Correlations for Pretest–Posttest Attitude Reliabilities as a Function of Volunteer Status (After Rosnow and Rosenthal, 1966)

	Profraternity Argument	Antifraternity Argument	Control Group
Volunteers	.49	.76	−.52
Nonvolunteers	.99[a]	.98[a]	.95[a]

[a] $p < .05$.

tial support for this idea when we asked a comparison group of undergraduate women from the same population to rate their impressions of the communicator's attitude toward fraternities. On a nine-point bipolar scale anchored at the negative end with the label "extremely antifraternity," the mean rating by these subjects was -1.1 (less than zero at $p < .05$), which reinforced the argument that our volunteers could have been more responsive to the communication that was congruent with their perceptions of the experimenter's attitude and less responsive to the incongruent argument. Consistent with this interpretation was an additional finding, which is shown in Table 5-2, that the average reliability in before–after attitudes of the volunteers ($\rho = .35$) was significantly lower than the average reliability in attitudes of the nonvolunteers $\rho = .97$). Although the volunteers' attitudes were appreciably less reliable than the attitudes of the nonvolunteers ($p < .0005$), there were no significant effects on reliability of the treatment conditions within subjects of either volunteer or nonvolunteer status. That the volunteers were heterogeneous in their attitude change could be tentatively interpreted as evidence of their greater willingness to be influenced in whatever direction they felt was demanded by the situation. From these thin findings, we could now hypothesize that volunteers may be more sensitive and accommodating to demand characteristics than captive nonvolunteers, and a second exploratory study was designed to examine this possibility.

Study 2

In this follow-up experiment, attitudes were observed in a situation in which the major directional response cues were contained in the communications themselves, and thus, the experimenter's private views on controversial issues were not a source of competing experimental expectations (Rosnow, Rosenthal, McConochie, and Arms, 1969). If our interpretation of study 1 were correct, it would follow that volunteers should be more compliant in their attitude responses when they were clear on the demand characteristics of the situation.

In order to manipulate the clarity of directional response demands, one-sided and two-sided personality sketches were substituted for the fraternity arguments of the first study. It was reasoned that equipollent two-sided communications, because they contained contradictory response cues, would obscure the directional demand characteristics of the situation. This time, the subjects were 263 captive undergraduate men and women, 53 of whom were verbal volunteers for a psychology experiment. At random, the students were assigned to one of five treatment groups, and all were presented the following introductory passage to read about a fictitious character named Jim (adapted from research on impression formation by Luchins, 1957):

> In everyday life we sometimes form impressions of people based on what we read or hear about them. On a given school day Jim walks down the street, sees a girl he knows, buys some stationery, stops at the candy store.

One group of subjects then read a short, extraverted personality sketch designed to portray Jim as friendly and outgoing; a second group read an introverted sketch, picturing him as shy and unfriendly. In two other groups, both communications were presented in a counterbalanced sequence, and the fifth group of subjects, which received only the introductory passage, served as a nondirectional control. In each case, the subjects had to rate Jim on four 9-point bipolar attitude scales for friendliness, forwardness, sociability, and aggressiveness. If our hypothesis were correct, we should expect more extreme congruent attitudes among volunteers than nonvolunteers who were exposed to the one-sided communications (where response cues were straightforward and consistent) and no appreciable attitude differences between volunteers and nonvolunteers in the two communication groups where response cues were contradictory.

Table 5-3.   Composite Attitude Scores of Volunteers and Nonvolunteers After Reading a One-Sided or Two-Sided Personality Sketch. (After Rosnow, Rosenthal, McConochie, and Arms, 1969)[a]

Treatment	Volunteers	Nonvolunteers
Extraverted (E) minus control	+6.8	+3.7
Introverted (I) minus control	−7.2	−5.9
EI minus control	−2.3	+0.3
IE minus control	−0.5	−0.5

[a] The more highly positive or negative the score, the more extreme were the subjects' attitudes, positive scores favoring the extraverted characterization and negative scores, the introverted characterization.

The results are summarized in Table 5-3, which shows for volunteers and nonvolunteers the difference between the average total score in the control group and the average total score in each of the four experimental groups. Although the overall effects were not significantly greater among volunteers than nonvolunteers, the trend of the findings was in the predicted direction, and the interaction of volunteering with positive versus negative one-sided communications showed that volunteers were significantly ($p < .05$) more susceptible to one-sided communications than were nonvolunteers. In addition, the effect size was even larger than that of the previously described study. Thus, when the personality sketch was slanted in the positive direction, it was the volunteers who became more positive in their attitudes; and when the communication was slanted in the negative direction, it was the volunteers who became more negative. Completely consistent with the demand clarity interpretation were the results with the opposing communications. These stimuli were generally ineffective regardless of whether they were compared to the control group or to each other.

Study 3

Encouraged by these data trends, we toyed with the clarity notion once more before formalizing the hypothesis and putting it to a more stringent experimental test. This time, we wondered if a successful deception study might not function in a manner similar to the two-sided communication in study 2, in effect obfuscating the directional response demands of the situation. An opportunity to test this idea arose when Roberta Marmer McConochie, then a graduate student in communications research at Boston University, agreed to tack on the voluntarism variable in a thesis experiment involving a demonstrably successful cognitive dissonance deception (Rosnow, Rosenthal, McConochie, and Arms, 1969).

There were two phases to the deception, which was carried out on 109 undergraduate women in a student dormitory at Boston University (60 volunteers and 49 nonvolunteers). In the first phase, the subjects all participated in what was represented to them as a national opinion survey. Embedded in the lengthy opinion questionnaire were 12 statements that the students rated on an 11-point scale to indicate how important they perceived such ideas as whether there should be more no-grade courses at universities, courses in sex education, student unionization, instruction on the use and control of hallucinatory drugs, and so on. One month later, another experimenter, who represented himself as a researcher from Boston University's Communication Research Center, told the students that the Center was conducting a follow-up to some of the questions from the national survey. Each student was handed a questionnaire (specially designed for her) in which were listed 2 of the 12 statements rated earlier. Since, according to Festinger's (1957) theory, important decisions or decisions where the unchosen alternative is relatively attractive should produce more cognitive dissonance than unimportant decisions or decisions where the unchosen alternative is unattractive, McConochie studied both these factors. Importance was manipulated by deceiving some of the subjects into believing that Boston University planned to put into practice one of the ideas listed in the questionnaire and that the students' preferences would be taken into account by the administration when making its final choice. Attractiveness of the unchosen alternative was manipulated by selecting ideas for the students to choose between which had been rated similarly (relatively "attractive") or dissimilarly (relatively "unattractive") on the initial questionnaire. After the students revealed their preferences, they once again rated all 12 items for importance. The dissonance theory prediction was that they should spread apart the values of the choice alternatives in direct proportion to the amount of cognitive dissonance they experienced.

Table 5-4. Reduction of Postdecision Dissonance by Changing the Importance of the Chosen and Unchosen Alternatives for Volunteers and Nonvolunteers (After Rosnow, Rosenthal, McConochie and Arms, 1969)[a]

| | Change from First to Second Rating for: | | |
| | Chosen | Unchosen | Net |
Experimental Variables	Alternative	Alternative	Change
Volunteers			
Low importance			
Low attractiveness	+0.1	+0.4	−0.3
High attractiveness	+0.3	−1.9	+2.2[b]
High importance			
Low attractiveness	+0.2	−0.7	+0.9
High attractiveness	+0.6	−1.6	+2.2[b]
Nonvolunteers			
Low importance			
Low attractiveness	−0.5	+0.1	−0.6
High attractiveness	+1.2	−1.3	+2.5[b]
High importance			
Low attractiveness	+0.4	−0.7	+1.1
High attractiveness	+2.1	−0.3	+2.4[b]

[a] Positive scores indicate an increase in importance, and negative scores a decrease. Net change is the change for the chosen alternative minus the change for the unchosen, which indicates the net spreading-apart of the alternatives following the choice. A positive net change is evidence of dissonance reduction.
[b] Net change significantly greater than zero, $p < .05$.

The results of the study, which are shown in Table 5-4, did suggest differences between volunteers and nonvolunteers. The attractiveness variable especially (but also the importance variable) appeared to have less effect on volunteers than on nonvolunteers with regard to the chosen alternative. For the unchosen alternative, volunteers showed a greater effect of attractiveness than did nonvolunteers. Consistent with this interpretation, there was a highly significant four-way interaction in a voluntarism by importance by attractiveness by repeated measures analysis of variance of the change data ($p < .001$). This was hardly a predicted interaction to be sure, but it indicated nevertheless that volunteering can make a difference. Of course, since cognitive dissonance researchers do not usually look separately at the alternatives but only at the net change data, an overall decision about the success of the manipulation would be only indirectly affected by subjects' volunteer status. Other than this complex interaction, no other interaction with voluntarism was statistically significant (every $F < 1$). However, consistent with the dissonance predictions, there was a greater spreading apart of the choice alternatives in the high than in the low attractiveness condition ($p < .001$) as well as in the high versus low importance conditions ($p = .11$). Clearly, volunteer status does not always directly interact with other experimental variables to bias research conclusions, although it may affect validity in an indirect way. (How differential sensitivity to demand characteristics could cope with a difference under high but not low importance was unclear.)

TYPE-I AND TYPE-II ERROR OUTCOMES

In Chapter 4, we derived hypothetical type-I and type-II error outcomes from relationships between volunteer status and certain dependent variables. Our exploratory findings, flimsy though they were, pointed now to a way of testing the notion experimentally. When questionnaires are employed as before-and-after measures in attitude research, such as in study 1, it is plausible that the pretest in conjunction with the treatment may sensitize the subject so that he approaches the treatment differently than if he had not been pretested. Repeated attitude measurements should easily convey to the subject that some attitude change is expected, particularly if the measurements are obviously related to the experimental treatment (Orne, 1962a); however, whether or not the subject complied with this demand characteristic should depend on his motivation.

Whether pretest sensitization was a potential source of invalidity in attitude research is a question that has aroused considerable theoretical and empirical concern over the years (Campbell and Stanley, 1966; Hovland, Lumsdaine, and Sheffield, 1949; Lana, 1969; Ross and Smith, 1965; Solomon, 1949). Surprisingly, the results of a dozen or more laboratory studies were remarkably consistent in revealing either no appreciable systematic effects of pretesting (Lana, 1959a,b; Lana and Rosnow, 1968) or a moderate dampening effect (Brooks, 1966; Lana, 1964, 1966; Lana and Rosnow, 1963; Nosanchuk and Marchak, 1969; Pauling and Lana, 1969). Summarizing these results, Lana concluded that "when pretest measures exert any influence at all in attitude research, the effect is to produce a Type II error, which is more tolerable to most psychological researchers than is an error of the first kind" (1969, p. 139).

Our exploratory findings on voluntarism led us to wonder whether the null and depressive effects in this body of research on pretest sensitization could have been caused by the failure to distinguish between motivational sets among subjects, for the results were based almost exclusively on the reactions of captive audiences. The actual subject samples might be visualized as pools of captive nonvolunteers mixed in some unknown proportion with potential volunteers. Since the ratio of nonvolunteers to volunteers frequently favors the former in college populations, the samples might have consisted largely of nonvolunteer types, or those subjects likely *not* to comply very strongly with demand characteristics. Furthermore, in the few instances in attitude research where a facilitative effect of pretesting was seen, the subjects were all rather willing participants—either volunteers or involved, presumably eager and highly motivated "nonvolunteers" (Crespi, 1948; Hicks and Spaner, 1962; Star and Hughes, 1950). It therefore followed that the directional effect of pretesting on subjects' approaches to a treatment in attitude research might be predicated upon their original willingness to participate as research subjects. Since our exploratory studies suggested that volunteers may be more compliant with demand characteristics than nonvolunteers, it could be hypothesized that the effect of using a before–after design on volunteers should be in the direction of a type-I error, whereas the effect with nonvolunteers should be in the type-II direction. In other words, a facilitative effect of pretesting was predicted for volunteers' responses to the treatment, and a dampening effect was predicted for nonvolunteers.

Research Procedure

To test these hypotheses, Rosnow and Suls (1970) randomly assigned 146 undergraduate men and women, including 50 verbal volunteers, four forms of a booklet containing the various pretest and treatment combinations in the design developed by Solomon (1949), as shown in Table 5-5. Thus, group I was administered a pretest questionnaire, followed by the experimental communication. Group II received the same pretest but an irrelevant control communication. Group III received the experimental communication and no pretest, and group IV, only the control communication. All the subjects were then

Table 5-5.   Design of the Rosnow and Suls Pretest Sensitization Experiment (After Solomon, 1949)

Treatment	Pretest	
	Yes	No
Experimental communication	Group I	Group III
Control communication	Group II	Group IV

simultaneously administered a posttest questionnaire that was identical to the pretest. Using this basic research design, it was possible to calculate the amount of attitude change for the experimental group (group I) that was caused by the summative action of the pretest (Pr), extraneous events (Ex), the experimental treatment (Tr), and the interaction between the pretest and the succeeding events in time (Int). Given the functional relationships (after Solomon, 1949)

$$Y_1 = f(\text{Pr} + \text{Ex} + \text{Tr} + \text{Int}),$$
$$Y_2 = f(\text{Pr} + \text{Ex}),$$
$$Y_3 = f(\text{Ex} + \text{Tr}),$$
$$Y_4 = f(\text{Ex}).$$

where Y_1–Y_4 represent the mean posttest scores in groups I–IV, respectively, the interaction between the pretest and succeeding temporal events was determined by the following subtractive-difference formula:

$$d = Y_1 - (Y_2 + Y_3 - Y_4)$$

where d might be positive or negative, depending upon the psychological effects of the pretest on the way the subject approached the experimental treatment. A positive difference score would imply a facilitative effect of pretesting and a negative difference would imply a depressive effect.

The 388-word experimental communication, which was represented as an excerpt from an editorial by a contributing science editor of the *New York Times,* discussed the scientific and social implications of the purported discovery of a new element called galaxium and the implications of nuclear research in general. It reported that an American nuclear physicist warned that the new element was difficult to handle because of its constantly changing nuclear structure, and that when changes occurred, radioactive particles were emitted into the surrounding atmosphere, resulting in harmful effects to living tissues. The communication added that an economist said that continued large-scale federal financial support of nuclear research could produce a sharp decline in the value of American currency and that the resulting inflation would lower the standard of living in the United States. The communication also warned that further nuclear research might produce another force for mankind to fear and misuse, and it concluded with the statement, "We have enough to worry about now without devoting our minds to the production of an even more overwhelming destructive power." The 348-word control communication, also represented as an excerpt from the *Times,* was on the subject of sexual promiscuity among college students.

The pretest and posttest questionnaires were identical, each containing four attitude statements along with instructions to the subjects to indicate their agreement or disagreement on a nine-point bipolar scale. Corresponding to the tricomponential conceptualization of attitude (Chein, 1948; Katz and Stotland, 1959; Kothandapani, 1971; Krech, Crutchfield, and Ballachey, 1962), one item tapped the affective component of attitude; another item, the conative component; a third, the cognitive; the fourth, a combination of affective and cognitive components. The four items were as follows:

1.   *Affective:* Nuclear scientists in this country are responsible men who should be allowed to do their research without interference from people in other fields.

2.   *Conative:* If asked to do so, I would probably be willing to sign a petition protesting the federal government's large-scale support of nuclear research.

3.   *Cognitive:* Continued large-scale funding of nuclear research will most likely result in a lowering of the standard of living in the United States.

4.   *Affective–cognitive:* Continued large-scale nuclear research will bring the world closer to destruction.

Responses to each item were scored on the basis of a scale ranging from 1 (strong disagreement with the view advocated in the experimental communication) to 9 (strong agreement).

Results

Before proceeding to the main analyses, two preliminary assumptions had to be considered. One assumption was that the treatment groups were initially comparable, and the other assumption had to do with the effectiveness of the experimental communication. There were several possible analyses that could be undertaken to test the two assumptions. One means by which to validate the first was to compare the pretest scores in groups I and II with the posttest scores in group IV. If the assumption of initial comparability were correct, there should be no appreciable differences between these three groups of attitude scores. Results of a series of unweighted-means analyses of variance supported the contention of initial comparability for three out of four questionnaire items. There were no overall differences obtained for items 1, 2 and 4 (every $F < 1$), although differences significant beyond the .05 level were obtained for item 3. A supplementary check on the assumption of initial comparability was to determine whether there were any pretest differences between volunteers and nonvolunteers in groups I and II versus the posttest scores in group IV. These results were consistent with the first analysis, disclosing differences between volunteers and nonvolunteers significant at the conventional level only for item 3 and negligible differences associated with the other three items. Hence, with the exception of the subjects' attitudes regarding the cognitive statement, it could be concluded that the groups were initially comparable in their attitudes for items 1, 2, and 4. Since the preliminary assumption of initial intergroup comparability was not met for item 3, this item was eliminated from the main analysis.

To provide an overall check on the second assumption, that the experimental communication was effective, correlated t tests were computed on the pretest versus posttest scores of subjects in groups I and II. The results were supportive of the preliminary assumption. Significant attitude gains in the expected direction were found in the group that had been subjected to the experimental communication for all three remaining items. Therefore, it could be concluded that the experimental communication was an effective attitude-change agent.

Given that the assumptions of initial comparability in attitudes and potency of the experimental treatment were satisfactorily met, a $2 \times 2 \times 2$ analysis of variance was computed on the summed posttest attitude scores for the acceptable items. The three factors in the analysis were (1) whether the subjects had been pretested or not, (2) whether they received the experimental or control communication, and (3) their volunteer status. Should the experimental hypotheses be correct, a three-way interaction was expected. Evidence of a simple pretesting-by-treatment effect would be a two-way interaction between factors 1 and 2. As predicted, the three-way interaction was statistically significant beyond the conventional level (effect size $= .41\sigma$). The two-way interaction, consistent with the earlier experimental findings, was insignificant ($F < 1$). To determine the overall direction of posttest differences, a subtractive-difference procedure was applied to the composite posttest means using the formula derived before, or $d = Y_1 - (Y_2 + Y_3 - Y_4)$. The results,

Table 5-6. Summary of Posttest Means and Results of Subtractive-Difference Procedure with Volunteers and Nonvolunteers (After Rosnow and Suls, 1970)

Attitude Item	Volunteers	Nonvolunteers
1	$6.6 - (4.6 + 5.8 - 5.1) = 1.3$	$5.2 - (6.1 + 5.7 - 5.1) = -1.5$
2	$5.7 - (4.8 + 5.2 - 5.5) = 1.2$	$5.0 - (5.9 + 5.7 - 5.5) = -1.1$
4	$6.6 - (4.0 + 5.4 - 5.5) = 2.7$	$3.9 - (5.7 + 5.2 - 4.4) = -2.6$

which are shown separately for each item in Table 5-6, provided strong support for the experimental hypotheses. The composite difference scores for volunteers and nonvolunteers were all opposite in sign and of similar magnitudes. This finding could certainly explain why the earlier research failed to yield the pretesting-by-treatment interaction. Differences between willing and unwilling subjects could have canceled each other, thereby producing small and insignificant two-way interactions.

Conclusions

The findings thus demonstrated that the directionality of the effect of pretesting on subjects' reactions to a communication in attitude-change research could be largely predicated upon their original willingness to participate as research subjects. The main finding was that pretested volunteer subjects were more accommodating, and pretested nonvolunteers less accommodating, to an attitude manipulation. This suggests that using a before–after design can lead to overestimates of the attitudinal effects of persuasive communications when the subjects are motivated positively pursuant to the demand characteristics of the situation and to underestimates when they are captive nonvolunteers.

We must mention, however, that recently there has also been an alternative explanation to account for the failure to isolate the simple interaction between the effect of pretesting and that of exposure to a persuasive communication. This alternative view, the commitment hypothesis, argues that subjects may become "frozen" in their original positions when they have to commit themselves on a serious controversial issue (Lana and Menapace, 1971; Pauling and Lana, 1969). Hence, to the extent that giving one's opinions may arouse evaluation anxieties about seeming too gullible if one were subsequently to change them very much, a person should become more firmly entrenched in his initial position. Some support for this interpretation was provided by Lana and Menapace (1971) in a study of adult rehabilitation patients whose opinions on hospital conditions were measured before and after they underwent routine hospitalization. Demand characteristics were manipulated by informing some of the patients that the researcher expected their opinions to change during the course of their hospital stay and that they would be tested again later on to determine whether they had actually changed their minds. Commitment was varied by having the patients declare their initial opinions either aloud to the researcher or else silently to themselves. The results of the study would seem to favor the commitment hypothesis in that there was less opinion change among patients who were made aware of the researcher's expectations and had "publicly" committed themselves than among those aware patients who had originally stated their feelings privately. Excluding the possibility of a boomerang effect in the aware group because of the blatancy of the demand characteristics, it may also be possible to reconcile these results with the demand hypothesis by postulating that different factors may predominate in different situations. Thus, while commitment may be a dominant variable in motivational conflicts of the sort investigated by Lana and Menapace, the demand hypothesis may be favored in experimental situations where there are no deep personal conflicts between evaluative cues and task-orienting cues. As the debate raises an empirical question, we were able to pit these two competing hypotheses against one another in the usual laboratory context simply by manipulating the subjects' anonymity of response (Rosnow, Holper, and Gitter, 1973). On the one hand, the commitment hypothesis would predict a greater likelihood of pretest-by-treatment interaction under comparable conditions of anonymity than nonanonymity, since it follows that nonanonymous subjects would be more committed to their pretest opinions and therefore less responsive to the treatment than anonymous subjects. On the other hand, the demand characteristics hypothesis would predict that nonanonymous subjects, being more easily identifiable as "good" or "bad" subjects, would be more apt to comply with experimental demands than anonymous subjects, and so, there would be a lesser facilitative effect of pretesting under anonymity than nonanonymity conditions. In this case, using the same four-group design and stimuli as in the study by Rosnow and Suls, the results did indeed favor the demand hypothesis with the predicted subtractive-difference effect being greater for subjects who were treated nonanonymously ($p < .08$).

We have now seen that in before–after attitude-change experiments the probability of type-I errors appears greater when the subjects are willing participants and that the probability of type-II errors appears greater when the subjects have the characteristics of nonvolunteers. More important, though, the results of the Rosnow and Suls study implied that pretesting may have the capacity to distort the relationships that emerge between independent and dependent variables in attitude-change studies when the subjects' motivational sets are taken into account, thereby jeopardizing the validity of inferred causal relationships. Given the volunteer's strong inclination to comply with task-orienting cues, now a stronger case could also be made that voluntarism operates as a motivation mediator. An opportunity to test the idea more directly arose next in an experiment on verbal operant conditioning.

THE "GOOD SUBJECT" IN VERBAL-CONDITIONING RESEARCH

The experimental task in this study was the well-known Taffel conditioning procedure in which the experimenter's use of the word *good* serves as a verbal reinforcement for the subject's emission of I–WE responses, a procedure detailed in Chapter 4 in connection with Resnick and Schwartz' ethical forewarning study. This popular experimental procedure had been employed in over 300 verbal-conditioning studies (Greenspoon, 1962; Kanfer, 1968; Krasner, 1958; Salzinger, 1959; Williams, 1964), with the rather consistent finding that *good* tended to facilitate I–WE sentences. What is it about the Taffel procedure that produces a change in verbal behavior? Researchers have been sharply divided on the answer. From a behavioristic viewpoint it has been argued that verbal behavior, like other forms of behavior, comes under the control of the reinforcing stimulus. Cognitive theorists maintain that it is the subject's awareness of the reinforcement contingency that is necessary for changes in verbal behavior to occur. Discussions generated by these contrasting theoretical orientations have been summarized by Spielberger and DeNike (1966) and Kanfer (1968), and Kanfer raised the interesting possibility that inherent methodological complications may be an inadvertent source of confounding artifact.

Given this perplexing state of affairs, it was thought that a fruitful alternative approach might be to view the procedure from the phenomenology of the research subject. Proceeding on the assumption that the typical subject in this experiment could regard his participation as a problem-solving task in which he tried to guess its purpose and the experimenter's intent (Dulany, 1962; Krasner, 1962), it follows that once having arrived at a plausible explanation, the subject must next determine whether to respond to the perceived coercive demands of the situation. Certainly in this particular case the demand characteristics seem simple and straightforward. Even despite a subject's not having been expressly instructed to this effect, he should readily infer that an I-WE response is required in order to elicit the experimenter's verbal approval. Furthermore, since most of the studies had used volunteers, one would think that the very subjects most frequently used in this research might be those most apt to comply with this salient coercive demand.

Research Procedure

The general procedure was conducted in two phases (Goldstein, Rosnow, Goodstadt, and Suls, 1972). First, undergraduate women in sections of an introductory psychology class were casually instructed about verbal conditioning procedures as a regular part of their classroom lecture. (Recall Resnick and Schwartz's finding that extensive forewarning resulted in countercompliant conditioning behavior.) Second, several days later 23 verbal volunteers and 22 nonvolunteers were drawn from among these informed students and from other sections that were experimentally naïve, and all the subjects were individually subjected to the standard Taffel conditioning procedure. Immediately afterward, each subject was ushered into an adjoining room by another experimenter, who administered Dulany's (1962) awareness questionnaire. This popular questionnaire was designed to assess three distinct classes of the subject's hypotheses about the experiment and his intention to act upon his beliefs: a reinforcement hypothesis (awareness of the reinforcement contingency), a behavioral hypothesis (his awareness of expected, or "correct," behaviors), and his behavioral intention (his motivation to act upon his hypothesis). The decision to use separate experimenters was predicated on our desire to minimize any bias in the administration and recording of awareness responses and to encourage the subjects to express their honest opinions. To safeguard against expectancy effects, both experimenters were kept unaware of the subjects' volunteer status throughout the study, and the second experimenter received no information about the quality of the subjects' conditioning performances.

Results

For convenience of analysis, the 80 conditioning trials were divided into four equal blocks, the first block of 20 defining the operant base rate for the critical I–WE responses and blocks labeled 1, 2, and 3 constituting learning segments also of 20 trials each (see Fig. 5-1). A comparison of volunteers and nonvolunteers at the operant level revealed no appreciable initial differences between the two groups. To provide a difference measure of conditioning, the mean rate of emission of I–WE responses at the operant level was subtracted from that in block 3. The data showed mean increases of 6.6 critical responses for volunteers and a corresponding increase of 2.9 for nonvolunteers, the difference in gain scores being significant beyond the .05 level with an effect size of $.72\sigma$. A repeated measures analysis of variance of volunteer status and all four blocks also disclosed significant differences in the emission of critical responses, and there was a significant interaction effect as well, the rate of increase being markedly higher among volunteers than nonvolunteers.

A secondary data analysis was calculated in which volunteer status was one factor and prior information about the treatment was a second factor. As shown in Fig. 5-1, naïve nonvolunteers conditioned less successfully than either informed or naïve volunteers ($p < .05$). The results of a 2 × 2 analysis of variance for conditioning (block 3 minus the operant block) yielded one significant effect: volunteers conditioned better than nonvolunteers ($p < .05$). Hence, prior information about the treatment was apparently of less importance ($F < 1$) than the subjects' volunteer status. We should note at this point, however, that the absence of a boomerang conditioning effect among informed volunteers is not, as it might seem on the surface, necessarily at odds with Resnick and Schwartz's finding (see Chapter 4) if one hypothesizes a curvilinear relationship between the clarity of demand characteristics and demand compliance. Here, prior information exposure was casually induced in the context of a regular classroom lecture, whereas Resnick and Schwartz explicitly forewarned their subjects about the nature of the experimental procedures in a methodically obtrusive manner inspired by the provisional APA ethical guidelines. We shall refer to this inverted **U**-shaped function again in the next chapter.

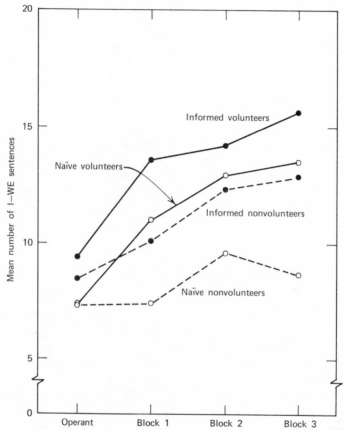

Fig. 5-1. Mean number of I–WE sentences constructed by informed and naive subjects (after Goldstein, Rosnow, Goodstadt, and Suls, 1972).

Regarding the Dulany questionnaire responses for awareness, there were no significant differences between volunteers and nonvolunteers for the reinforcement hypothesis or the behavioral hypothesis ($F < 1$), although volunteers, as anticipated, more often reported intentions to produce the correct response class (effect size $= .67\sigma, p < .05$). Prior information exposure had no significant effects on any of the awareness measures (which was not unexpected given the straightforward demands operating in this situation). Of course, our use of a postexperimental awareness measure carried certain problems of interpretation (cf. Greenspoon and Brownstein, 1967; Spielberger and DeNike, 1966). Such measures are typically used to corroborate hypotheses about awareness as an intervening factor in verbal conditioning. Aside from the epistemological difficulties inherent in such ex post facto reasoning is the problem of interpreting just what an awareness measure actually measures. Responses to an awareness interview, like those to sentence construction cards in the Taffel task, are also subject to conscious control and could be correlated with performance change. Subjects might intentionally report low or high awareness as a means of expressing or withholding their cooperation from an experimenter. This is an important problem that awaits more definitive inquiry, particularly in its broader implications for demand controls in general.

Finally, it is worth mentioning that a study by Kennedy and Cormier (1971) also implies differences in verbal conditioning rates as a function of the mode of recruitment. These investigators compared three groups of subjects on the Taffel task—a group of unpaid volunteers, a group of subjects who were recruited for $2, and a group of required participants. While overall they found no appreciable difference between groups by an analysis of variance, combining two of them and then recalculating differences in conditioning rates shows that the unpaid volunteers exceeded the other groups on an order of magnitude of better than 3:1 (7.9 versus 2.3, effect size $= .28\sigma$, $z = 1.39$).

WHEN COMPLIANCE SHIFTS TO SELF-DEFENSE

The sixth study in this series (Rosnow, Goodstadt, Suls, and Gitter, 1973) provided an independent test of a provocative finding by Sigall, Aronson, and Van Hoose (1970) challenging the ubiquitous belief in the cooperative nature of psychological research subjects. These investigators had reported a complicated deception experiment in which there were two sets of cues occurring simultaneously in one of the treatment conditions, one set of cues ostensibly related to the demand characteristics of the treatment and a competing set that conveyed the idea that demand compliance would result in the respondent being unfavorably evaluated on an important psychological dimension. Instead of cooperating with the experimenter, the subjects responded in the direction they would have seen as promoting a favorable image. The results were interpreted as evidence of the prepotency of ego-defensive motives when demand compliance is incongruent with a favorable self-presentation. The present study explored the responsiveness of willing and unwilling subjects in circumstances where there were conflicting task- and ego-orienting cues.

Research Procedure

The subjects were 123 undergraduate women from the introductory psychology course, 59 of whom were verbal volunteers. Two response demands were intended to operate concurrently in the study, one communicating manipulatory intent and the other, the expected direction of the subjects' responding. As our earlier research had suggested that before–after procedures may effectively convey manipulatory intent, this simple routine was adopted for transmitting the first demand cue. Directionality was communicated by exposing subjects to the one-sided extraverted or introverted personality sketches of "Jim" used in the earlier exploratory research (study 2). The before-and-after questionnaires now contained three 9-point scales on which the subject recorded the degree to which she perceived Jim to be friendly or unfriendly, forward or shy, social or unsocial, and the pretest was preceded by the same explanatory passage used in the earlier investigation.

Subjects were unobtrusively assigned to four groups, two of which received the extraverted characterization and two of which received the introverted message; half the groups participated in a "complementary" condition and half the groups participated in a "competing" condition. In devising these two conditions, our intent was to convey in a subtle, but unequivocal, way that compliance with demand characteristics could result in a favorable or unfavorable image, depending on the experimental condition. Hence, an indirect means of imparting this information was sought that, although straightforward and attention-getting, would not be so transparent as to reveal the true nature of the deception. For this purpose a young actor was employed who was planted in each of the classes as another student. In the *complementary condition* the actor interrupted the experimenter while test booklets were being explained and said that he heard from a friend in another class who had already participated in the study that the experimenter was trying to prove that "only people with really high IQ's are able to come up with the correct impression of someone from a short paragraph." To the confederate's question whether this was really the aim of the study, the experimenter said he would answer later, when the experiment was completed. Thus, demand compliance should have been perceived as congruent with the desire to project a favorable image. In the *competing condition,* the opposite intent was conveyed by having the confederate say that he had heard that the experimenter was trying to prove that "only people with really low IQ's would even attempt to form impressions of a person just from a short description." In this case, demand compliance should have been perceived as incongruent with the desire to present a favorable image.

Results

The results of the experiment are shown in Fig. 5-2, which summarizes the data separately for volunteers and nonvolunteers. The valences associated with change scores (see vertical axis) indicate whether opinion changes were in the direction implied by demand characteristics. It can be seen that in three cases out of four there were sharp decreases in demand compliance from the complementary to the competing condition, the one reversal (which was statistically insignificant) being among volunteers who received the extraverted sketch. Where there was any change significant beyond the .05 level, it was in the predicted direction. Consistent with this observation, there was a significant statistical interaction of message directionality and the conflicting cues factor in a three-way analysis of variance ($p < .05$) and a borderline main effect for the conflicting cues factor ($p < .06$).

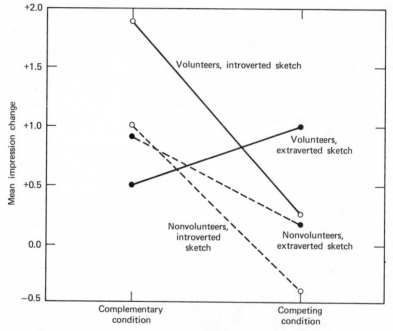

Fig. 5-2.   Mean impression changes of volunteers and nonvolunteers. Positive and negative signs are independent of the direction of the stimulus. Positive scores simply denote gains in whatever direction, positive *or* negative, was communicated by an extraverted or introverted sketch, and negative scores reveal demand countercompliance (after Rosnow, Goodstadt, Suls, and Gitter, 1973).

Based on discussions by Green (1963) and Silverman (1970), it was thought that volunteers would be more strongly impelled by coercive demands, and nonvolunteers, by ego-defensive cues. Contrary to expectation there was only a very negligible voluntarism by conflicting cues interaction in the three-way analysis of variance ($F < 1$) and also a nearly zero triple interaction. However, there may be a hint of the hypothesized relationship in the fact that one group of volunteers responded slightly counter to evaluative cues. Since the same treatment was simultaneously administered to both volunteers and nonvolunteers, it would be difficult to explain this exception as a failure of the treatment.

The results also provided an opportunity to check on our earlier finding that volunteers are more compliant with demand characteristics than nonvolunteers. While there was no conventionally significant main effect of volunteer status or a voluntarism by message directionality interaction, it can be seen that there was a tendency in the predicted direction. Volunteers in three out of four conditions exhibited greater congruent change than nonvolunteers. Moreover, even though two out of four cases were quite insignificant ($t < 1$ for extraverted–complementary and introverted–competing conditions), relationships in the two cases that were statistically significant or approached the conventional level repeated our previous experimental finding (one-tailed $p < .01$, effect size $= .96\sigma$ for extraverted–competing and one-tailed $p < .10$, effect size $= .56\sigma$ for introverted–complementary). Taken together with the earlier findings, these results would certainly support the idea of a greater motivational tendency among volunteers than nonvolunteers to play the role of good subject.

ROLE EXPECTATIONS OF VOLUNTEERS AND NONVOLUNTEERS

To summarize our findings thus far, the results of the preceding six studies provided compelling evidence of the subtle threat stemming from volunteer status as an artifact stimulus variable to the validity of inferred causal relationships. They showed, moreover, a definite link between voluntarism and the motivation mediator alluded to in the previous chapter. However, while they may also seem to imply differences in role perceptions between volunteers and nonvolunteers that could account for their energetic or sluggish experimental behaviors, the evidence on this score, being of an indirect nature, is at best circumstantial and one would prefer to ask subjects themselves what their role expectations are. Hence, it was with this idea in mind that the final study in this series was designed (Aiken and Rosnow, 1973).

In our earlier discussions we mentioned that there has been some controversy centering on the role that subjects adhere to for research participation and what their experimental motivations are. One position holds that research subjects respond to demand characteristics because they hope and expect "that the study in which they are participating will in some material way contribute to human welfare in general" (Orne, 1962, p. 778). Consistent with this notion was Straits, Wuebben, and Majka's (1972, p. 516) conclusion, having factor analyzed the reports of respondents who simulated research participation, that "subjects are apparently willing to forego 'hedonistic' considerations for 'altruistic' goals such as those of advancing science and helping the experimenter." An alternative view attributes role behaviors to expectations of obedience to authority. For example, Fillenbaum (1966, p. 537) characterized experimental behaviors as "dutifully going along with the instructions," and Sigall, Aronson, and Van Hoose (1970, p. 9) speculated, "Subjects are obedient in the sense that if they are instructed to do something, they fulfill that request." A similar idea was contained in Kelman's (1972) analysis of the rights of subjects in terms of relative power and legitimacy. The subject is compliant owing to his perception of experimenters as legitimate authorities to be obeyed and of himself "as having no choice, particularly since the investigators are usually higher in status and since the agencies sponsoring and conducting research may represent (or at least appear to represent) the very groups on which the subjects are dependent" (Kelman, 1972, p. 990). A third view implies that role behaviors may be a function of subjects' heightened approval needs in response to evaluative expectations that are endemic to behavioral research participation. The typical subject, it is hypothesized, approaches the typical experiment with the expectation of being evaluated on some pertinent psychological dimension and guides his behavior accordingly (Rosenberg, 1965, p. 29).

Which of these interpretations best defines the predominant role expectation of subjects for standard experimental research—the altruism hypothesis, the obedience to authority hypothesis, or the evaluation hypothesis—and are there differences in role expectations between voluntary and nonvoluntary subjects? These were the questions to which this final study in the series was addressed. Since we sought verbal reports that were not themselves blatantly biased by the operation of demand characteristics, the study employed a kind of "projective" method of inquiry and scaling procedure that brought together the altruism, obedience, and evaluation hypotheses to paint a multidimensional picture of subjects' expectations for experimental research participation.

Research Procedure

Again, the subjects were drawn from sections of an introductory psychology class and identified as volunteers or nonvolunteers by the identical procedure used in the preceding studies. The recruitment procedure produced a list of 53 volunteers and 100 nonvolunteers.

All the subjects were given computer output sheets on which to respond directly by judging each of 55 unique pairs of 11 different stimuli that were presented in a complete paired-comparison schedule. One stimulus, the target situation stated simply, "being a subject in a psychology experiment." The remaining 10 stimuli were designed either to represent experiences related to the three role hypotheses or to serve as control situations for tapping positive or negative affect. The 10 comparison stimuli and 5 conditions they represented were as follows:

Altruism hypothesis
1. giving anonymously to charity
2. working free as a laboratory assistant

Obedience to authority hypothesis
3. obeying a no-smoking sign
4. not arguing with the professor

Evaluation hypothesis
5. taking a final exam
6. being interviewed for a job

Positive control
7. spending the evening with a good friend
8. taking a walk in the woods

Negative control
9. going to school on the subway
10. having to work on a weekend or holiday.

The instructions to the subjects began:

There are many situations in which you might find yourself which are quite similar in the expectations you have about them. For example, playing in a tennis match or being in a debating contest evoke similar competitive expectations. In contrast, there are other situations which are probably quite different in the expectations you have about them. For example, jogging around the block versus watching television after a hard day of work evoke obviously different expectations, the first being very active, the second being very passive.

The subjects were then instructed to consider other pairs of experiences like these and to rate them on how similar the experiences were in the expectations the subjects had about them. A 15-point scale was provided for this purpose, with 15 representing maximum similarity ("very similar expectations") and one representing maximum dissimilarity ("very dissimilar expectations"). After practicing on some sample pairs, the subjects rated the similarity of their expectations for the 55 pair members made up of the 11 different stimuli. Each subject received the pairs in a different random sequence to control for order effects. For the purpose of assessing reliability of judgment, the subjects were then administered a second output sheet containing 15 pairs chosen from across the pair sequence and asked to repeat their judgments.

Data Analysis

For each subject, a Pearson product–moment correlation was computed on original versus repeated judgments to the 15 reliability pairs. The median reliability coefficient among volunteers was .68 ($p < .01$), and among non-volunteers it was .48 ($p < .05$). Since the inclusion of unreliable protocols could tend to obscure or confound differences between groups, only those volunteers and nonvolunteers whose protocols were reliable at r ($df = 13$) = .51, $p = .05$, were retained for further analysis. Thirteen volunteer protocols were discarded for failure to meet this criterion, and 52 nonvolunteer protocols. The median reliability coefficients of the remaining 40 volunteers and 48 nonvolunteers were .77 ($p < .01$) and .79 ($p < .01$).

In passing, we should perhaps note that the difference in reliabilities was significant well beyond the conventional level ($\chi^2 = 9.6, p < .002$), although what this means is not very clear at this point. Could some of the volunteer subjects, being brighter and higher in the need for social approval than the nonvolunteers, have been trying to appear more consistent? Alternatively, might the volunteers have shown greater care in answering questions? Further research may shed light on these questions.

Of the 55 total judgments each subject made, 10 were direct assessments of the target stimulus ("being a subject in a psychology experiment") with the comparison stimuli. From these judgments five scores were computed for each subject, the scores representing the similarity of each of the five comparison categories (altruism, obedience, evaluation, positive control, negative control) to the target stimulus. Within each category this score was the sum of the judged similarities of the paired situations in that category to the target stimulus. These results, which are shown in Table 5-7, reveal that the category with highest similarity to the target stimulus among both volunteers and nonvolunteers was that corresponding to Orne's altruism hypothesis. A 2×5 un-weighted means analysis of variance of group (volunteer, nonvolunteer) $\times$ category (altruism hypothesis . . . negative control), followed by post hoc analysis, confirmed this finding. The significant category main effect of F (4, 344) = 21.4, $p < .001$, indicated differential similarity of the various categories to the target stimulus. That there was no interaction effect, F (4, 344) = 1.8, $p > .10$, indicated that category profiles were similar across groups. Lastly, the group main effect reflects the higher mean judgments of the volunteers over the nonvolunteers, F (1, 86) = 12.4, $p < .001$, which repeats the finding in our second exploratory study, described earlier. (Whether in the first case this means that "being a subject" has greater semantic meaning for volunteers than for nonvolunteers is an intriguing question and awaits further exploration.) As regards the post hoc analysis of category means using the Newman–Keuls technique, the altruism category, as stated above, was seen as

Table 5-7.   Judged Similarity of the Target Stimulus to Five Categories of Paired Experiences (After Aiken and Rosnow, 1973)[a]

Subject's Volunteer Status	Experiential Categories				
	Altruism Hypothesis	Obedience Hypothesis	Evaluation Hypothesis	Positive Control	Negative Control
Volunteers	20.3	12.8	14.5	15.1	12.7
	(7.1)	(7.2)	(6.8)	(8.8)	(5.8)
Nonvolunteers	16.9	9.4	14.5	10.0	9.4
	(7.4)	(6.9)	(6.5)	(6.9)	(6.1)

[a]The maximum possible score was 30. The higher the score, the greater was the perceived similarity in role expectations between the target stimulus ("being a subject in a psychology experiment") and the combined category stimuli. Standard deviations are indicated in parentheses.

significantly more similar to the target stimulus than all other categories ($p < .01$ in all cases). The evaluation category was closer to the target situation than was the positive control category ($p < .05$), the obedience to authority category ($p < .01$), or the negative control category ($p < .01$), and no differences were noted between these last three categories.

Next, multidimensional scaling (MDS) was used to explore the structure underlying subjective similarity judgments between all situations. MDS is conceptually similar to factor analysis in that the purpose of MDS is to extract the dimensions (analogous to factors) underlying sets of interstimulus similarities (analogous to intervariable correlations). In addition, MDS furnishes for each stimulus its projections on the dimensions of the underlying configuration (analogous to factor loadings). As in factor analysis, the number of dimensions chosen to represent the structure of a set of judgments depends on the goodness-of-fit of a solution to the original judgments as well as on the interpretability of the dimensions of the solution. For the present MDS application, the mean judged similarity to each category pair was calculated separately for volunteers and nonvolunteers. These mean judgments were then analysed with the TORSCA nonmetric MDS procedure (Young, 1968). Four-, three-, two-, and one-dimensional solutions were derived separately for volunteers and nonvolunteers so that goodness-of-fit could be examined as a function of solution dimensionality. The measure of fit in the TORSCA procedure, stress (Kruskal, 1964), is actually a "badness-of-fit" measure in that the larger the stress, the poorer the fit. Stress curves for the volunteer and nonvolunteer solutions showed elbows at two dimensions, thus indicating that two dimensions were appropriate for representing the original judgments of both groups. Among volunteers the stress values were .18, .08, .05, and .03 for the one-through-four-dimensional solutions respectively, and among nonvolunteers the corresponding stress values were .21, .09, .06, and .02.

The raw judgments of the 88 individual subjects were next rescaled with the INDSCALE MDS procedure (Carroll and Chang, 1970), a technique to treat subjects and stimuli simultaneously. By using this procedure, a single stimulus configuration is recovered. The configuration is that unique solution which best represents the judgments of all individual subjects. For each subject, weights are simultaneously calculated that best represent the importance of each dimension to the subject. The procedure thus assumes that there is a common set of stimulus dimensions available to all observers but that individual subjects perceive particular stimulus dimensions as more-or-less salient when they judge the similarity between stimulus pairs. From this scaling procedure, three kinds of information are obtained: (1) a unique stimulus configuration with projections of the stimuli on the dimensions thereof; (2) for each individual a set of weights, one for each dimension of the stimulus configuration, which represents the extent to which the various stimulus dimensions are reflected in the subjects' judgments; and (3) a measure of goodness-of-fit for each subject's original judgments to the common stimulus configuration as weighted by the subject's unique dimension weights.

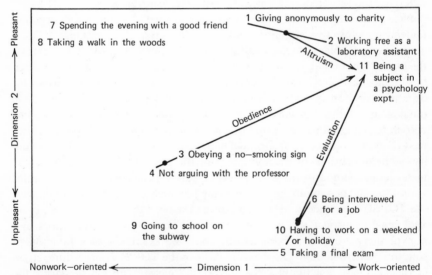

Fig. 5-3. Two-dimensional INDSCALE solution based on individual judgments of 88 subjects. Lines labeled "altruism," "evaluation," and "obedience" show the actual relative distances between these three categories and the target stimulus ("being a subject in a psychology experiment"). The proximity between any pair of situations reflects the perceived similarity in role expectations for the pair members (after Aiken and Rosnow, 1973).

The two-dimensional stimulus configuration derived for the INDSCALE procedure is shown in Fig. 5-3. The first dimension can be interpretated as work orientation, with the nonwork experiences of "taking a walk in the woods" and "spending the evening with a good friend" at one extreme and the highly work-oriented experiences at the other. The second dimension can be interpreted as affective, with "giving anonymously to charity" at one extreme and "taking a final exam" at the other. In the scaling solution the ordering of distances of the altruism, evaluation, and obedience categories from the target stimulus was reported before. Altruism stimuli, it can now be seen, were closest to the target stimulus, followed by the evaluation and obedience to authority stimuli. The correlations of individual subjects' original judgments and weighted distances derived from scaling were significant for all subjects (for 87 out of 88 subjects, $p < .01$; for the last subject, $p < .05$). Among volunteers the median correlation was .67 with a semi-interquartile range of .10 and for nonvolunteers the median correlation was .65 with a .06 semi-interquartile range. In sum, the judgments of all individual subjects could be represented in the common stimulus configuration given in Fig. 5-3.

Lastly, we turn to the question of whether volunteers and nonvolunteers could be differentiated on the basis of the weight placed on each dimension in making their judgments. For this purpose the dimension weights of individual subjects derived from the INDSCALE procedure were examined to test for differentiation of groups on the basis of dimension salience. This analysis revealed that the nonvolunteers placed more weight on the work-orientation dimension that did the volunteers, with mean weights of .36 and .28, respectively, $F(1, 86) = 9.3, p < .01$. And the volunteers placed slightly more weight on the pleasant–unpleasant dimension than did the nonvolunteers, with mean weights of .55 versus .49, and $F(1,86) = 3.3, p < .10$. As a final check, using the weights for the two dimensions as predictors in a discriminant analysis of volunteers versus nonvolunteers, the groups were significantly differentiated by the combination of weights, $F(2,85) = 4.7, p < .05$. However, only weights assigned to the work-orientation dimension contributed to the distinction between groups, and $F < 1$ for the affective dimension.

SUMMARY OF THE RESEARCH FINDINGS AND CONCLUSIONS

To reiterate the earlier conclusion, the results of the six experimental studies can be seen as evidence of the subtle threat deriving from voluntarism as an artifact-independent variable to the validity of inferred causal relationships. Volunteers were consistently more accommodating than nonvolunteers as long as the demand characteristics were presented clearly, and this motivational difference had the capacity to distort the relationships emerging between independent and dependent variables.

In the study on error outcomes, it was discovered that the systematic biasing effect of pretesting subjects in before–after attitude research was to increase the likelihood of type-I decisions when the subjects are willing participants and to promote type-II decisions when they are captive nonvolunteers. (We use "type-I" in this context as shorthand for obtaining significant effects of an independent variable in a sample when such effects would not be significant in a more representative sample and "type II" for obtaining no significant effects in a sample when such effects would be significant in a more representative sample.) A biasing behavioral effect of voluntarism was also obtained in the fifth experiment, on verbal conditioning, although the results, when considered in the light of Resnick and Schwartz's findings, implied to us that demand clarity may operate in a curvilinear fashion with demand compliance. This is an important theoretical assumption to which we return in the next chapter. As regards the sixth experimental study, further support was provided for the Sigall, Aronson, and Van Hoose hypothesis that subjects, given a strongly felt conflict between their perceptions of demand characteristics and presenting a good appearance, may tend to opt for the latter behavioral alternative. Contrary to expectation, there was no strong evidence that nonvolunteers were any more responsive to ego-defensive cues than volunteers, although there was at least a hint of this possibility.

Given these experimental findings, what can be said now about the pervasive influence of voluntarism as a potential artifact-independent variable? In view of the fact that several hundred studies have used the verbal conditioning paradigm on volunteer subjects (Resnick and Schwartz, 1973), and who knows how many hundreds of social influence studies have used the before–after opinionnaire design, the fact of having isolated this artifact in these broad domains of experimental inquiry should at least suggest the variable's potential pervasiveness. However, to focus on the factor of pervasiveness to the exclusion of other important criteria may be misleading in the implications for the conceptualization of artifacts in general. Thus, in the next chapter we argue that artifact stimuli may not typically function as autonomous variables able to be ranked according to their pervasiveness as independent sources of systematic error. Probably like any other variable in social psychology, artifact stimuli also interact in complex ways, their pervasiveness as independent contaminants depending on what other factors are operating. This point will be emphasized in the next chapter in generating an integrative model of the artifact influence process in which volunteer status is postulated to be one of an array of intervening factors.

Turning finally to the seventh study and the question posed earlier concerning which of three views best defines the customary role expectations of subjects for experimental research, those findings revealed elements of all three conceptions in the spectrum of role expectations that subjects associated with research participation. No single formulation was exclusively valid or invalid, although there was a strong indication that altruistic and evaluative situations, in that order, bore the closest resemblance to the target stimulus with substantially less similarity in role expectations noted between situations tapping obedience to authority. These results provide compelling support both for Orne's contention that the typical subject associates altruistic expectations with the experience of participating in a psychology experiment as well as for Rosenberg's conception of the experience as being heavily weighted by evaluative role expectations. As regards differences between willing and unwilling subjects, the results showed that nonvoluntary subjects put significantly heavier emphasis on a work-oriented dimension than did volunteers, whereas the volunteers placed more weight on an affective dimension. That nonvolunteers tended to amplify the distinction between situations involving work and nonwork activities and judged research participation more as a work-oriented experience seems consistent with a finding by Straits and Wuebben (1973) that it is the negative aspects of experimental participation that are likely to be more salient for nonvoluntary subjects (with the reverse result occurring among volunteers). The collective findings may help to explain why nonvolunteers can be so unenthusiastic about participating as research subjects as well as their generally sluggish behavior when they are unpaid, captive subjects; that is, being compelled to work when there is no personal monetary gain attached to the effort could be seen as promoting uncooperative behavior in subjects who are perhaps already more attuned to the negative aspects of the "work" situation.

CHAPTER 6

An Integrative Overview

We have been discussing how the subject's volunteer status may determine his role enactment and thereby affect the tenability of research findings based on that behavior. While it is probably true that all social-influence theories bear to some extent on this issue, William McGuire's (1968a, 1969b) information-processing formulation has provided us with an illuminating vantage point from which to examine the interaction of factors such as voluntarism, demand clarity, and the like, in influencing subjects' role behaviors.

This hybrid model visualizes the social influence process as a six-step Markov chain (communication → attention → comprehension → yielding → retention → behavior), the dependent variable being influenceability, or what is broadly interpreted as a tendency to change in response to social pressure. Hence, altering one's opinions on a matter-of-fact or a matter-of-taste are included, as are judgments and movements in reaction to group pressures and normative expectancies. The fundamental postulate of the theory is that influenceability is a positive function of two requisite mediational steps: effective reception of the stimulus (through attention and comprehension) and yielding to what was understood. Influenceability is affected insofar as the subject adequately receives the stimulus and yields to the point received, and any additional variables are thought to affect influenceability indirectly by acting on receptivity, yielding, or a residual factor representing the probability of all other relevant processes.

Given that influenceability may be liberally generalized to encompass the subject's reaction to demand characteristics, an abbreviated and slightly modified version of McGuire's model can be fitted to the data on experimental artifacts. In the proposed view, the status of voluntarism as an artifact-independent variable is seen as one of an array of usually uncontrolled stimuli that operate on a few main intervening variables affecting demand compliance. We begin this chapter with an outline of the postulated artifact-influence model and conclude with a discussion of alternatives for dealing with the ensuing methodological problem. (A survey of general factors jeopardizing the validity of various experimental and quasi experimental designs can be found in the monograph by Campbell and Stanley, 1966, and more recently in a chapter by Cook and Campbell, 1974.)

THE ARTIFACT-INFLUENCE MODEL

The central thesis of the proposed view is that there are three mutually exclusive and exhaustive states of behavior that are the end products of three conjoint mediators, and artifact-independent variables affect the ultimate outcomes of studies by indirectly impinging on the behavioral states at any of the mediating points (Rosnow and Aiken, 1973). Table 6-1 defines the three mutually exclusive and exhaustive states of overt behavior corresponding to this liberalized conception of influenceability. In essence, a trichotomy of role enactments is postulated, consisting of compliant behavior, noncompliant behavior, and countercompliant behavior. It is theorized that these behavioral states are the end products of the mediating variables defined in Table 6-2 and that artifact-determining stimuli, such as the subject's volunteer status, affect role behaviors only indirectly by acting on the appropriate mediating variable. Thus, a subject could adequately receive the demand characteristics operating in an experimental situation or some proportion thereof, or he could be unreceptive or unclear about what demands were operating. Second, his motivation to comply with such demands could range from acquiescence to counteracquiescence. Third, he might or might not have the capability of responding to the demand characteristics he received. Very generally speaking, the three motivational states in Table 6-2 correspond to Willis' (1965) familiar concepts of conformity, anticonformity, and independence, although with regard to the third motivational state, no distinction will be drawn between unmotivated and motivated nonacquiescence as both should lead to the same behavioral outcome (cf. Kelvin, 1971; Stricker, Messick, and Jackson, 1970).

Table 6-1.   Mutually Exclusive and Exhaustive Behavioral Influenceability States Pursuant to the Demand Characteristics of an Experiment

State of behavior	Notation	Description
Compliant behavior	B^+	Cooperative behavior in capitulation to the demand characteristics of the situation.
Noncompliant behavior	B^0	Behavior overtly unaffected by the demand characteristics of the situation.
Countercompliant behavior	B^-	Behavior antithetical to the demand characteristics of the situation.

The theoretical sequences leading to the three behavioral outcomes are depicted in Fig. 6-1 in the form of a tree diagram. There is only one branch of the tree that leads to compliance with demand characteristics. This branch, labeled 1, requires adequate reception, a positive motivation, and the capability to pursue that motivation. There is also only one branch that leads to counter-compliance with demand characteristics. This branch, labeled 3, requires adequate reception, a counteracquiescent motivation, and the capability to express that negative motivation behaviorally. All the remaining paths lead to non-compliance. Path 6 is limited by the receptivity state; path 5, by the motivational state; and paths 2 and 4, by the capability state. If the subject failed to perceive any demand characteristics, he could not possibly act on them (path 6). If he received demand characteristics but was unmotivated to act on them, they could not affect his experimental behavior (path 5). If the subject perceived demand characteristics, was motivated in an acquiescent direction, and yet was unable to comply, the demand characteristics could not influence his experimental behavior (path 2). Neither could they distort his experimental reaction if he received them and was motivated in a counteracquiescent direction but lacked the capacity to manifest his negative motivation behaviorally (path 4). The complete artifact-influence sequence is thus conceptualized as a five-step chain when compliance or countercompliance is the end product.

Table 6-2.   Mutually Exclusive and Exhaustive Subject States for Each of Three Mediating Variables

Mediator	State	Notation	Description
Receptivity	Adequate	R^+	Subject effectively receives demand characteristics.
	Inadequate	R^0	Subject fails to receive, or inadequately receives, demand characteristics.
Motivation	Acquiescent	A^+	Subject is in an acquiescent mood pursuant to demand characteristics.
	Nonacquiescent	A^0	Subject is not motivated to respond overtly to demand characteristics.
	Counteracquiescent	A^-	Subject is in a counteracquiescent mood pursuant to demand characteristics.
Capability	Capable	C^+	Subject is capable of manifesting his demand motivation behaviorally.
	Incapable	C^0	Subject is incapable of manifesting his demand motivation behaviorally.

STEPS IN THE ARTIFACT INFLUENCE PROCESS

Origins of Demand Characteristics

In coining the term *demand characteristics* (which comprise both uncontrolled explicit and implicit task-orienting cues), Orne (1962a, p. 779) speculated on their varied origins in rumors and campus scuttlebutt (cf. Wuebben, 1967; Taub and Farrow, 1973), in information conveyed during the original solicitation for subjects, in the person of the experimenter and the experimental setting, and in the experimental procedure itself. It was shown in the preceding chapter that when an attitude questionnaire is given twice with some intervening persuasive communication, this may convey manipulatory intent, a type of implicit demand characteristic also anticipated by Orne. The subject's preconceptions of the experimental situation as a function of his prior experimental experiences could be another unexpected source of demand characteristics —as, for example, in the subject's preconceived ideas about the characteristics of hypnotic behavior (Orne, 1959, 1970). (Recall in Chapter 4 our mention of the experiment in which catalepsy of the dominant hand was concocted as a characteristic of hypnosis.) Other sources of demand characteristics could be the experimenter's sex and scientific experience, his personality and expectations, and his modeling behavior (Kintz, Delprato, Mettee, Persons and Schappe, 1965; Rosenthal, 1966, 1967, 1969).

Modeling cues may arise when the investigator projects his own views onto the subject. While it is difficult to predict the direction and magnitude of modeling effects in laboratory experimentation, in survey research they are usually positive but variable in magnitude (Rosenthal, 1966, p. 112 ff.). The interpretation of the variability of direction in modeling effects that seems best supported by the evidence, although still not firmly established, is that a happier, more pleasant, less tense experimenter will tend to model his subjects negatively, whereas less pleasant, more tense experimenters will produce positive modeling effects. Exactly why this should be is not clear, although it is possible to speculate on the phenomenon within the framework of reinforcement theory. The emotional tone conveyed by the experimenter could be a stimulus source of satisfaction or dissatisfaction that, by (unwittingly) rewarding or punishing the subject for his experimental behavior, also helps to shape it in a particular fashion (cf. Jones and Cooper, 1971). If there is a methodological lesson to be learned from the informative research on modeling behavior in children, it is that demand characteristics are cognitively processed and that compliance will depend on the cognitive and emotional linkages with such behavior in the subject's mind (cf. Bryan and London, 1970; Rosenhan, 1969; Rosenhan and White, 1967). However, in order to be cognitively processed, first the cues must be adequately received.

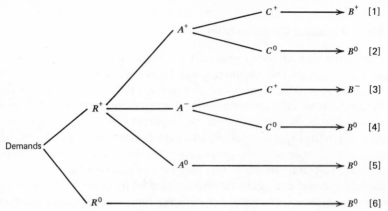

Fig. 6-1. Sequences of determining states leading to compliance, noncompliance, and counter-compliance (after Rosnow and Aiken, 1973).

Receptivity

A number of studies point tentatively to such factors as the scientific atmosphere of the experimental setting and the sheer amount of the subject's experience or prior knowledge as possible determinants of the facility for recognizing and interpreting demand characteristics (Goodstadt, 1971; Holmes, 1967; Holmes and Applebaum, 1970;Milgram, 1965; Stumberg, 1925; cf. discussion by Weber and Cook, 1972). The experimenter's professional manner may serve to legitimize for the subject his cooperative behavior (Rosenthal, 1966, p. 258), and recent findings, which lend support to this idea, suggest that the practiced experimenter, by his professional behavior, will prompt his subjects to perceive the experiment in a more scientific light (Straits, Wuebben, and Majka, 1972).

Silverman, Shulman, and Wiesenthal (1970) had introductory psychology students participate in two experiments. In the first, they were either deceived and debriefed or else took part in an ordinary memory study without deception. For their second participation, which occurred one week later, the subjects were all given a series of tests to check on how compliant with demand characteristics they now were. What is relevant to the present discussion from the standpoint of the receptivity mediator is that the deception apparently sensitized the subjects to possible ulterior evaluation cues in the second experimental session. In conformity research, suspiciousness of deception (which could be enhanced by communication between subjects) appears to predominate among young male subjects and to correlate positively with social desirability, ascendance, self-esteem, and intelligence (Stricker, Messick, and Jackson, 1967). Other work suggests an even more basic and intuitive principle for the operation of this initial mediator in the artifact-influence chain, which is that insofar as demand characteristics are simple and straightforward, they are likely to be clearly received (Adair and Schachter, 1972; Silverman, 1968). However, research also implies that role behaviors may be as much a function of the blatancy as the clarity of demand characteristics (a point to which we return shortly).

Motivation

The studies in Chapter 5 suggested that the second mediator in the artifact-influence chain, the subject's motivation, may be influenced by his original willingness to participate. In that series of studies in which volunteer status was the independent variable and the clarity of demand characteristics was held roughly constant across levels of verbal voluntarism in each experiment, willing subjects exhibited role behaviors implying greater acquiescence than captive nonvolunteers. It is difficult to explain such behavior simply as a self-selection of conformist people in volunteer situations, as the relationship between voluntarism and conformity (Chapter 2), while not conclusive, suggested that volunteers were, if anything, less conforming than nonvolunteers. Self-selection on the basis of high social desirability or need for approval is, however, a very real possibility.

A cognitive dissonance hypothesis that volunteering induces self-justification needed to cooperate is one plausible alternative. Silverman (1965) has developed this interesting idea, reasoning that subjects are motivated to make the experimental outcome successful in order to justify the time and effort they will have had to expend. Hence, any reward for participating in the experiment, whether it be monetary or psychological, should reduce this dissonance and the need to comply with demand characteristics. Unfortunately, the evidence on this score is mixed. Weitz (1968) did a standard experimenter-expectancy manipulation using Harvard undergraduates, in which paid and unpaid voluntary and nonvoluntary subjects were exposed to positive and negative expectancy demands. As one would predict from cognitive dissonance theory, compliance with demand characteristics was greatest among the unpaid volunteers. In fact, there was a strong boomerang effect for the paid volunteers. However, when a similar experiment was carried out by Mackenzie (1969) using high school students, his results were quite the opposite of a cognitive dissonance outcome. In this case, the paid volunteers showed considerable demand compliance, almost as much as a group of unpaid nonvolunteers. Silverman also reminds us that the cognitive dissonance interpretation is contrary to Ward and Sandvold's (1963) notion that salary increases the subject's sense of obligation and thus makes him more amenable to the experimenter's demands.

Certainly there are other plausible explanations besides cognitive dissonance theory for volunteers' usually strong predilection to comply with demand characteristics. From Bem's (1970) theory that behavior determines attitudes, one might posit that the act of volunteering could be cognitively interpreted by subjects as overt evidence of their own acquiescence, a cognition that feeds on itself and to which they submit in responding to the demand characteristics of the situation. Volunteering may be the foot in the door that opens the way to further compliance (cf. Freedman and Fraser, 1966). Alternatively, given that altruistic role expectations may be strongly associated with psychological research participation in our culture (cf. final study in Chapter 5), perhaps volunteers are compliant as a function of salient social expectancies. Since, from another point of view, helping behavior can be seen as instrumentally rewarding in terms of the psychological benefits accrued by the donor (cf. Foa, 1971; Handfinger, 1973; Weiss, Buchanan, Alstatt and Lombardo, 1971), possibly demand compliance serves a similar function for some research subjects (cf. Eisenman, 1972).

As long as there is not a conflict between demand compliance and the desire to project a favorable image, the fact of having been made to feel apprehensive about being evaluated also seems to bolster acquiescence tendencies. Minor (1970; cf. Johnson, 1973a) succeeded in producing experimenter expectancy effects only when his subjects were made to feel ego-involved in their performances. Henchy and Glass (1965) found that the presence of an audience enhanced the emission of dominant responses at the expense of subordinate responses only under conditions where the audience was perceived as an evaluative element of the situation. Several studies have shown that anonymous subjects are less compliant with demand characteristics than subjects who can be individually identified by the experimenter (Rosnow, Goodstadt, Suls and Gitter, 1973; Rosnow, Holper, and Gitter, 1973; Silverman, 1968). If all these different manipulations were linked to Rosenberg's (1965, 1969) concept of evaluation apprehension, but merely involved different levels of evaluation anxiety, the collective results might imply a monotonic relationship with acquiescence when task- and ego-orienting cues are operating in harmony. However, when evaluation apprehension and demand characteristics are strongly in conflict—as in the sixth study in Chapter 5 and in the experiment by Sigall, Aronson, and Van Hoose (1970; see also Page, 1971a)—this seems to dampen acquiescence, with deceptions sometimes increasing the tendency for favorable self-presentations and decreasing demand compliance (Silverman, Shulman, and Wiesenthal, 1970).

The experiment by Resnick and Schwartz (Chapter 4), when viewed together with the verbal-conditioning results with informed and naïve volunteers and nonvolunteers in Chapter 5, implies another condition in which negative motivations may prevail. Subjects who feel their freedom to act is constrained by demand characteristics may approach the experimental situation from a counteracquiescent set. Thus, in a follow-up to Horowitz's study on fear arousal, discussed in Chapter 4, Horowitz and Gumenik (1970) systematically replicated the procedure in light of implications of Brehm's (1966) reactance theory, which would predict boomerang effects for subjects denied freedom of choice. This time, volunteers and nonvolunteers for a previous study were either given or not given an opportunity to select the particular required experiment in which to participate. The subjects who were allowed a choice showed greater acceptance of the recommendations of the fear appeal as the level of emotional arousal was increased from low to high, whereas the nonvolunteers who hadn't any freedom in the selection of experiments reacted in the opposite way.

In other research on demand motivation, Rubin and Moore (1971) found suspicious subjects with low authoritarian scores likely to react against perceived demands, and there is a hint that the emotional tone of subjects' attitudes toward psychology may correlate with their motivational set when participating in a psychological experiment (Adair, 1969, 1970; Adair and Fenton, 1970). There are other variables as well which may ultimately be shown to have a depressive effect on motivations. Modeling cues were mentioned earlier as possibly affecting subjects' instrumental role behaviors (cf. Feldman and Scheibe, 1972; Silverman, Shulman, and Wiesenthal, 1972). Klinger (1967) showed that nonverbal cues from an experimenter who appeared more achievement-motivated elicited significantly more achievement-motivated responses from his subjects. Evidence of counterconditioning behavior was identified in subjects labeled as psychopathic or sociopathic (Cairns, 1961; Johns and Quay, 1962; Quay and Hunt, 1965), an effect that could perhaps also generalize to anti-establishment role behaviors in the research situation. The experimenter's manner and temperament, the subject's suspicion about the nature of the research or his frustrating earlier experiences, and his perception of role expectancies—these are promising candidates and await more definitive examination (cf. Brock and Becker, 1966; Cook, Bean, Calder, Frey, Krovetz, and Reisman, 1970; Fillenbaum, 1966; Grabitz-Gniech, 1972; Gustafson and Orne, 1965; Marquis, 1973; McGuire, 1969a; Silverman and Kleinman, 1967; Silverman and Shulman, 1969, 1970; Silverman, Shulman and Wiesenthal, 1970).

Capability

Residual factors affecting the subject's capability to enact a particular role behavior could include specific situational determinants having a pervasive effect on the entire subject pool as well as idiosyncratic characteristics (cf. Rosenzweig, 1952). If a critical response is beyond the subject's reaction threshold, he should be incapable of responding to demand characteristics whatever his levels of receptivity and motivation. By the same token, if his latitude of movement was artificially restrained by observational or measurement boundaries, demand compliant behavior should be nil. A subject in a before–after attitude experiment might end up noncompliant, for example, if his pretest response were so extreme that he could not respond more extremely in the direction of the manipulation on the posttest.

A subject might also be biologically incapable of complying with the experimenter's wishes or expectations. Not all volunteers will be capable of conforming to some coercive demands no matter how intensely motivated and knowledgeable they are. Although it has been documented that some nonhypnotized control subjects can perform the "human-plank trick" on being instructed to do so by a competent investigator (Barber, 1969; Orne, 1962b), no doubt even the most acquiescent volunteer would fail to comply with this experimental demand if he lacked the sheer physical stamina to lie suspended in midair with only his head and feet resting on supports. However, because the self-selection process in research volunteering tends to weed out incapability—just as incompetence is weeded out by self-selection in volunteering for extraexperimental altruistic acts (Kazdin and Bryan, 1971)—this mediating factor may be of little practical consequence for understanding the antecedents of role behaviors in psychological experimentation. Furthermore, most experienced investigators are usually attuned to these obvious limitations and are very careful to select research settings that are well within the bounds of their subjects' capabilities. The settings that have been traditionally chosen by laboratory researchers may favor not only elicitation of the desired critical responses within the subjects' normal capabilities but also any undesired responses to demand characteristics lurking in those situations.

Behavior

In the parent formulation it is presumed that independent variables relate to influenceability primarily through the combined mediation of receptivity and yielding (McGuire, 1968b). The artifact-influence model visualizes artifact stimuli as relating to demand behaviors mainly through the combined mediation of receptivity and motivation. For example, Fig. 6-2 expresses the postulated relationship between the demand clarity factor briefly discussed in the preceding chapter and role behavior pursuant to the demand characteristics of the situation. The inverted U-shaped function alluded to earlier can now be envisioned as the product of a positive association with receptivity and a negative association with motivation; that is, demand receptivity is postulated as increasing with an increase in demand clarity, while acquiescence is postulated as decreasing with an increase in demand clarity. When cues are so patently obtrusive as to restrict seriously the subject's latitude of movement, the resulting increase in psychological reactance should have a dampening effect on motivations, even to the point of arousing a counteracquiescent set. We assume that other artifact stimuli affect role behaviors in a similar combinatorial fashion by indirectly impinging on these primary mediating states.

The factor of evaluation apprehension can also be reinterpreted with the help of the combinatorial rule. Assuming that receptivity would remain roughly level throughout, where task- and ego-orienting cues are operating harmoniously evaluation apprehension may bolster motivations to comply. In this case, demand compliance would be congruent with the subject's desire to project a favorable image and there should be a positive association with motivation (see Fig. 6-3a). Alternatively, when incongruent task- and ego-orienting cues coexist, evaluation apprehension may have a depressive effect on motivations. In this case, demand compliance would be incongruent with the subject's desire to project a favorable image, and following from data already discussed, ego-defensive needs should emerge as the predominant motivating force. With receptivity again at a roughly constant level, there would be a negative association with motivation (Fig. 6-3b).

One can infer the simple relationship between these mediating states and demand behavior in a study by Koenigsberg (1971) using the verbal-conditioning paradigm, although the results do not bear directly on our postulated combinatorial effects. In this study, subjects were divided into four groups on the basis of their responses to a postexperimental awareness–motivation questionnaire. Some of the subjects in each group had been conditioned by an experimenter with positive expectancies for their behavior and the others, by an experimenter having negative expectations, although we are concerned here

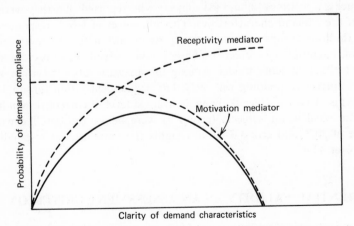

Fig. 6-2. Postulated curvilinear relationship (shown by a solid line) between demand clarity and demand compliance.

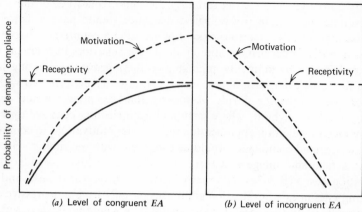

Fig. 6-3. Postulated curvilinear relationships (shown by solid lines) between evaluation apprehension (*EA*) and demand compliance when (a) task- and ego-orienting cues are operating harmoniously and (b) task- and ego-orienting cues are operating nonharmoniously.

only with the classification main effect. There are some difficulties in interpretation because of possible ambiguities in his grouping of responses. However, the four groups might be classified as (1) subjects who were aware of the demand characteristics and were positively motivated (e.g., "I felt that I was doing what he wanted me to" and "I thought it might be of some benefit to him."); (2) subjects with a counteracquiescent motivational set (e.g., "I did not wish him to control my thinking."); (3) a conglomerate of nonacquiescent subjects and subjects operating on poor receptivity (e.g., "I didn't recognize a pattern and didn't worry about following a pattern" and "I started to make it balance out at times."); and (4) subjects who reported that they were unaware of the demand characteristics. The differences in I–WE responding between the four groups were statistically significant at the .01 level, and the order of magnitude of correct responses could probably have been predicted by the artifact-influence model. Among the unaware subjects (group 4), the level of correct responding was 39.3. The acquiescent group (group 1) surpassed this "baseline" mean, giving an average level of correct responding of 52.6; the recalcitrant subjects (group 2) were below the baseline with an average of 30.7; and group 3 fell at roughly the same level of responding as group 4 or 41.4.

INFERENTIAL VALIDITY AS AN ASSESSMENT CRITERION

In cataloguing the predominant artifact stimuli that distort dependent measures in behavioral research, our assumption has been that these confounding factors (of which the subject's volunteer status was considered to be one) operated via a few mediating variables. A practical advantage of this integrative position is that rather than having to concern oneself with juggling an unmanageable number of control procedures for specifically coping with each artifact stimulus separately, it is possible to conceptualize the artifact problem from a broader perspective and seek ways of establishing the tenability of research findings at a more workable level of analysis. The concept of *inferential validity* provides one convenient, practicable criterion for assessing the tenability of inferred causal relationships in behavioral research.

The object of experimental research in psychology is to observe psychological processes in a precisely controlled standard situation where it is possible to manipulate some given independent variable or interfere carefully with some normally occurring relationship while holding everything else constant. To be able to draw legitimate inferences from such findings to situations outside the research setting presumes that the experimental conditions adequately reflect the actual processes under investigation. Questions of inferential validity ask whether conclusions drawn from a set of research data are also tenable in the corresponding naturalistic environment where the subject's behavior is not influenced by situationally localized *experimental* cues (Rosnow and Aiken, 1973).

Whether conclusions from experimental studies are inferentially valid should, according to this view, hinge fundamentally on the subject's awareness of the nature of the situation and how his behavior is guided by this knowledge; that is, insofar as the subject is responsive to the investigative aura of the laboratory or field setting in which he finds himself, he is probably attuned to localized cues on the basis of which he can generate hypotheses about the aims or expectations of the research. In general, we are assuming that role-restricting experimental contingencies of the sort just discussed can initially come to bear only if the subject becomes aware of the special nature of the situation. His awareness may directly or indirectly stem from cues that he received before or during the treatment or experimental manipulation or that were contained somehow in the research setting itself. Awareness might also be the result of inadvertent measurement or observation cues or of forewarning by the investigator about some aspect of the setting because of the investigator's ethical concerns. Since in actual practice manipulation and measurement are usually very closely intertwined in an obvious way, the same role-mediating contingencies could be operating throughout a research study. We turn now to procedures aimed either at bypassing the inferential invalidity problem or at partialing out systematic error that may have contributed to a biased experimental outcome.

Field Research With Unobtrusive Measures

Using very young or abnormally unsophisticated subjects, while it might lead to a low level of awareness, would also automatically limit the generality of the research data (Rosenzweig, 1933; Stricker, Messick and Jackson, 1969, p. 349). An approach that aims to skirt the artifact problem while also encouraging a high degree of robustness has been to use techniques of disguised experimentation in natural, nonlaboratory settings (Campbell, 1969). The assumption is that by emphasizing naturalistic social demands and not laboratory demand characteristics, the subject's motivations and capabilities pursuant to the latter will not become an issue affecting his responses to the former. Webb, Campbell, Schwartz and Sechrest (1966) have provided an excellent treatment of this research strategy as well as a compelling rationale for the greater utilization of unobtrusive measures. Instead of a single, critical experiment on a problem, they have recommended a sequence of linked investigations, each of which examines some different substantive outcropping of the hypothesis. Through triangulation of the data, the experimenter can logically strip away plausible rival explanations for his findings.

The field experimental approach was used by Rosenbaum (1956; Rosenbaum and Blake, 1955) in research on the prepotency of social pressures as a determinant of volunteering behavior. Several students at the University of Texas were seated at desks in a library. In one condition an accomplice seated at the same desk as a student agreed to participate in the experimenter's research. In another condition the accomplice refused to participate; in the control condition the accomplice was absent. Significantly more students volunteered in the first condition than in the control, and significantly fewer students volunteered in the second condition than in the control. Thus, in a naturalistic experiment on experimental recruiting, it was demonstrated that witnessing another person volunteer or refuse to volunteer strongly influenced the observer's own decision to volunteer.

In other applications of this approach, Gelfand, Hartmann, Walder and Page (1973) studied the kinds of people who report shoplifters by having a confederate actually stuff drugstore merchandise into her handbag while other customers were around. Doob and Gross (1968) explored an aspect of frustration–aggression by having someone drive up to a signal-controlled intersection and remain stopped for a time in order to provoke a horn-honking response from the car behind. Mann and Taylor (1969) studied positioning in long queues for football tickets, Batman shirts, and chocolate bars to investigate the effect of people's motives upon their estimates of how many others were standing in line ahead of them. Milgram, Bickman, and Berkowitz (1969) examined the drawing power of different sized crowds on a busy Manhattan street by having confederates stop for a minute and look up at a sixth-floor window. Hartmann (1936) explored the effect on voting patterns of emotional and rational Socialist party leaflets distributed during a local election in Pennsylvania in which his own name was on the ballot. As one can readily discern, this research approach has inspired many ingenious studies (cf. Bickman and Henchy, 1972; Evans and Rozelle, 1973; Swingle, 1973), although, in general, field research has still seen comparatively limited usage among social psychologists (Fried, Gumpper, and Allen, 1973). However, while field experimentation accompanied by unobtrusive measurement is a methodology that certainly has the potential for contributing theoretically enlightening findings, it is also true in practice that it seldom permits the degree of precision in the measurement of dependent variables afforded by laboratory research. Mindful of this possible limitation, other investigators have turned to the use of experimental deceptions as a way of capturing some degree of naturalistic realism in their research. When a good deception manipulation is effectively set into operation, it should arouse the subjects in much the same way they would be affected by a complex of naturalistic stimuli (cf. Aronson and Carlsmith, 1968; Rosenzweig, 1933, p. 346 $f.$).

Laboratory Deceptions

Quite different kinds of deceptions were incorporated in some of the scenarios reported in the preceding chapter. It will be recalled that some subjects in the third exploratory study (on cognitive dissonance) were intended to believe that their university had commissioned the survey because the administration was interested in putting one of the ideas into practice the following year. In this case, the rationale for using deception was to determine whether it might function in the way a two-sided communication seemed to work in the previous exploratory study, in effect to obfuscate laboratory demand characteristics.

Stricker (1967) discovered that nearly one-fifth of the research appearing in 1964 in four major social psychological journals involved some form of deception, and Menges (1973) found the same percentage in a survey of articles published during 1971 in a more varied assortment of psychological journals. Besides concerns about the ethicality of this approach to social inquiry, the question has been asked repeatedly whether researchers can really be certain about who the "true" deceiver is in their studies. It is important to have effective guidelines for evaluating the results of deception studies (cf. Orne, Thackray, and Paskewitz, 1972; Stricker, Messick, and Jackson, 1969), particularly inasmuch as subjects are often reluctant to confess their awareness of being deceived or of having prior information (Levy, 1967; Newberry, 1973; Taub and Farrow, 1973).

Concerned about this problem, Orne (1969) proposed the use of "quasi-control" subjects for ferreting out the potential biasing effects of role mediating variables in situations of this sort. Quasi-control subjects, who typically are from the same population as the research subjects, step out of their traditional role (the experimenter–subject interaction being redefined to make quasi-control subjects "co-investigators" instead of manipulated objects) and clinically reflect upon the context in which an experiment was conducted. They are asked to speculate on ways in which the context might influence their own and research subjects' behaviors.

One quasi-control approach employs research subjects who function as their own controls. The procedure involves eliciting from the subjects by judicious and exhaustive inquiry, either in a postexperimental interview or in an interview conducted after a pilot study, their perceptions and beliefs about the experimental situation without making them unduly suspicious or inadvertently cuing them about what to say. Recently, there has been some attention paid to testing different postexperimental inquiry procedures that seek to optimize the likelihood of detecting demand awareness (Page, 1971b, 1973). There is, of course, the recurrent problem of demand characteristics in the inquiry itself, a potential hazard that researchers will have to be mindful of when adopting this strategy. A second quasi-control procedure is preinquiry, in which control subjects are provided with information about the experiment that is equivalent to that available to an actual research subject and they are asked to imagine themselves to be research subjects (cf. Straits, Wuebben, and Majka, 1972). Another alternative is like the second in that the experimental situation is simulated for control subjects whose task is to imagine how they might behave if the situation were real, but in this case blind controls and quasi-controls are simultaneously treated by an experimenter who the subjects know is unaware of their status.

The present theoretical orientation suggests a bit of structure that could be imposed on the questions presented to a quasi-control subject, such as inviting him to comment on feelings of acquiscence and evaluation apprehension and on his perceptions of cues revealing the experimenter's expectations. The main deficiency of the procedure is that it provides only a very rough estimate of awareness of demand contingencies, still leaving the investigator with the knotty problem of trying to determine the extent to which his dependent measure was actually contaminated by uncontrolled factors of the type described.

In an effort to bypass this last problem, the "bogus pipeline" was conceived by Jones and Sigall (1971) as a testable paradigm for assuring more objectively valid data by directly incorporating deception in the dependent measurement. The format of the bogus pipeline is comparable to most self-rating attitude measures except that the subject is led to believe that a physiological monitoring device can reliably catch him when he is lying. Claims for the efficacy of this measurement paradigm currently rest on its power to attenuate social desirability responses in the expression of negative interpersonal sentiments (Sigall and Page, 1971, 1972). While assurances of inferential validity and measurement sensitivity are debatable at this stage (Jones and Sigall, 1973; Ostrom, 1973), the approach does provide an imaginative first step for trying to circumvent the artifact problem in laboratory behavioral measures of attitude and affect. In seeking alternatives to deception manipulations, other investigators have resorted to role play and laboratory simulations as a way of trying vicariously to duplicate naturalistic realism without sacrificing the precision afforded by experimental control.

Role Play

An illustration of the use of role play was a study by Greenberg (1967) that replicated earlier social psychological findings on anxiety and affiliation. In a well-known series of experiments by Schachter (1959), subjects were allowed to wait with others or to wait alone before participating in a research project. For some subjects (the "high-anxiety" group) the anticipated project was described as involving painful electric shocks, while for others (the "low-anxiety" group) it was represented as involving no physical discomfort. Significantly more of the high-anxiety subjects chose to wait with others in a similar plight, a finding that inspired the conclusion that misery likes not only company but company that is equally miserable. Another finding in the research was that anxious firstborns and only-children showed this propensity to affiliate with others more so than did laterborns. In Greenberg's role-play study, the subjects were instructed to act as if the situation were real and they were audience to a scenario that was closely modeled after that employed in the original experiments. Although the statistical significance of Greenberg's role-play findings was mixed, the direction of his results was completely consistent with the earlier experimental findings.

There have been several more exploratory inquiries on role play since Greenberg's study (Darroch and Steiner, 1970; Horowitz and Rothschild, 1970; Wicker and Bushweiler, 1970; Willis and Willis, 1970), and the issue has drawn considerable discussion pro and con. However, opinions remain divided on the efficacy of role play as a dependable substitute for experimental research, some favoring it on moral or methodological grounds (Brown, 1962, p. 74; Kelman, 1967; Ring, 1967; Schultz, 1969) and others opposing it (Aronson and Carlsmith, 1968; Carlson, 1971; Freedman, 1969; McGuire, 1969; Miller, 1972). At this point, the exploratory findings are not sufficiently definitive to swing the consensus of scientific opinion one way or the other. Intuitively, one might speculate that role play will ultimately be shown to have only very restricted applicability as a methodological substitute for deception research. That there have already been differences discovered between role play and deception studies does not establish which methodology has the greater potential for inferential validity, since all the studies so far have concentrated on the comparative reliability of the two approaches. Even if role play should be preferred on ethical grounds (which is a debatable conclusion), this would not in and of itself guarantee that resulting data were inferentially valid. Perhaps the effectiveness of the role-play methodology can be improved by incorporating emotionally involving role enactments (e.g., Janis and Mann, 1965), by introducing incentives or other factors that might strengthen a subject's personal commitment to his pretend behavior (cf. Boies, 1972; Elms, 1969), or by programming greater congruence between role demands and the personalities of the actors (Moos and Speisman, 1962; O'Leary, 1972). The issue of inferential validity is an empirical question, and while role play may prove to have some limited potential as an experimental substitute, the validity question certainly merits further careful inquiry before the role-play procedure is universally sanctioned (cf. Holmes and Bennett, 1974; Orne, 1971).

Dual Observation

Up to this point we have been discussing some strategies for circumventing the inferential invalidity problem (1) by doing research in field settings with unobtrusive measures so that the subjects are blind to the investigative nature of the situation, (2) by employing laboratory deceptions having the capability of engrossing subjects in the same way that a complex of naturalistic social stimuli would, or (3) by using role simulations as a vicarious means of capturing naturalistic realism without sacrificing the precision of laboratory control. We also described two measurement approaches for dealing with this problem, one aimed at teasing out the potential biasing effects of role-mediating demand characteristics (Orne's quasi-control procedure) and the other designed to avoid confounding artifacts by directly incorporating deception into the dependent measurement (Jones and Sigall's bogus pipeline procedure). There is an alternative measurement paradigm that is more deeply rooted in the present theoretical position. It is the method of *dual observation,* which aims at estimating the inferential invalidity of experimental findings.

The conception of dual observation is simply to "reobserve" the original critical responses outside the laboratory in an atmosphere where the subject is not cognizant of whatever experimental implications of his behavior could have affected his initial responding (Rosnow and Aiken, 1973). This does not mean that he must be unaware of being observed, only that he does not connect the fact of his now being observed with the experiment or the experimenter.

In most cases, the difference between observations (minus the effects of random error or other nuisance variables) could provide an estimate of the invalidity that is a function of the totality of demand-associated artifacts operating in the experimental setting.

In effect, the approach is to manipulate the subject's response set, and in this respect it is similar to other useful measurement procedures also altering response set. The use of anonymity in measurement or of a bogus pipeline deception are other good examples of inducing a special response set in subjects. Indeed, establishing a particular set that is inclined to produce more valid, reliable, or representative responses is a familiar idea that has been examined both by experimental and social psychologists. Brunswik (1956, Pp. 93 ff.) discussed the possibility of separating subjects' attitudes statistically within the specific framework of perception. The phenomenological research he described experimented with creating a naïve perceptual attitude and comparing the effects against an analytical attitude. In half the cases he had the subject take a critical, or "betting," stance, and in half the cases he had the subject take an uncritical set. More recently, Jourard (1968, 1969) has argued that disclosure by experimenters should result in more honest responding by subjects, and Hood and Back (1971) found self-disclosure to the experimenter to be a prevalent tendency among volunteer subjects (cf. Cozby, 1973; Lyons, 1970, p. 25). However, what is distinctive about dual observation is that it is based on the notion of repeated measurement of the laboratory-dependent variable under conditions in which the original demand contingencies should no longer be affecting the subject's response set.

By way of illustration, a qualitative variation of this procedure was the multiple observation stratagem employed in a study of laboratory posthypnotic suggestion by Orne, Sheehan, and Evans (1968). Highly suggestible subjects who were under hypnosis and a control group that simulated hypnosis were given the suggestion that for the following 48 hours they would respond by touching their forehead every time they heard the word *experiment.* Initially, the experimenters tested the suggestion in the experimental setting, and then, to gauge the inferential validity of their laboratory findings, they observed the dependent variable again, this time unbeknownst to the subject presumably, by having a secretary in the waiting room confirm the time for which the subject was scheduled "to come for the next part of the *experiment.*" Later, she asked him whether it was all right to pay him "now for today's *experiment* and for the next part of the study tomorrow." On the following day she met the subject with the question, "Are you here for Dr. Sheehan's *experiment?*"

One might also imagine dual observation being used to test the inferential validity of a verbal-conditioning interview, a laboratory opinion-change procedure, or any of a wide variety of experimental paradigms. By reobserving the critical responses under conditions where the original theoretical contingencies were no longer salient or relevant or where they were unclear, absent, or ignored, it should be possible to assess the inferential validity of the original experimental behaviors. Insko (1965) studied verbal conditioning by having his assistants telephone students at the University of Hawaii and read statements to them about the possibility of celebrating a springtime Aloha Week. Half the subjects were reinforced with approval ("good") whenever they gave a positive response, and the other half were positively reinforced whenever they gave a negative response. One week later, an item about Aloha Week was surreptitiously embedded in a "Local Issues Questionnaire" that undergraduates filled out during class. Aronson (1966) experimented with using confederates to coax information about an experimental participation from their friends. Evans and Orne (1971) spied on subjects when the experimenter had left the room by employing an old, but little used, method of observation. Instead of the all too familiar one-way mirror, they watched the subject from behind a framed silk-screen painting that fitted into the natural decor of the room. The painting, which covered a hole in the wall, acted as a one-way screen when the observer looked from the dark to the lighter side. Variations of these and other techniques could easily be adapted for use in assessing the inferential invalidity of experimental findings. There are, of course, ethical implications to be considered in the use of dual observation, and experimenters must weigh the advantages and disadvantages of the paradigm.

REPRESENTATIVE RESEARCH DESIGN

There is one final aspect to the methodological issue we have been discussing. It concerns procedures for assuring (or being able to specify) the generality of causal experimental relationships given that the relationships are in fact inferentially valid. We are referring to the robustness of causal relationships, which was a focus of attention in Chapter 4.

In the specific case of the volunteer subject, the generality question translates into ways of assuring greater participation by nonvoluntary subjects. We mentioned in Chapter 1 that psychologists in academic institutions have achieved some measure of success in reducing volunteer sampling bias by the practice of requiring undergraduate majors to spend a specified number of hours serving as research subjects. However, which experiment he participates in is often left to the student in order not to encroach too much on his freedom of choice. While the practice of compulsory participation undoubtedly draws more nonvoluntary subjects into the overall sampling pool, their participation in any one experiment will not be a random event. Brighter students might sign up for learning experiments; gregarious students, for social interaction studies;

men, for unconventional experiments. For this reason, and because the APA code may be interpreted by some as officially countermanding this practice, new procedures may have to be tested for reducing volunteer bias by motivating the more traditionally nonvolunteer types of individuals to volunteer for experimental participation. The sociological and statistical literature on survey research is rich with suggestions for ameliorating volunteer sampling error, although some of the correction procedures travel hand in hand with other methodological problems. For example, research by Norman (1948) and Wallin (1949) implies that an increase in the potential respondent's degree of acquaintance with the investigator will lead to an increase in the likelihood of volunteering (see also Chapter 3). Similarly, an increase in the perceived status of the investigator should result in greater cooperation (Norman, 1948; Poor, 1967; see also Chapter 3). Although acquaintance with the experimenter might reduce volunteer bias by drawing more subjects into the sampling urn, it is conceivable that another type of error might be introduced as a result. Because there is evidence that experimenter-expectancy effects increase in likelihood the better acquainted that experimenters and subjects are (Rosenthal, 1966), in this case one would need to decide which type of error he would rather live with as well as which type could be more easily controlled.

A more subtle aspect to this problem was defined by Egon Brunswik; it concerns restrictions imposed on the generality of research conclusions as a function of the nonrepresentativeness of the research design that specified how the data were to be collected and partitioned. In the classical design, all the variables on the stimulus side are held constant except for the independent variable, x, and effects are then observed on the subject side upon the dependent variable, y. Expressed in the semantics of causal analysis, the rationale for the studies on artifact can thus be seen as proceeding from the assumption that the independent variable in the statement $y = f(x)$ is contaminated by unspecified determinants also affecting the dependent variable, the essence of the artifact problem stemming from the indeterminacy of the specification of what actually constitutes x and not-x (Boring, 1969). In the case of robustness, the problem usually concerns the extent to which a causal relationship is generalizable on the subject side; such generalizability should be proportional to the adequacy of the sampling procedures of all the relevant population variables. Brunswik (1947, 1955), however, pointed out another interesting issue that is a concomitant of the latter problem. Since research designs drawn from the classical design may impose restrictions on stimulus representativeness, causal generalization may also be limited as much on the stimulus side as on the subject side. To correct for this deficiency, Brunswik proposed that researchers sample from among stimuli and situations as well as from among subject populations.

Hammond (1948, 1951, 1954) has discussed the utility of this approach as it applies to clinical experimentation in particular. To illustrate its present applicability, suppose that we wished to test the hypothesis that male and female volunteers and nonvolunteers are differentially responsive to the experimental expectations of male and female investigators. If we proceeded from the classical design, we might seek a representative sample of volunteer and nonvolunteer subjects of both sexes and then assign them to a male or female experimenter whose experimental orientation was prescribed beforehand using a counterbalanced procedure. However, the extent to which any inferentially valid conclusions were generalizable to other subjects, other experimenters, and other experimental situations would be influenced by the fact that the only element representatively sampled was the subject variable. Since our design did not representatively sample from among populations of experimenters and situations, it could be hazardous to generalize beyond these meager limits. Generalizability could be further affected, however, if there were other relevant variables unrepresented that fell on neither the stimulus nor the subject side. For example, there could be biases in the interpretation of our data stemming from the ways in which psychologists of different political ideologies or different cultural or biographical backgrounds fulfilled their scientific role (Innes and Fraser, 1971; Pastore, 1949; Sherwood and Nataupsky, 1968). Indeed, one might conceive of a hierarchical regression of relevant distal and proximal variables worth representing. While it is obviously impossible to sample every potentially relevant variable in a study, Brunswik's contribution was to help us avoid a double standard in scrutinizing subject generality while ignoring the generality of other significant elements of the research situation.

CHAPTER 7

Summary

Nearly 30 years have passed since Quinn McNemar cautioned researchers that the routine practice of sampling populations of convenience was causing our science of human behavior to become "the science of the behavior of sophomores." Yet if recent data are representative, showing that from 70–90% of studies on normal adults have drawn subjects from the collegiate setting, that old warning may still ring true. Indeed, McNemar's assessment may eventually prove too sanguine, as not only do the data suggest an increase in the percentage of research subjects who are college students, but recent ethical concerns make one wonder if the behavioral science of the near future may have to draw its data exclusively from an elite subject corps of informed volunteers. The extent to which a useful, comprehensive science of human behavior can be based upon the behavior of such self-selected and investigator-selected subjects is an empirical question of broad importance, and the preceding chapters have dwelled on various significant aspects of this problem.

RELIABILITY OF VOLUNTEERING

How reliable is the act of volunteering to be a research subject? If volunteering were an unreliable event, we could not expect to find any stable relationships between it and various personal characteristics of willing and unwilling subjects, nor would it be logical to presume to study the experimental effects of voluntarism when it can be presented as an independent variable in the research paradigm. However, there are many personal characteristics that do relate predictably to the act of volunteering. Moreover, statistical measures of reliability tend to be satisfactorily high whether the measure of volunteering is simply stating one's willingness to participate or whether it is defined in terms of volunteering for sequentially different types of research tasks. From the available data, the median overall reliability for volunteering was computed as .52, which, by way of comparison, is identical to the median reliability of subtest intercorrelations as reported by Wechsler for the WAIS.

For studies requesting volunteers for the same task the median reliability was .80, and for studies asking for volunteers for different tasks it was .42. Although the number of studies on the reliability of volunteering is not large (10 studies), the findings do suggest that volunteering, like IQ, may have both general and specific predictors. Some people volunteer reliably more than others for a variety of tasks, and these reliable individual differences may be further stabilized when the particular task for which volunteering was requested is specifically considered.

ASSESSING THE NONVOLUNTEER

How do researchers determine the attributes of those who do not volunteer to participate? Several procedures have been found useful, and they can be grouped into one of two types, the exhaustive and the nonexhaustive.

In the exhaustive method, all potential subjects are identified by their status on all the variables on which volunteers and nonvolunteers are to be compared. They may be tested first and then recruited, as when the investigator begins with an archive of data on each person and then, sometimes years later, makes a request for volunteers. For example, incoming freshmen are routinely administered a battery of tests in many colleges, and these data can then be drawn upon in future comparisons. Another variation is to recruit subjects and then test them. In this case, subjects for behavioral research are solicited, usually in a college classroom context, and the names of the volunteers and nonvolunteers are sorted out by using the class roster; shortly thereafter, a test or some other material is administered to the entire class by someone ostensibly unrelated to the person who recruited the volunteers.

In the nonexhaustive method, data are not available for all potential subjects, but they are available for those differing in likelihood of finding their way into a final sample. Thus, one variation of the method uses the easy-to-recruit subject, although, because true nonvolunteers are not available, it requires extrapolation on a gradient of volunteering. The procedure in this case is to tap a population of volunteer subjects repeatedly so as to compare second-stage volunteers with first-stage volunteers, and so on. If repeated volunteers, for example, were higher in the need for social approval than one-time volunteers, then by extrapolating these data roughly to the zero level of volunteering it could be tentatively concluded that nonvolunteers might be lower still in approval need. Another variation gets at the hard-to-recruit subject by repeatedly increasing the incentive to volunteer, a method frequently used in survey research to tease more respondents into the sampling urn. Still another variation focuses on the slow-to-reply subject. In this case only a single request for volunteers is issued, and latency of volunteering is the criterion for dividing up the waves of respondents, as well as the basis for extrapolating to nonrespondents.

VOLUNTEER CHARACTERISTICS

Examining studies that used these various procedures for assessing the nonvolunteers, we drew the following conclusions about characteristics that may reliably differentiate willing and unwilling subjects:

Conclusions Warranting Maximum Confidence

1. Volunteers tend to be better educated than nonvolunteers, especially when personal contact between investigator and respondent is not required.
2. Volunteers tend to have higher social-class status than nonvolunteers, especially when social class is defined by respondents' own status rather than by parental status.
3. Volunteers tend to be more intelligent than nonvolunteers when volunteering is for research in general but not when volunteering is for somewhat less typical types of research such as hypnosis, sensory isolation, sex research, small-group and personality research.
4. Volunteers tend to be higher in need for social approval than nonvolunteers.
5. Volunteers tend to be more sociable than nonvolunteers.

Conclusions Warranting Considerable Confidence

6. Volunteers tend to be more arousal-seeking than nonvolunteers, especially when volunteering is for studies of stress, sensory isolation, and hypnosis.
7. Volunteers tend to be more unconventional than nonvolunteers, especially when volunteering is for studies of sex behavior.
8. Females are more likely than males to volunteer for research in general, but less likely than males to volunteer for physically and emotionally stressful research (e.g., electric shock, high temperature, sensory deprivation, interviews about sex behavior.)
9. Volunteers tend to be less authoritarian than nonvolunteers.
10. Jews are more likely to volunteer than Protestants, and Protestants are more likely to volunteer than Catholics.

11. Volunteers tend to be less conforming than nonvolunteers when volunteering is for research in general but not when subjects are female and the task is relatively "clinical" (e.g., hypnosis, sleep, or counseling research.)

Conclusions Warranting Some Confidence

12. Volunteers tend to be from smaller towns than nonvolunteers, especially when volunteering is for questionnaire studies.
13. Volunteers tend to be more interested in religion than nonvolunteers, especially when volunteering is for questionnaire studies.
14. Volunteers tend to be more altruistic than nonvolunteers.
15. Volunteers tend to be more self-disclosing than nonvolunteers.
16. Volunteers tend to be more maladjusted than nonvolunteers, especially when volunteering is for potentially unusual situations (e.g., drugs, hypnosis, high temperature, or vaguely described experiments) or for medical research employing clinical rather than psychometric definitions of psychopathology.
17. Volunteers tend to be younger than nonvolunteers, especially when volunteering is for laboratory research and especially if they are female.

Conclusions Warranting Minimum Confidence

18. Volunteers tend to be higher in need for achievement than nonvolunteers especially among American samples.
19. Volunteers are more likely to be married than nonvolunteers, especially when volunteering is for studies requiring no personal contact between investigator and respondent.
20. Firstborns are more likely than laterborns to volunteer, especially when recruitment is personal and when the research requires group interaction and a low level of stress.
21. Volunteers tend to be more anxious than nonvolunteers, especially when volunteering is for standard, nonstressful tasks and especially if they are college students.
22. Volunteers tend to be more extraverted than nonvolunteers when interaction with others is required by the nature of the research.

SITUATIONAL DETERMINANTS

What are the variables that tend to increase or decrease the rates of volunteering obtained? The answer to this question has implications both for the theory and practice of the behavioral sciences. If we can learn more about the situational determinants of volunteering, we will also have learned more about the social psychology of social-influence processes and, in terms of methodology, be in a better position to reduce the bias in our samples that derives from volunteers being systematically different from nonvolunteers on a variety of personal characteristics. As with the previous list of conclusions, our inventory of situational determinants was developed inductively, based on an examination of a fairly sizable number of research studies:

Conclusions Warranting Maximum Confidence

1. Persons more interested in the topic under investigation are more likely to volunteer.
2. Persons with expectations of being more favorably evaluated by the investigator are more likely to volunteer.

Conclusions Warranting Considerable Confidence

3. Persons perceiving the investigation as more important are more likely to volunteer.
4. Persons' feeling states at the time of the request for volunteers are likely to affect the probability of volunteering. Persons feeling guilty are more likely to volunteer, especially when contact with the unintended victim can be avoided and when the source of guilt is known to others. Persons made to "feel good" or to feel competent are also more likely to volunteer.
5. Persons offered greater material incentives are more likely to volunteer, especially if the incentives are offered as gifts in advance and without being contingent on the subject's decision to volunteer. Stable personal characteristics of the potential volunteer may moderate the relationship between volunteering and material incentives.

Conclusions Warranting Some Confidence

6. Personal characteristics of the recruiter are likely to affect the subject's probability of volunteering. Recruiters higher in status or prestige are likely to obtain higher rates of volunteering, as are female recruiters. This latter relationship is especially modifiable by the sex of the subject and the nature of the research.
7. Persons are less likely to volunteer for tasks that are more aversive in the sense of their being painful, stressful, or dangerous biologically or psychologically. Personal characteristics of the subject and level of incentive

offered may moderate the relationship between volunteering and task aversiveness.

8.   Persons are more likely to volunteer when volunteering is viewed as the normative, expected, appropriate thing to do.

Conclusions Warranting Minimum Confidence

9.   Persons are more likely to volunteer when they are personally acquainted with the recruiter. The addition of a "personal touch" may also increase volunteering.

10.   Conditions of public commitment may increase rates of volunteering when volunteering is normatively expected, but they may decrease rates of volunteering when nonvolunteering is normatively expected.

SUGGESTIONS FOR REDUCING VOLUNTEER BIAS

Our assessment of the literature dealing with the situational determinants of volunteering led us to make a number of tentative suggestions for the reduction of volunteer bias. Implementing these suggestions may serve not only to reduce volunteer bias but also to make us more thoughtful in the planning of the research itself. Our relations with potential subjects may become increasingly reciprocal and human and our procedures may become more humane. Our suggestions follow in outline form:

1.   Make the appeal for volunteers as interesting as possible, keeping in mind the nature of the target population.

2.   Make the appeal for volunteers as nonthreatening as possible so that potential volunteers will not be "put off" by unwarranted fears of unfavorable evaluation.

3.   Explicitly state the theoretical and practical importance of the research for which volunteering is requested.

4.   Explicitly state in what way the target population is particularly relevant to the research being conducted and the responsibility of potential volunteers to participate in research that has potential for benefiting others.

5.   When possible, potential volunteers should be offered not only pay for participation but small courtesy gifts simply for taking time to consider whether they will want to participate.

6.   Have the request for volunteering made by a person of status as high as possible, and preferably by a woman.

7.   When possible, avoid research tasks that may be psychologically or biologically stressful.

8.   When possible, communicate the normative nature of the volunteering response.

9. After a target population has been defined, an effort should be made to have someone known to that population make the appeal for volunteers. The request for volunteers itself may be more successful if a personalized appeal is made.

10. In situations where volunteering is regarded by the target population as normative, conditions of public commitment to volunteer may be more successful; where nonvolunteering is regarded as normative, conditions of private commitment may be more successful.

AN ETHICAL DILEMMA

The 1973 APA code of ethical guidelines for research with human subjects indirectly raises an issue as to whether compliance with the letter of the law might jeopardize the tenability of inferred causal relationships. A verbal-conditioning study by Resnick and Schwartz was presented as illustrative of one horn of the dilemma in that volunteer subjects who were forewarned of the nature of the research along the lines of the APA standards showed a boomerang effect in the conditioning rate—a reaction quite contrary to our present laws of verbal learning. The ethical dilemma results from the likelihood that fully informed voluntarism, while it may satisfy the moral concern of researchers, may be contraindicated for the scientific concern in many cases; and experimenters must weigh the social ethic against the scientific ethic in deciding which violation would constitute the greater moral danger.

Other research, by Sullivan and Deiker, was reassuring at least from the point of view of the societal concern in implying that professional psychologists may be ultraconservative watchdogs because of their stringent ethical views. However, if the current social temper of the times persists, an already complicated issue may become further compounded in the future as greater restrictions are placed on the kinds of recruitment conditions that are ethically permissible.

ROBUSTNESS OF RESEARCH FINDINGS

In light of these developments emphasizing more use of fully informed consent procedures in recruiting subjects for behavioral research, it is important to be aware of the threat to the generalizability of data from using voluntary subjects exclusively. For example, to the extent that a pool of volunteers differed from the population at large, the resulting positive or negative bias would lead to overestimates or underestimates of certain population parameters. Suppose we relied entirely on volunteer subjects to standardize norms for a new test of social approval. Since volunteers tend to be higher in approval need than nonvolunteers, our estimated population mean would be artificially inflated by this procedure. Of course it is also possible to conceive of situations where population means were underestimated because only volunteers were used. The important point is that routinely sampling volunteer subjects could lead to estimates of population parameters that were seriously in error.

Another way in which volunteer status can affect the generalizability of inferences has to do with the naturalistic motivations of human beings. Insofar as volunteer status as an organismic variable was related to the dependent variable of an investigation, the study of voluntarism could be the substantive basis for the research. From this slightly different perspective, volunteer status can be seen as merely another organismic variable like all the myriad variables affecting human behavior. A good case in point was Horowitz's study on the effects of fear-arousal on attitude change. He noticed that research that used voluntary subjects tended to produce a positive relationship between fear-arousal and attitude change and that research using captive subjects tended toward the inverse relationship. Reasoning that volunteers and nonvolunteers may be differentially disposed to felt emotional–persuasive demands, he set about to demonstrate the difference in persuasibility of these two types of subjects by assigning them either to a condition of high or low fear-arousal. Consistent with his hypothesis, the attitude-change data clearly indicated that voluntarism was an important organismic variable for assessing the generality of the fear-arousal relationship. The important point in this case was the empirical emphasis on the fact that behavioral data must always be interpreted within the motivational context in which they occurred.

THE ARTIFACT PROBLEM

Artifacts are systematic errors stemming from specifiable uncontrolled conditions and can be traced to the social nature of the behavioral research process. Our own empirical study of volunteer artifacts has stressed their occurrence in experimental contexts, although to the extent that demand characteristics may be operating outside the laboratory in psychological research, there is reason to believe that volunteer status can also be isolated as a mediating source of nonexperimental artifacts.

The way in which voluntarism can affect causal inferences in this case has to do with threats to the tenability of inferred causal relationships stemming from the occurrence of demand characteristics; and a series of experiments to demonstrate and to probe this effect was discussed. For example, it was possible to imagine the effects of subjects' volunteer status interacting with other variables to increase either the likelihood of obtaining significant effects of an independent variable in a selectedr sample when such effects would not be significant in a more representative sample (type I) or the likelihood of obtaining no significant effects in a selected sample when such effects would be significant in a more representative sample (type II). These types of confounding were demonstrated when volunteers and nonvolunteers participated in an attitude-change experiment using the familiar four-group design by Solomon for determining a pretest-by-treatment interaction, and the results may also have helped to unravel a puzzle about why previous studies in the area had failed to demonstrate the biasing effect of pretesting.

Other research in this program of experiments used the verbal operant conditioning paradigm to suggest that volunteers may be more accommodating to demand characteristics than nonvolunteers, and this motivational difference was shown overall to have the capacity to distort the relationships emerging between independent and dependent variables. Contrary to expectation, however, there was no strong evidence that nonvolunteers were any more responsive to ego-defensive cues than volunteers, though there was at least a hint of this possibility.

MOTIVATIONAL ELEMENTS

Other research was addressed to the question of the role expectations of voluntary and nonvoluntary subjects. Since verbal reports were sought that were not themselves blatantly confounded by the operation of demand characteristics, an indirect method of "projective" inquiry was used in which several hypotheses could be brought together to paint a multidimensional picture of subjects' expectations for experimental research participation. Multidimensional scaling revealed altruistic and evaluative expectancies (in that order) to be the predominant role expectations associated with research participation, thus supporting the theoretical views of both Orne and Rosenberg. The nonvolunteers tended to amplify the distinction between situations involving work and nonwork activities and judged research participation more as a work-oriented experience. Viewed in the light of findings by Straits and Wuebben that it is the negative aspects of experimental participation which are likely to be more salient for nonvoluntary subjects (with the reverse result occurring among volunteers), the collective data suggested one reason why nonvolunteers can be so unenthusiastic about participating as research subjects, as well as their generally sluggish task behavior when they are unpaid, captive subjects. Being compelled to work at a task where there is no personal monetary incentive attached to the effort may promote uncooperative behaviors in subjects who are perhaps already more attuned to the negative aspects of the "work" situation.

AN ARTIFACT-INFLUENCE MODEL

We spoke of pervasiveness in connection with volunteer artifacts; however, to focus on this factor to the exclusion of other important criteria may also be misleading in the implications for the conceptualization of artifacts in general. Artifact-producing stimuli may not typically function as autonomous variables capable of being rank-ordered according to their pervasiveness as independent sources of systematic error. Probably like any other variables, they also interact in complex ways, their pervasiveness as independent contaminants depending on what other factors are operating. This point was emphasized in presenting an integrative model of the artifact-influence process in which volunteer status was postulated to be one of an array of intervening factors. The theoretical model presumed three mutually exclusive and exhaustive states of behavior (compliance, countercompliance, and noncompliance with demand characteristics) and posited that artifact-independent variables, such as the subject's volunteer status, affect the ultimate outcomes of studies by indirectly impinging on the behavioral states at any of three mediating points. How some combinations of artifact stimuli may relate to demand behaviors through the combined mediation of receptivity and motivation was shown. For example, the factor of evaluation apprehension could be reinterpreted with the aid of the combinatorial rule by assuming a positive association with motivation when task- and ego-orienting cues are operating harmoniously and a negative association with motivation when these cues are in conflict. Finally, various procedures were discussed either for circumventing the artifact problem or for teasing out any biasing effect when the difficulty cannot be avoided.

Appendix

Since the preparation of this book, we have gained access to a number of additional studies that provide information about characteristics of volunteers. Table A-1 lists these studies under the appropriate characteristics, in the order in which the characteristics are discussed in the book. Studies are listed as supporting a relationship if the result was significant at .05 or if a clear but nonsignificant trend was obtained. On the whole, the addition of these studies tends to increase our confidence in the pattern of volunteer characteristics described in our summary.

In addition to the studies of Table A-1 we also gained access to several studies relevant to our understanding of the situational determinants of volunteering. Thus, Robinson and Agisim (1951) found that enclosing 25 cents with their mailed questionnaires increased their returns substantially. They also found that when the return envelope bore a postage stamp rather than a business reply permit, returns were nearly 8% greater.

Maas (1956) surveyed former university students and found that potential respondents who had been asked to volunteer before were significantly more likely to participate than were those who had never before been approached; the effect size was .35σ

In their research, Doob and Ecker (1970) compared the rates of volunteering obtained by an experimenter wearing or not wearing an eyepatch. When volunteering involved no future contact with the experimenter, the "stigmatized" experimenter obtained a much higher volunteering rate (69%) than did the "unstigmatized" experimenter (40%). However, when volunteering required further interaction with the stigmatized experimenter, his success rate dropped to 34% (compared to the 32% of the unstigmatized experimenter with whom further interaction was required).

Politz and Brumbach (1947) reported that respondents to a survey of radio listening habits were reliably more likely to listen to the radio stations studied than were the nonrespondents.

Miller, Pokorny, Valles, and Cleveland (1970) showed that former alcoholic patients were significantly more likely to cooperate with requests for follow-up interviews if their social, marital, and vocational adjustment was more satisfactory (effect size > .38σ).

Finally, the very recent and interesting study by Parlee (1974) suggests the possibility that levels of estrogen or progesterone in women might be significant correlates of volunteering.

Table A-1   Additional Studies of Volunteer Characteristics

SEX
   Females volunteer more
      Ferree, Smith, and Miller (1973)
      Schaie, Labouvie, and Barrett (1973)
      Streib (1966)
   No difference
      Dreger and Johnson (1973)
      Loewenstein, Colombotos, and Elinson (1962)
SOCIABILITY
   Volunteers more sociable
      Donnay (1972)
      Loewenstein, Colombotos, and Elinson (1962)
   No difference
      Dreger and Johnson (1973)
EXTRAVERSION
   Volunteers more extraverted
      Burdick and Stewart (1974)
      McLaughlin and Harrison (1973)
      Silverman and Margulis (1973)[a]
   Volunteers less extraverted
      Ramsay (1970)
ACHIEVEMENT NEED
   Volunteers more achievement motivated
      Burns (1974)
APPROVAL NEED
   Volunteers more approval motivated
      Schofield (1974)
AUTHORITARIANISM
   Volunteers less authoritarian
      Loewenstein, Colombotos, and Elinson (1962)
      Silverman and Margulis (1973)[a]
CONVENTIONALITY
   No difference
      Dreger and Johnson (1973)
ANXIETY
   Volunteers less anxious
      Dreger and Johnson (1973)
PSYCHOPATHOLOGY
   Volunteers more maladjusted
      Burdick and Stewart (1974)
   No difference
      Dreger and Johnson (1973)
      Loewenstein, Colombotos, and Elinson (1962)
      McLaughlin and Harrison (1973)
      Streib (1966)

INTELLIGENCE
  Volunteers more intelligent
    Donnay (1972)
    Riegel, Riegel, and Meyer (1967)
    Schaie, Labouvie, and Barrett (1973)
  Volunteers less intelligent
    Maas (1956)
EDUCATION
  Volunteers better educated
    Loewenstein, Colombotos, and Elinson (1962)
    Streib (1966)
SOCIAL CLASS
  Volunteers higher in social class
    Politz and Brumbach (1947)
    Robinson and Agisim (1951)
    Speer and Zold (1971)
    Streib (1966)
  No difference
    Burdick and Stewart (1974)
    Loewenstein, Colombotos, and Elinson (1962)
    Riegel, Riegel, and Meyer (1967)
AGE
  Volunteers younger
    Ferree, Smith, and Miller (1973)
    Jones, Conrad, and Horn (1928)
    Loewenstein, Colombotos, and Elinson (1962)
    Riegel, Riegel, and Meyer (1967)
  No difference
    Robinson and Agisim (1951)
MARITAL STATUS
  No difference
    Robinson and Agisim (1951)
RELIGION
  Protestants volunteer more than Catholics
    Streib (1966)
  No difference
    Loewenstein, Colombotos, and Elinson (1962)

[a] Volunteers for personality assessment research compared to volunteers for color preferences research.

References

Abeles, N., Iscoe, I., and Brown, W. F. (1954–1955). Some factors influencing the random sampling of college students. *Public Opinion Quarterly*, **18**, 419–423.

Ad Hoc Committee on Ethical Standards in Psychological Research (1973). *Ethical Principles in the Conduct of Research with Human Participants*. Washington, D. C.: American Psychological Association.

Adair, J. G. (1970a). Pre-experiment attitudes toward psychology as a determinant of subject behavior. Paper read at Canadian Psychological Association, Winnipeg, May.

Adair, J. G. (1970b). Preexperiment attitudes towards psychology as a determinant of experimental results: Verbal conditioning of aware subjects. *Proceedings of the 78th American Psychological Association Meeting, 5, 417–418.*

Adair, J. G. (1972a). Coerced versus volunteer subjects. *American Psychologist*, **27**, 508.

Adair, J. G. (1972b). Demand characteristics or conformity?: Suspiciousness of deception and experimenter bias in conformity research. *Canadian Journal of Behavioural Science*, **4**, 238–248.

Adair, J. G. (1973). *The Human Subject: The Social Psychology of the Psychological Experiment*. Boston: Little, Brown.

Adair, J. G. and Fenton, D. P. (1970). Subjects' attitudes toward psychology as a determinant of experimental results. Paper presented at the Midwestern Psychological Association meeting, Cincinnati, Ohio.

Adair, J. G. and Fenton, D. P. (1971). Subject's attitudes toward psychology as a determinant of experimental results. *Canadian Journal of Behavioural Science*, **3**, 268–275.

Adair, J. G., and Schachter, B. S. (1972). To cooperate or to look good?: The subjects' and experimenters' perceptions of each others' intentions. *Journal of Experimental Social Psychology*, **8**, 74–85.

Adams, M. (1973). Science, technology, and some dilemmas of advocacy. *Science*, **180**, 840–842.

Adams, S. (1953). Trends in occupational origins of physicians. *American Sociological Review*, **18**, 404–409.

Aderman, D. (1972). Elation, depression, and helping behavior. *Journal of Personality and Social Psychology*, **24**, 91–101.

Adorno, T. W.; Frenkel-Brunswik, E.; Levinson, D. J.; and Sanford, R. N. (1950). *The Authoritarian Personality*. New York: Harper.

Aiken, L. S., and Rosnow, R. L. (1973). Role expectations for psychological research participation. Unpublished manuscript, Temple University.

Alexander, C. N., Jr., and Knight, G. W. (1971). Situated identities and social psychological experimentation. *Sociometry*, **34**, 65–82.

Alexander, C. N., Jr., and Sagatun, I. (1973). An attributional analysis of experimental norms. *Sociometry*, **36**, 127–142.

Alexander, C. N., Jr., and Weil, H. G. (1969). Players, persons, and purposes: Situational meaning and the prisoner's dilemma game. *Sociometry*, **32**, 121–144.

Alexander, C. N., Jr., Zucker, L. G., and Brody, C. L. (1970). Experimental expectations and autokinetic experiences: Consistency theories and judgmental convergence. *Sociometry*, **33**, 108–122.

Allen, V. L. (1966). The effect of knowledge of deception on conformity. *Journal of Social Psychology*, **69**, 101–106.

Alm, R. M., Carroll, W. F., and Welty, G. A. (1972). The internal validity of the Kuhn–McPartland TST. *Proceedings of the American Statistical Association*, Pp. 190–193.

Altus, W. D. (1966). Birth order and its sequelae. *Science*, **151**, 44–49.

Alumbaugh, R. V. (1972). Another "Malleus maleficarum"? *American Psychologist*, **27**, 897–899.

Anastasiow, N. J. (1964). A methodological framework for analyzing nonresponses to questionnaires. *California Journal of Educational Research*, **15**, 205–208.

Argyris, C. (1968). Some unintended consequences of rigorous research. *Psychological Bulletin*, **70**, 185–197.

Aronson, E. (1966). Avoidance of inter-subject communication. *Psychological Reports*, **19**, 238.

Aronson, E., and Carlsmith, J. M. (1968). Experimentation in social psychology. In G. Lindzey and E. Aronson, Eds., *The Handbook of Social Psychology*, rev. ed. Vol. II. Reading, Massachusetts: Addison-Wesley.

Aronson, E., Carlsmith, J. M., and Darley, J. M. (1963). The effects of expectancy on volunteering for an unpleasant experience. *Journal of Abnormal and Social Psychology*, **66**, 220–224.

Ascough, J. C., and Sipprelle, C. N. (1968). Operant verbal conditioning of autonomic responses. *Behavior Research and Therapy*, **6**, 363–370.

Atkinson, J. (1955). The achievement motive and recall of interrupted and completed tasks. In D. C. McClelland, Ed. *Studies in Motivation*. New York: Appleton-Century-Crofts, pp. 494–506.

Back, K. W., Hood, T. C., and Brehm, M. L. (1963). The subject role in small group experiments. Paper presented at the meetings of the Southern Sociological Society, Durham, North Carolina, April. Technical Report #12.

Ball, R. J. (1930). The correspondence method in follow-up studies of delinquent boys. *Journal of Juvenile Research*, **14**, 107–113.

Ball, R. S. (1952). Reinforced conditioning of verbal and nonverbal stimuli in a situation resembling a clinical interview. Unpublished doctoral diss. Indiana University.

Barber, T. X. (1969). *Hypnosis: A scientific approach. New York: Van Nostrand.*

Barefoot, J. C. (1969). Anxiety and volunteering. *Psychonomic Science,* **16**, 283–284.

Barker, W. J., and Perlman, D. (1972). Volunteer bias and personality traits in sexual standards research. Unpublished manuscript, University of Manitoba.

Barnette, W. L., Jr. (1950a). Report of a follow-up of counseled veterans: I Public Law 346 versus Public Law 16 clients. *Journal of Social psychology*, **32**, 129–142.

Barnette, W. L., Jr. (1950b). Report of a follow-up of counseled veterans: II Status of pursuit of training. *Journal of Social Psychology*, **32**, 143–156.

Bass, B. M. (1967). Social behavior and the orientation inventory: A review. *Psychological Bulletin*, **68**, 260–292.

Bass, B. M., Dunteman, G., Frye, R., Vidulich, R., and Wambach, H. (1963). Self, interaction, and task orientation inventory scores associated with overt behavior and personal factors. *Educational and Psychological Measurement* **23**, 101–116.

Baumrind, D. (1964). Some thoughts on ethics of research: After reading Milgram's *Behavioral Study of Obedience. American Psychologist*, **19**, 421–423.

Baumrind, D. (1971). Principles of ethical conduct in the treatment of subjects:

Reaction to the draft report of the Committee on Ethical Standards in Psychological Research. *American Psychologist*, **26**, 887–896.

Baumrind, D. (1972). Reactions to the May 1972 draft report of the ad hoc committee on ethical standards in psychological research. *American Psychologist*, **27**, 1083–1086.

Baur, E. J. (1947–1948). Response bias in a mail survey. *Public Opinion Quarterly*, **11**, 594–600.

Beach, F. A. (1950). The snark was a boojum. *American Psychologist*, **5**, 115–124.

Beach, F. A. (1960). Experimental investigations of species specific behavior. *American Psychologist*, **15**,1–18.

Bean, W. B. (1959). The ethics of experimentation on human beings. In S. O. Waife and A. P. Shapiro, Eds., *The Clinical Evaluation of New Drugs*. New York: Hoeber-Harper, Pp. 76–84.

Beckman, L., and Bishop, B. R. (1970). Deception in psychological research: A reply to Seeman. *American Psychologist*, **25**, 878–880.

Beecher, H. K. (1970). *Research and the individual: Human studies*. Boston: Little, Brown.

Bell, C. R. (1961). Psychological versus sociological variables in studies of volunteer bias in surveys. *Journal of Applied Psychology*, **45**, 80–85.

Bell, C. R. (1962). Personality characteristics of volunteers for psychological studies. *British Journal of Social and Clinical Psychology*, **1**, 81–95.

Belmont, L., and Marolla, F. A. (1973). Birth order, family size, and intelligence. *Science*, **182**, 1096–1101.

Belson, W. A. (1960). Volunteer bias in test-room groups. *Public Opinion Quarterly*, **24**, 115–126.

Belt, J. A., and Perryman, R. E. The subject as a biasing factor in psychological experiments. Paper read at meeting meetings S.W.P.A., St. Louis, April, 1970.

Bem, D. J. (1970). *Beliefs, Attitudes, and Human Affairs*. Belmont, Calif.: Brooks/Cole.

Bennett, C. M., and Hill, R. E., Jr. (1964). A comparison of selected personality characteristics of responders and nonresponders to a mailed questionnaire study. *Journal of Educational Research*, **58**, 178–180.

Bennett, E. B. (1955). Discussion, decision, commitment and consensus in "group decision." *Human Relations*, **8**, 251–273.

Benson, L. E. (1946). Mail surveys can be valuable. *Public Opinion Quarterly*, **10**, 234–241.

Benson, S., Booman, W. P., and Clark, K. E. (1951). A study of interview refusal. *Journal of Applied Psychology*, **35**, 116–119.

Bentler, P. M., and Roberts, M. R. (1963). Hypnotic susceptibility assessed in large groups. *International Journal of Clinical and Experimental Hypnosis*, **11**, 93–97.

Bergen, A. v., and Kloot, W. v. d. (1968–1969). Recruitment of subjects. *Hypothese: Tijdschrift voor Psychologie en Opvoedkunde*, **13**, no.1, 11–15.

Berkowitz, L., and Cottingham, D. R. (1960). The interest value and relevance of fear-arousing communication. *Journal of Abnormal and Social Psychology.* **60**, 37–43.

Bickman, L., and Henchy, T., Eds. (1972). *Beyond the Laboratory: Field Research in Social Psychology.* New York: McGraw-Hill.

Biddle, B. J., and Thomas, E. J., Eds. (1966). *Role Theory: Concepts and Research.* New York: Wiley.

Black, R. W., Schumpert, J., and Welch, F. (1972). A "partial reinforcement extinction effect" in perceptual–motor performance: Coerced versus volunteer subject populations. *Journal of Experimental Psychology*, **92**, 143–145.

Blake, R. R., Berkowitz, H., Bellamy, R. Q., and Mouton, J. S. (1956). Volunteering as an avoidance act. *Journal of Abnormal and Social Psychology,* **53**, 154–156.

Boice, R. (1973). Domestication. *Psychological Bulletin*, **80**, 215–230.

Boies, K. G. (1972). Role playing as a behavior change technique: Review of the empirical literature. *Psychotherapy: Theory, Research and Practice*, **9**, 185–192.

Boring, E. G. (1969). Perspective: Artifact and control. In R. Rosenthal and R. L. Rosnow, Eds., *Artifact in Behavioral Research.* New York: Academic Press.

Boucher, R. G., and Hilgard, E. R. (1962). Volunteer bias in hypnotic experimentation. *American Journal of Clinical Hypnosis*, **5**, 49–51.

Bradt, K. (1955). The usefulness of a post card technique in a mail questionnaire study. *Public Opinion Quarterly*, **19**, 218–222.

Brady, J. P., Levitt, E. E., and Lubin, B. (1961). Expressed fear of hypnosis and volunteering behavior. *Journal of Nervous and Mental Disease*, **133**, 216–217.

Bragg, B. W. (1966). Effect of knowledge of deception on reaction to group pressure. Unpublished master's thesis, University of Wisconsin.

Brehm, J. W. (1966). *A Theory of Psychological Reactance.* New York: Academic Press.

Brehm, M. L., Back, K. W., and Bogdonoff, M. D. (1964). A physiological effect of cognitive dissonance under stress and deprivation. *Journal of Abnormal and Social Psychology*, **69**, 303–310.

Brightbill, R., and Zamansky, H. S. (1963). The conceptual space of good and poor hypnotic subjects: A preliminary exploration. *International Journal of Clinical and Experimental Hypnosis*, **11**, 112–121.

Britton, J. H., and Britton, J. O. (1951). Factors in the return of questionnaires mailed to older persons. *Journal of Applied Psychology*, **35**, 57–60.

Brock, T. C., and Becker, G. (1965). Birth order and subject recruitment. *Journal of Social Psychology*, **65**, 63–66.

Brock, T. C., and Becker, L. A. (1966). "Debriefing" and susceptibility to subsequent experimental manipulations. *Journal of Experimental Social Psychology*, **2**, 314–323.

Brooks, W. D. (1966). Effects of a persuasive message upon attitudes: A methodological comparison of an offset before–after design with a pretest–posttest design. *Journal of Communication*, **16**, 180–188.

Brower, D. (1948). The role of incentive in psychological research. *Journal of General Psychology*, **39**, 145–147.

Brown, R. (1962). Models of attitude change. In R. Brown, E. Galanter, E. H. Hess, and G. Mandler, *New Directions in Psychology*, Vol. I. New York: Holt, Rinehart, and Winston.

Bruehl, D. K. (1971). A model of social psychological artifacts in psychological experimentation with human subjects. Unpublished doctoral diss. University of California at Berkeley.

Bruehl, D. K., and Solar, D. (1970). Systematic variation in the clarity of demand characteristics in an experiment employing a confederate. *Psychological Reports*, **27**, 55–60.

Bruehl, D. K., and Solar, D. (1972). Clarity of demand characteristics in an experimenter expectancy experiment. Paper presented at the Western Psychological Association meeting, Portland, Oregon.

Brunswik, E. (1947). *Systematic and Representative Design of Psychological Experiments*. Berkeley: University of California Press.

Brunswik, E. (1955). Representative design and probabilistic theory in a functional psychology. *Psychological Review*, **62**, 193–217.

Brunswik, E. (1956). *Perception and the Representative Design of Psychological Experiments*. Berkeley: University of California Press.

Bryan, J. H., and London, P. (1970). Altruistic behavior by children. *Psychological Bulletin*, **73**, 200–211.

Buckhout, R. (1965). Need for approval and attitude change. *Journal of Psychology*, **60**, 123–128.

Burchinal, L. G. (1960). Personality characteristics and sample bias. *Journal of Applied Psychology*, **44**, 172–174.

Burdick, H. A. (1956). The relationship of attraction, need achievement, and certainty to conformity under conditions of a simulated group atmosphere. Unpublished doctoral diss. University of Michigan.

Burdick, J. A., and Stewart, D. Y. (1974). Differences between "Show" and "No Show" volunteers in a homosexual population. *Journal of Social Psychology*, **92**, 159–160.

Burns, J. L. (1974). Some personality attributes of volunteers and of nonvolunteers for psychological experimentation. *Journal of Social psychology*, **92**, 161–162.

Cairns, R. B. (1961). The influence of dependency inhibition on the effectiveness of social reinforcement. *Journal of Personality*, **29**, 466–488.

Campbell, D. T. (1957). Factors relevant to the validity of experiments in social settings. *Psychological Bulletin*, **54**, 297–312.

Campbell, D. T. (1969). Prospective: Artifact and control. In R. Rosenthal and R. L. Rosnow, Eds., *Artifact in Behavioral Research*. New York: Academic Press.

Campbell, D. T., and Stanley, J. C. (1966). *Experimental and Quasi-experimental Designs for Research*. Chicago: Rand McNally.

Capra, P. C., and Dittes, J. E. (1962). Birth order as a selective factor among volunteer subjects. *Journal of Abnormal and Social Psychology*, **64**, 302.

Carlson, R. (1971). Where is the person in personality research? *Psychological Bulletin*, **75**, 203–219.

Carr, J. E., and Wittenbaugh, J. A. (1968). Volunteer and nonvolunteer characteristics in an outpatient population. *Journal of Abnormal Psychology*, **73**, 16–17.

Carroll, J. D., and Chang, J. (1970). Analysis of individual differences in multidimensional scaling via an n-way generalization of Eckhart–Young decomposition. *Psychometrika*, **35**, 282–319.

Chapanis, A. (1967). The relevance of laboratory studies to practical situations. *Ergonomics*, **10**, 557–577.

Chein, I. (1948). Behavior theory and the behavior of attitudes: Some critical comments. *Psychological Review*, **55**, 175–188.

Christie, R. (1951). Experimental naïveté and experiential naïveté. *Psychological Bulletin*, **48**, 327–339.

Clark, K. E. (1949). A vocational interest test at the skilled trades level. *Journal of Applied Psychology*, **33**, 291-303.

Clark, K. E. et al. (1967). Privacy and behavioral research. *Science,*155, 535–538.

Clausen, J. A., and Ford, R. N. (1947). Controlling bias in mail questionnaires. *Journal of the American Statistical Association,* 42, 497–511.

Cochran, W. G. (1963). *Sampling techniques.* 2nd ed. New York: Wiley.

Cochran, W. G., Mosteller, F., and Tukey, J. W. (1953). Statistical problems of the Kinsey report. *Journal of the American Statistical Association,* 48, 673–716.

Coe, W. C. (1964). Further norms on the Harvard Group Scale of Hypnotic Susceptibility, Form A. *International Journal of Clinical and Experimental Hypnosis, 12, 184–190.*

Coe, W. C. (1966). Hypnosis as role enactment: The role demand variable. *American Journal of Clinical Hypnosis,* 8, 189–191.

Coffin, T. E. (1941). Some conditions of suggestion and suggestibility. *Psychological Monographs,* 53, no. 4 (Whole no. 241).

Cohen, J. (1969). *Statistical Power Analysis for the Behavioral Sciences.* New York: Academic Press.

Cohler, B. J., Woolsey, S. H., Weiss, J. L.. and Grunebaum, H. H. (1968). Childrearing attitudes among mothers volunteering and revolunteering for a psychological study. *Psychological Reports,* 23, 603–612.

Conroy, G. I., and Morris, J. R. (1968). Psychological health among volunteers, non-volunteers and no shows. Paper presented at Southeastern Psychological Association Meeting, Roanoke, Va. April.

Cook, S. W., Kimble, G. A., Hicks, L. H., McGuire, W. J., Schoggen, P. H., and Smith, M. B. (1971). Ethical standards for psychological research. *APA Monitor,* 2, no. 7, 9–28.

Cook, S. W., Kimble, G. A., Hicks, L. H., McGuire, W. J., Schoggen, P. H., and Smith M. B. (1972). Ethical standards for research with human subjects. *APA Monitor,* 3, i-xix.

Cook, T. D., Bean, J. R., Calder, B. J., Frey, R., Krovetz, M. L., and Reisman, S. R. (1970). Demand characteristics and three conceptions of the frequently deceived subject. *Journal of Personality and Social Psychology,* 14, 185–194.

Cook, T. D., and Campbell, D. T. (1974). The design and conduct of quasi-experiments and true experiments in field settings. In M.D. Dunnette, Ed., *Handbook of Industrial and Organizational Psychology.* Chicago: Rand-McNally, in press.

Cope, C. S., and Kunce, J. T. (1971). Unobtrusive behavior and research methodology. *Journal of Counseling Psychology,* 18, 592–594.

Cope, R. G. (1968). Nonresponse in survey research as a function of psychological characteristics and time of response. *Journal of Experimental Education*, **36**, 32–35.

Cox, D. E., and Sipprelle, C. N. (1971). Coercion in participation as a research subject. *American Psychologist*, **26**, 726–728.

Cozby, P. C. (1973). Self-disclosure: A literature review. *Psychological Bulletin*, **79**, 73–91.

Craddick, R. A., and Campitell, J. (1963). Return to an experiment as a function of need for social approval. *Perceptual and Motor Skills*, **16**, 930.

Crespi, L. P. (1948). The interview effect in polling. *Public Opinion Quarterly*, **12**, 99–111.

Croog, S. H., and Teele, J. E. (1967). Religious identity and church attendance of sons of religious intermarriages. *American Sociological Review*, **32**, 93–103.

Crossley, H. M., and Fink, R. (1951). Response and nonresponse in a probability sample. *International Journal of Opinion and Attitude Research*, **5**, 1–19.

Crowne, D. P., and Marlowe, D. (1964). *The Approval Motive*, New York: Wiley.

Cudrin, J. M. (1969). Intelligence of volunteers as research subjects. *Journal of Consulting and Clinical Psychology*, **33**, 501–503.

Damon, A. (1965). Discrepancies between findings of longitudinal and cross-sectional studies in adult life: Physique and physiology. *Human Development*, **8**, 16–22.

Darroch, R. K., and Steiner, I. D. (1970). Role playing: An alternative to laboratory research? *Journal of Personality*, **38**, 302–311.

Deming, W. E. (1944). On errors in surveys. *American Sociological Review*, **9**, 359–369.

Dewolfe, A. S., and Governale, C. N. (1964). Fear and attitude change. *Journal of Abnormal and Social Psychology*, **69**, 119–123.

Diab, L. N., and Prothro, E. T. (1968). Cross-cultural study of some correlates of birth order. *Psychological Reports*, **22**, 1137–1142.

Diamant, L. (1970). Attitude, personality, and behavior in volunteers and nonvolunteers for sexual research. *Proceedings, 78th Annual Convention, American Psychological Association*, Pp. 423-424.

Dillman, D. A. (1972). Increasing mail questionnaire response for large samples of the general public. Agricultural Research Center Scientific Paper No. 3752. Washington State University. Also in *Public Opinion Quarterly*, **36**, 254–257.

Dittes, J. E. (1961). Birth order and vulnerability to differences in acceptance. *American Psychologist,* **16,** 358 (Abstract).

Dohrenwend, B. S., and Dohrenwend, B. P. (1968). Sources of refusals in surveys. *Public Opinion Quarterly,* **32,** 74–83.

Dohrenwend, B. S.; Feldstein, S.; Plosky, J.; and Schmeidler, G. R. Factors interacting with birth order in self-selection among volunteer subjects. *Journal of Social Psychology,* **72,** 125–128.

Dollard, J. (1953). The Kinsey report on women: "A strangely flawed masterpiece." *New York Herald Tribune,* Sept. 13, 1953, Section 6.

Donald, M. N. (1960). Implications of nonresponse for the interpretation of mail questionnaire data. *Public Opinion Quarterly,* **24,** 99–114.

Donnay, J. M. (1972). L'affiliation: Son substrat dynamique et ses implications sur le plan comportemental et intellectuel. *Psychologica Belgica,* **12,** 175–187.

Doob, A. N., and Gross, A. E. (1968). Status of frustrator as an inhibitor of horn-honking responses. *Journal of Social Psychology,* **76,** 213–218.

Doob, A. N., and Ecker, B. P. (1970). Stigma and compliance. *Journal of Personality and Social Psychology,* **14,** 302–304.

Dreger, R. M., and Johnson, W. E., Jr. (In press). Characteristics of volunteers, non-volunteers, and no-shows in a clinical follow-up. *Journal of Consulting and Clinical Psychology.*

Dulany, D. E. (1962). The place of hypotheses and intentions: An analysis of verbal control in verbal conditioning. In C. E. Eriksen, Ed., *Behavior and Awareness.* Durham, N. C.: Duke University Press.

Ebert, R. K. (1973). The reliability and validity of a mailed questionnaire for a sample of entering college freshmen. Unpublished doctoral diss. Temple University.

Eckland, B. K. (1965). Effects of prodding to increase mailback returns. *Journal of Applied Psychology,* **49,** 165–169.

Edgerton, H. A.; Britt, S. H.; and Norman, R. D. (1947). Objective differences among various types of respondents to a mailed questionnaire. *American Sociological Review,* **12,** 435–444.

Edwards, C. N. (1968a). Characteristics of volunteers and nonvolunteers for a sleep and hypnotic experiment. *American Journal of Clinical Hypnosis,* **11,** 26–29.

Edwards, C. N. (1968b). Defensive interaction and the volunteer subject: An heuristic note. *Psychological Reports,* **22,** 1305–1309.

Efran, J. S., and Boylin, E. R. (1967). Social desirability and willingness to participate in a group discussion. *Psychological Reports,* **20,** 402.

Eisenman, R. (1972). Experience in experiments and change in internal–external control scores. *Journal of Consulting and Clinical Psychology*, **39**, 434–435.

Eisenman, R. (1965). Birth order, aesthetic preference, and volunteering for an electric shock experiment. *Psychonomic Science*, **3**, 151–152.

Ehrlich, A. (1974). The age of the rat. *Human Behavior*, **3**, 25–28.

Ellis, R. A.; Endo, C. M.; and Armer, J. M. (1970). The use of potential nonrespondents for studying nonresponse bias, *Pacific Sociological Review*, **13**, 103–109.

Elms, A. C., Ed., (1969). *Role Playing, Reward, and Attitude Change*. New York: Van Nostrand.

Epstein, Y. M.; Suedfeld, P.; and Silverstein, S. J. (1973). The experimental contract: Subjects' expectations of and reactions to some behaviors of experimenters. *American Psychologist*, **28**, 212–221.

Esecover, H.; Malitz, S.; and Wilkens, B. (1961). Clinical profiles of paid normal subjects volunteering for hallucinogenic drug studies. *American Journal of Psychiatry*, **117**, 910–915.

Etzioni, A. (1973). Regulation of human experimentation. *Science*, **182**, 1203.

Evans, F. J., and Orne, M. T. (1971). The disappearing hypnotist: The use of simulating subjects to evaluate how subjects perceive experimental procedures. *International Journal of Clinical and Experimental Hypnosis*, **19**, 277–296.

Evans, R. I., and Rozelle, R. M., Eds., (1973). *Social Psychology in Life*. Boston: Allyn and Bacon.

Eysenck, H. J. (1967). *The Biological Basis of Personality*. Springfield, Ill.: Charles C. Thomas.

Feldman, R. S., and Scheibe, K. E. (1972). Determinants of dissent in a psychological experiment. *Journal of Personality*, **40**, 331–348.

Ferber, R. (1948–1949). The problem of bias in mail returns: A solution. *Public Opinion Quarterly*, **12**, 669–676.

Ferree, M. M.; Smith, E. R.; and Miller F. D. (1973). Is sisterhood powerful? A look at feminist belief and helping behavior. Unpublished manuscript, Harvard University.

Ferriss, A. L. (1951). A note on stimulating response to questionnaires. *American Sociological Review*, **16**, 247–249.

Festinger, L. (1957). *A Theory of Cognitive Dissonance*. Evanston, Ill.: Row, Peterson; Reissued by Stanford University Press, 1962.

Fillenbaum, S. (1966). Prior deception and subsequent experimental performance: The "faithful" subject. *Journal of Personality and Social Psychology*, **4**, 532–537.

Fischer, E. H., and Winer, D. (1969). Participation in psychological research: Relation to birth order and demographic factors. *Journal of Consulting and Clinical Psychology*, **33**, 610–613.

Fisher, S.; McNair, D. M.; and Pillard, R. C. (1970). Acquiescence, somatic awareness and volunteering. *Psychosomatic Medicine*, **32**, 556.

Foa, U. G. (1971). Interpersonal and economic resources.*Science*, **171**, 345–351.

Ford, R. N., and Zeisel, H. (1949). Bias in mail surveys cannot be controlled by one mailing. *Public Opinion Quarterly*, **13**, 495–501.

Foster, R. J. (1961). Acquiescent response set as a measure of acquiescence. *Journal of Abnormal and Social Psychology*, **63**, 155–160.

Francis, R. D., and Diespecker, D. D. (1973). Extraversion and volunteering for sensory isolation. *Perceptual and Motor Skills*, **36**, 244–246.

Franzen, R., and Lazarsfeld, P. F. (1945). Mail questionnaire as a research problem. *Journal of Psychology*, **20**, 293–320.

Fraser, S. C., and Zimbardo, P. G. (n.d.) Subject compliance: The effects of knowing one is a subject. Unpublished manuscript. New York University.

Freedman, J. L. (1969). Role playing: Psychology by consensus. *Journal of Personality and Social Psychology*, **13**, 107–114.

Freedman, J. L., and Fraser, S. C. Compliance without pressure: The foot-in-the-door technique. *Journal of Personality and Social Psychology*, **4**, 195–202.

Freedman, J. L.; Wallington, S. A.; and Bless, E. (1967). Compliance without pressure: The effect of guilt. *Journal of Personality and Social Psychology*, **7**, 117–124.

French, J. R. P. (1963). Personal communication. Aug. 19.

Frey, A. H., and Becker, W. C. (1958). Some personality correlates of subjects who fail to appear for experimental appointments. *Journal of Consulting Psychology*, **22**, 164.

Frey, P. W. (1973). Student ratings of teaching: Validity of several rating factors. *Science*, **182**, 83–85.

Fried, S. B.; Gumpper, D. C.; and Allen, J. C. (1973). Ten years of social psychology: Is there a growing commitment to field research? *American Psychologist*, **28**, 155–156.

Friedman, H. (1968). Magnitude of experimental effect and a table for its rapid estimation. *Psychological Bulletin*, **70**, 245–251.

Frye, R. L., and Adams, H. E. (1959). Effect of the volunteer variable on leaderless group discussion experiments. *Psychological Reports*, 5, 184.

Gannon, M. J., Nothern, J. C., and Carroll, S. J., Jr. (1971). Characteristics of nonrespondents among workers. *Journal of Applied Psychology*, 55, 586–588.

Gaudet, H., and Wilson, E. C. (1940). Who escapes the personal investigator? *Journal of Applied Psychology*, 24, 773–777.

Gelfand, D. M., Hartmann, D. P., Walder, P., and Page, B. (1973). Who reports shoplifters?: A field-experimental study. *Journal of Personality and Social Psychology*, 25, 276–285.

Geller, S. H., and Endler, N. S. (1973). The effects of subject roles, demand characteristics, and suspicion on conformity. *Canadian Journal of Behavioural Science*, 5, 46–54.

Gergen, K. J. (1973). The codification of research ethics: Views of a doubting Thomas. *American Psychologist*, 28, 907–912.

Glinski, R. J., Glinski, B. C., and Slatin, G. T. (1970). Nonnaivety contamination in conformity experiments: Sources, effects, and implications for control. *Journal of Personality and Social Psychology*, 16, 478–485.

Goldstein, J. H., Rosnow, R. L., Goodstadt, B. E., and Suls, J. M. (1972). The "good subject" in verbal operant conditioning research. *Journal of Experimental Research in Personality*, 6, 29–33.

Goodstadt, B. E. (1971). When coercion fails. Unpublished doctoral diss. Temple University.

Grabitz-Gniech, G. (1972). Versuchspersonenverhalten: Erklärungsansätze aus Theorien zum sozialen Einfluss. *Psychologische Beiträge*, 14, 541–549.

Green, D. R. (1963). Volunteering and the recall of interrupted tasks. *Journal of Abnormal and Social Psychology*, 66, 397–401.

Greenberg, A. (1956). Respondent ego-involvement in large-scale surveys. *Journal of Marketing*, 20, 390–393.

Greenberg, M. S. (1967). Role playing: An alternative to deception? *Journal of Personality and Social Psychology*, 7, 152–157.

Greene, E. B. (1937). Abnormal adjustments to experimental situations. *Psychological Bulletin*, 34, 747–748 (Abstract).

Greenspoon, J. (1951). The effect of verbal and nonverbal stimuli on the frequency of members of two verbal response classes. Unpublished doctoral diss., Indiana University.

Greenspoon, J. (1962). Verbal conditioning and clinical psychology. In A. J. Bachrach, Ed., *Experimental Foundations of Clinical Psychology*. New York: Basic Books.

Greenspoon, J., and Brownstein, A. J. (1967). Awareness in verbal conditioning. *Journal of Experimental Research in Personality*, **2**, 295–308.

Gustafson, L. A., and Orne, M. T. (1965). Effects of perceived role and role success on the detection of deception. *Journal of Applied Psychology*, **49**, 412–417.

Gustav. A. (1962). Students' attitudes toward compulsory participation in experiments. *Journal of Psychology*, **53**, 119–125.

Haas, K. (1970). Selection of student experimental subjects. *American Psychologist*, **25**, 366.

Haefner, D. P. (1956). Some effects of guilt-arousing and fear-arousing persuasive communications on opinion change. Unpublished doctoral diss. University of Rochester.

Hammond, K. R. (1948). Subject and object sampling—a note. *Psychological Bulletin*, **45**, 530–533.

Hammond, K. R. (1951). Relativity and representativeness. *Philosophy of Science*, **18**, 208–211.

Hammond, K. R. (1954). Representative vs. systematic design in clinical psychology. *Psychological Bulletin*, **51**, 150–159.

Hancock, J. W. (1940). An experimental study of four methods of measuring unit costs of obtaining attitude toward the retail store. *Journal of Applied Psychology*, **24**, 213–230.

Handfinger, B. M. (1973). Effect of previous deprivation on reaction for helping behavior. Paper presented at the Eastern Psychological Association meeting, Washington, D. C..

Hansen, M. H., and Hurwitz, W. N. (1946). The problem of non-response in sample surveys. *Journal of the American Statistical Association*, **41**, 517–529.

Hartmann, G. W. (1936). A field experiment on the comparative effectiveness of "emotional" and "rational" political leaflets in determining election results. *Journal of Abnormal and Social Psychology*, **31**, 99–114.

Havighurst, C. C. (1972). Compensating persons injured in human experimentation. *Science*, **169**, 153–169.

Hayes, D. P., Meltzer, L., and Lundberg, S. (1968). Information distribution, interdependence, and activity levels. *Sociometry*, **31**, 162–179.

Heckhausen, H., Boteram, N., and Fisch, R. (1970). Attraktivitätsänderung der Aufgabe nach Misserfolg. *Psychologische Forschung*, **33**, 208–222.

Heilizer, F. (1960). An exploration of the relationship between hypnotizability and anxiety and/or neuroticism. *Journal of Consulting Psychology*, **24**, 432–436.

Henchy, T., and Glass, D. C. (1968). Evaluation apprehension and the social facilitation of dominant and subordinate responses. *Journal of Personality and Social Psychology*, **10**, 446–454.

Hendrick, C., Borden, R., Giesen, M., Murray, E. J, and Seyfried, B. A. (1972). Effectiveness of ingratiation tactics in a cover letter on mail questionnaire response. *Psychonomic Science*, **26**, 349–351.

Hicks, J. M., and Spaner, F. E. (1962). Attitude change and mental hospital experience. *Journal of Abnormal and Social Psychology*, **65**, 112–120.

Higbee, K. L., and Wells, M. G. (1972). Some research trends in social psychology during the 1960s. *American Psychologist*, **27**, 963–966.

Hilgard, E. R. (1965). *Hypnotic Susceptibility*. New York: Harcourt, Brace and World.

Hilgard, E. R. (1967). Personal communication. Feb. 6.

Hilgard, E. R., and Payne, S. L. (1944). Those not at home: Riddle for pollsters. *Public Opinion Quarterly*, **8**, 254–261.

Hilgard, E. R., Weitzenhoffer, A. M., Landes, J., and Moore, R. K. (1961). The distribution of susceptibility to hypnosis in a student population: A study using the Stanford Hypnotic Susceptibility Scale. *Psychological Monographs*, **75**, 8 (Whole no. 512).

Hill, C. T., Rubin, Z., and Willard, S. (1973). Who volunteers for research on dating relationships? Unpublished manuscript, Harvard University.

Himelstein, P. (1956). Taylor scale characteristics of volunteers and nonvolunteers for psychological experiments. *Journal of Abnormal and Social Psychology*, **52**, 138–139.

Holmes, D. S. (1967). Amount of experience in experiments as a determinant of performance in later experiments. *Journal of Personality and Social Psychology*, **2**, 289–294.

Holmes, D. S., and Applebaum, A. S. (1970). Nature of prior experimental experience as a determinant of performance in a subsequent experiment. *Journal of Personality and Social Psychology*, **14**, 195–202.

Holmes, D. S., and Bennett, D. H. (1974). Experiments to answer questions raised by the use of deception in psychological research: I. Role playing as an alternative to deception; II. Effectiveness of debriefing after a deception; III. Effect of informed consent on deception. *Journal of Personality and Social Psychology*, **29**, 358–367.

Holmes, J. G., and Strickland L. H. (1970). Choice freedom and confirmation of incentive expectancy as determinants of attitude change. *Journal of Personality and Social Psychology*, **14**, 39–45.

Hood, T. C. (1963). The volunteer subject: Patterns of self-presentation and the decision to participate in social psychological experiments. Unpublished master's thesis, Duke University.

Hood, T. C., and Back, K. W. (1967). Patterns of self-disclosure and the volunteer: The decision to participate in small groups experiments. Paper read at Southern Sociological Society, Atlanta, April.

Hood, T. C., and Back, K. W. (1971). Self-disclosure and the volunteer: A source of bias in laboratory experiments. *Journal of Personality and Social Psychology*, **17**, 130–136.

Horowitz, I. A. (1969). Effects of volunteering, fear arousal, and number of communications on attitude change. *Journal of Personality and Social Psychology*, **11**, 34–37.

Horowitz, I. A., and Gumenik, W. E. (1970). Effects of the volunteer subject, choice, and fear arousal on attitude change. *Journal of Experimental Social Psychology*, **6**, 293–303.

Horowitz, I. A., and Rothschild, B. H. (1970). Conformity as a function of deception and role playing. *Journal of Personality and Social Psychology*, **14**, 224–226.

Hovland, C. I., Lumsdaine, A. A., and Sheffield, F. D. (1949). *Experiments on Mass Communication*. Princeton, N. J.: Princeton University Press.

Howe, E. S. (1960). Quantitative motivational differences between volunteers and nonvolunteers for a psychological experiment. *Journal of Applied Psychology*, **44**, 115–120.

Hyman, H., and Sheatsley, P. B. (1954). The scientific method. In D. P. Geddes, Ed., *An Analysis of the Kinsey Reports*. New York: New American Library.

Innes, J. M., and Fraser, C. (1971). Experimenter bias and other possible biases in psychological research. *European Journal of Social Psychology*. **1**, 297–310.

Insko, C. A. (1965). Verbal reinforcement of attitude. *Journal of Personality and Social Psychology*, **2**, 621–623.

Insko, C. A., Arkoff, A., and Insko, V. M. (1965). Effects of high and low fear-arousing communication upon opinions toward smoking. *Journal of Experimental Social Psychology*, **1**, 256–266.

Jackson, C. W., Jr., and Kelley, E. L. (1962). Influence of suggestion and subject's prior knowledge in research on sensory deprivation. *Science*, **132**, 211–212.

Jackson, C. W., and Pollard, J. C. (1966). Some nondeprivation variables which influence the "effects" of experimental sensory deprivation. *Journal of Abnormal Psychology*, **71**, 383–388.

Jackson, J. A., Ed. (1972). *Role.* Cambridge: Cambridge University Press.

Jaeger, M. E.; Feinberg, H. K.; and Weissman, H. N. (1973). Differences between volunteers, nonvolunteers, and pseudovolunteers as measured by the Omnibus Personality Inventory. Paper presented at the Eastern Psychological Association meeting, Washington, D. C.

Janis, I. L. (1967). Effects of fear arousal on attitude change: Recent developments in theory and experimental research. In L. Berkowitz, Ed., *Advances in Experimental Social Psychology*, Vol. III. New York: Academic Press.

Janis, I. L., and Feshbach, S. (1953). Effects of fear-arousing communications. *Journal of Abnormal and Social Psychology*, **48**, 78–92.

Janis, I. L., and Gilmore, J. B. (1965). The influence of incentive conditions on the success of role playing in modifying attitudes. *Journal of Personality and Social Psychology*, **1**, 17–27.

Janis, I. L., and Mann, L. (1965). Effectiveness of emotional role-playing in modifying smoking habits and attitudes. *Journal of Experimental Research in Personality*, **1**, 84–90.

Janis, I. L., and Terwilliger, R. F. (1962). An experimental study of psychological resistances to fear-arousing communication. *Journal of Abnormal and Social Psychology*, **65**, 403–410.

Johns, J. H., and Quay, H. C. (1962). The effect of social reward on verbal conditioning in psychopathic and neurotic military offenders. *Journal of Consulting Psychology*, **26**, 217–220.

Johnson, R. W. (1973a). Inducement of expectancy and set of subjects as determinants of subjects' responses in experimenter expectancy research. *Canadian Journal of Behavioural Science*, **5**, 55–66.

Johnson, R. W. (1973b). The obtaining of experimental subjects. *Canadian Psychologist*, **14**, 208–211.

Jones, E. E., and Sigall, H. (1971). The bogus pipeline: A new paradigm for measuring affect and attitude. *Psychological Bulletin*, **76**, 349–364.

Jones, E. E., and Sigall, H. (1973). Where there is *ignis*, there may be fire. *Psychological Bulletin,* **79**, 260–262.

Jones, H. E.; Conrad, H.; and Horn, A. (1928). Psychological studies of motion pictures: II. Observation and recall as a function of age. *University of California Publications in Psychology*, **3**, 225–243.

Jones, R. A., and Cooper, J. (1971). Mediation of experimenter effects. *Journal of Personality and Social Psychology*, **20**, 70–74.

Jourard, S. M. (1968). *Disclosing Man to Himself.* Princeton, N. J.: Van Nostrand.

Jourard, S. M. (1969). The effects of experimenters' self-disclosure on subjects' behavior. In C. Spielberger, Ed., *Current Topics in Community and Clinical Psychology,* Vol I. New York: Academic Press.

Jourard, S. M. (1971). *Self-Disclosure: An Experimental Analysis of the Transparent Self.* New York: Wiley - Interscience.

Juhasz, J. B., and Sarbin, T. R. (1966). On the false alarm metaphor in psychophysics. *Psychological Record,* **16,** 323–327.

Jung, J. (1969). Current practices and problems in the use of college students for psychological research. *Canadian Psychologist,* **10,** 280–290.

Kaats, G. R., and Davis, K. E. (1971). Effects of volunteer biases in studies of sexual behavior and attitudes. *Journal of Sex Research,* **7,** 26–34.

Kaess, W., and Long, L. (1954). An investigation of the effectiveness of vocational guidance. *Educational and Psychological Measurement,* **14,** 423–433.

Kanfer F. H. (1968). Verbal conditioning: A review of its current status. In T. R. Dixon and D. L. Horton, Eds., *Verbal Behavior and General Behavior Theory.* Englewood Cliffs, N. J.: Prentice-Hall.

Katz, D., and Cantril, H. (1937). Public opinion polls. *Sociometry,* **1,** 155–179.

Katz, D., and Stotland, E. (1959). A preliminary statement to a theory of attitude structure and change. In S. Koch, Ed. *Psychology: A Study of a Science,* Vol. III. New York: McGraw-Hill.

Katz, J. (1972). *Experimentation with Human Beings: The Authority of the Investigator, Subject, Professions, and State in the Human Experimentation Process.* New York: Russell Sage Foundation (with the assistance of A. M. Capron and E. S. Glass).

Kauffmann, D. R. (1971). Incentive to perform counterattitudinal acts: Bribe or gold star? *Journal of Personality and Social Psychology,* **19,** 82–91.

Kavanau, J. L. (1964). Behavior: Confinement, adaptation, and compulsory regimes in laboratory studies. *Science,* **143,** 490.

Kavanau, J. L. (1967). Behavior of captive white-footed mice. *Science,* **155,** 1623–1639.

Kazdin, A. E., and Bryan, J. H. (1971). Competence and volunteering. *Journal of Experimental Social Psychology,* **7,** 87–97.

Kegeles, S. S. (1963). Some motives for seeking preventative dental care. *Journal of the American Dental Association,* **67,** 110–118.

Kelley, T. L. (1929). *Scientific Method.* Columbus: Ohio State University Press.

Kelman, H. C. (1965). Manipulation of human behavior: An ethical dilemma for the social scientist. *Journal of Social Issues,* **21**, 31–46.

Kelman, H. C. (1967). Human use of human subjects: The problem of deception in social psychological experiments. *Psychological Bulletin,* **67**, 1–11.

Kelman, H. C. (1968). *A Time to Speak.* San Francisco: Jossey Bass.

Kelman, H. C. (1972). The rights of the subject in social research: An analysis in terms of relative power and legitimacy. *American Psychologist,* **27**, 989–1016.

Kelvin, P. (1971). Socialization and conformity. *Journal of Child Psychology and Psychiatry,* **12**, 211–222.

Kennedy, J. J., and Cormier, W.H. (1971). The effects of three methods of subject and experimenter recruitment in verbal conditioning research. *Journal of Social Psychology,* **85**, 65–76.

Kerlinger, F. N. (1972). Draft report of the APA committee on ethical standards in psychological research: A critical reaction. *American Psychologist,* **27**, 894–896.

King, A. F. (1967). Ordinal position and the Episcopal Clergy. Unpublished bachelor's thesis, Harvard University.

King, D. J. (1970). The subject pool. *American Psychologist,* **25**, 1179–1181.

Kinsey, A. C, Pomeroy, W. B., and Martin, C. E. (1948). *Sexual Behavior in the Human Male.* Philadelphia: Saunders.

Kinsey, A. C., Pomeroy, W. B., Martin, C. E., and Gebhard, P. H. (1953). *Sexual Behavior in the Human Female.* Philadelphia: Saunders.

Kintz, B. L., Delprato, D. J., Mettee, D. R., Persons, C. E., and Schappe, R. H. (1965). The experimenter effect. *Psychological Bulletin,* **63**, 223–232.

Kirby, M. W., and Davis, K. E. (1972). Who volunteers for research on marital counseling? *Journal of Marriage and the Family,* **34**, 469–473.

Kirchner, W. K., and Mousley, N. B. (1963). A note on job performance: Differences between respondent and nonrespondent salesmen to an attitude survey. *Journal of Applied Psychology,* **47**, 223–224.

Kish, G. B., and Barnes, J. (1973). Variables that affect return rate of mailed questionnaires. *Journal of Clinical Psychology,* **29**, 98–100.

Kish, G. B., and Hermann, H. T. (1971). The Fort Meade Alcoholism Treatment Program. *Quarterly Journal of Studies on Alcohol,* **32**, 628–635.

Kish, L. (1965). *Survey Sampling.* New York: Wiley.

Kivlin, J. E. (1965). Contributions to the study of mail-back bias. *Rural Sociology,* **30**, 322-326.

Klinger, E. (1967). Modeling effects on achievement imagery. *Journal of Personality and Social Psychology,* **7,** 49–62.

Koenigsberg, R. A. (1971). Experimenter–subject interaction in verbal conditioning. Unpublished doctoral diss. New School for Social Research.

Kothandapani, V. (1971). Validation of feeling, belief, and intention to act as three components of attitude and their contribution to prediction of contraceptive behavior. *Journal of Personality and Social Psychology,* **19,** 321–333.

Krasner, L. (1958). Studies of the conditioning of verbal behavior. *Psychological Bulletin,* **55,** 148–170.

Krasner, L. (1962). The therapist as a social reinforcement machine. In H. Strupp and L. Luborsky, Eds., *Research in psychotherapy,* Vol II. Washington: American Psychological Association.

Krech, D., Crutchfield, R. S., and Ballachey, E. L. (1962). *Individual in Society.* New York: McGraw-Hill.

Kroger, R. O. (1967). The effects of role demands and test-cue properties upon personality test performance. *Journal of Consulting Psychology,* **31,** 304–312.

Kruglanski, A. W. (1973). Much ado about the "volunteer artifacts." *Journal of Personality and Social Psychology,* **28,** 348–354.

Kruglov, L. P., and Davidson, H. H. (1953). The willingness to be interviewed: A selective factor in sampling. *Journal of Social Psychology,* **38,** 39–47.

Kruskal, J. B.(1964). Multidimensional scaling by optimizing goodness of fit to a nonmetric hypothesis. *Psychometrika,* **29,** 1–27.

Laming, D. R. J. (1967). On procuring human subjects. *Quarterly Journal of Experimental Psychology,* **19,** 64–69.

Lana, R. E. (1959a). A further investigation of the pretest-treatment interaction effect. *Journal of Applied Psychology,* **43,** 421–422.

Lana, R. E. (1959b). Pretest-treatment interaction effects in attitudinal studies. *Psychological Bulletin,* **56,** 293–300.

Lana, R. E. (1964). The influence of the pretest on order effects in persuasive communications. *Journal of Abnormal and Social Psychology,* **69,** 337–341.

Lana, R. E. (1966). Inhibitory effects of a pretest on opinion change. *Educational and Psychological Measurement,* **26,** 139–150.

Lana, R.E. (1969). Pretest sensitization. In R. Rosenthal and R.L. Rosnow, Eds. *Artifact in Behavioral Research.* New York: Academic Press.

Lana, R.E., and Menapace, R.H. (1971). Subject commitment and demand characteristics in attitude change. *Journal of Personality and Social Psychology*, **20**, 136–140.

Lana, R. E. and Rosnow, R. L. (1963). Subject awareness and order effects in persuasive communications. *Psychological Reports*, **12**, 523–529.

Lana, R. E. and Rosnow, R. L. (1969). Effects of pretest-treatment interval on opinion change. *Psychological Reports*, **22**, 1035–1036.

Larson, R. F., and Catton, W. R., Jr.(1959). Can the mail-back bias contribute to a study's validity? *American Sociological Review*, **24**, 243–245.

Lasagna, L., and von Felsinger, J. M. (1954). The volunteer subject in research. *Science*, **120**, 359–361.

Latané, B., and Darley, J. M. (1970). *The Unresponsive Bystander: Why Doesn't He Help?* New York: Appleton-Century-Crofts.

Lawson, F. (1949). Varying group responses to postal questionnaires. *Public Opinion Quarterly*, **13**, 114–116.

Lehman, E. C., Jr. (1963). Tests of significance and partial returns to mailed questionnaires. *Rural Sociology*, **28**, 284–289.

Leik, R. K. (1965). "Irrelevant" aspects of stooge behavior: Implications for leadership studies and experimental methodology. *Sociometry*, **28**, 259–271.

Leipold, W. D., and James, R. L., (1962). Characteristics of shows and no-shows in a psychological experiment. *Psychological Reports*, **11**, 171–174.

Leslie, L. L. (1972). Are high response rates essential to valid surveys? *Social Science Research*, **1**, 323–334.

Lester, D. (1969). The subject as a source of bias in psychological research. *Journal of General Psychology*, **81**, 237–248.

Leventhal, H. (1970). Findings and theory in the study of fear communications. In L. Berkowitz, Ed., *Advances in Experimental Social Psychology*, Vol V. New York: Academic Press, 1970.

Leventhal, H., and Niles, P. (1964). A field experiment on fear-arousal with data on the validity of questionnaire measures. *Journal of Personality*, **32**, 459–479.

Leventhal, H., Singer, R., and Jones, S. (1965). Effects of fear and specificity of recommendation upon attitudes and behavior. *Journal of Personality and Social Psychology*, **2**, 20–29.

Levitt, E. E., Lubin B., and Brady, J. P.(1962). The effect of the pseudovolunteer on studies of volunteers for psychology experiments. *Journal of Applied Psychology*, **46**, 72–75.

Levitt, E. E., Lubin B., and Zuckerman, M. (1959). Note on the attitude toward hypnosis of volunteers and nonvolunteers for an hypnosis experiment. *Psychological Reports,* **5**, 712.

Levitt, E. E.; Lubin, B.; and Zuckerman, M. (1962). The effect of incentives on volunteering for an hypnosis experiment. *International Journal of Clinical and Experimental Hypnosis,* **10**, 39–41.

Levy, L. H. (1967). Awareness, learning, and the beneficent subject as expert witness. *Journal of Personality and Social Psychology,* **6**, 365–370.

Lewin, K. (1929). *Die Entwicklung der Experimentellen Willenspsychologie und die Psychotherapie.* Leipzig: Verlag von S. Hirzel.

Locke, H. J. (1954). Are volunteer interviewees representative? *Social Problems,* **1**, 143–146.

Loewenstein, R., Colombotos, J., and Elinson, J. (1962). Interviews hardest-to-obtain in an urban health survey. *Proceedings of the Social Statistics Section of the American Statistical Association,* 160–166.

London, P. (1961). Subject characteristics in hypnosis research: Part I. A survey of experience, interest, and opinion. *International Journal of Clinical and Experimental Hypnosis,* **9**, 151–161.

London, P., Cooper, L. M., and Johnson. H. J. (1962). Subject characteristics in hypnosis research. II. Attitudes towards hypnosis, volunteer status, and personality measures. III. Some correlates of hypnotic susceptibility. *International Journal of Clinical and Experimental Hypnosis,* **10**, 13–21.

London, P., and Rosenhan, D. (1964). Personality dynamics. *Annual Review of Psychology,* **15**, 447–492.

Loney, J. (1972). Background factors, sexual experiences, and attitudes toward treatment in two "normal" homosexual samples. *Journal of Consulting and Clinical Psychology,* **38**, 57–65.

Lowe, F. E., and McCormick, T. C. (1955). Some survey sampling biases *Public Opinion Quarterly,* **19**, 303–315.

Lubin, B., Brady, J. P., and Levitt, E. E. (1962a). A comparison of personality characteristics of volunteers and nonvolunteers for hypnosis experiments. *Journal of Clinical Psychology,* **18**, 341–343.

Lubin, B., Brady, J. P., and Levitt, E. E. (1962b). Volunteers and nonvolunteers for an hypnosis experiment. *Diseases of the Nervous System,* **23**, 642–643.

Lubin, B., Levitt, E. E., and Zuckerman, M. (1962). Some personality differences between responders and nonresponders to a survey questionnaire. *Journal of Consulting Psychology,* **26**, 192.

Luchins, A. S. (1957). Primacy-recency in impression formation. In C. I.

Hovland, W. Mandell, E. H.Campbell, T. C. Brock, A. S. Luchins, A. R. Cohen, W. J. McGuire, I. L. Janis, R. L. Feierabend, and N. H. Anderson, *The Order of Presentation in Persuasion.* New Haven: Yale University Press.

Lyons, J. (1970). The hidden dialogue in experimental research. *Journal of Phenomenological Psychology,* **1**, 19–29.

Maas, I. (1956). Who doesn't answer? *Bulletin of the British Psychological Society,* **29**, 33–34.

Macaulay, J., and Berkowitz, L. Eds. (1970). *Altruism and Helping Behavior.* New York: Academic Press.

MacDonald, A. P., Jr. (1969). Manifestations of differential levels of socialization by birth order. *Developmental Psychology,* **1**, 485–492.

MacDonald, A. P. Jr. (1972a). Characteristics of volunteer subjects under three recruiting methods: Pay, extra credit, and love of science. *Journal of Consulting and Clinical Psychology,* **39**, 222–234.

MacDonald, A. P., Jr. (1972b). Does required participation eliminate volunteer differences? *Psychological Reports,* **31**, 153–154.

Mackenzie, D. (1969). Volunteering, paralinguistic stress, and experimenter effects. Unpublished manuscript, Harvard University.

Mann, L., and Taylor, K. F. (1969). Queue counting: The effect of motives upon estimates of numbers in waiting lines. *Journal of Personality and Social Psychology,* **12**, 95–103.

Mann, Sister M. J. (1959). A study in the use of the questionnaire. In E. M. Huddleston, Ed. *Sixteenth Yearbook of the National Council on Measurements Used in Education.* New York: National Council on Measurements Used in Education, Pp. 171–179.

Marlatt, G. A. (1973). Are college students "real people"? *American Psychologist,* **28**, 852–853.

Marmer, R. S. (1967). The effects of volunteer status on dissonance reduction. Unpublished master's thesis, Boston University.

Marquis, P. C. (1973). Experimenter-subject interaction as a function of authoritarianism and response set. *Journal of Personality and Social Psychology,* **25**, 289–296.

Martin, D. C., Arnold, J. D, Zimmerman, T. F. and Richart, R. H. (1968). Human subjects in clinical research - a report of three studies. *New England Journal of Medicine,* **279**, 1426–1431.

Martin, R. M., and Marcuse, F. L. (1957). Characteristics of volunteers and nonvolunteers for hypnosis. *Journal of Clinical and Experimental Hypnosis,* **5**, 176–180.

Martin, R. M., and Marcuse, F. L. (1958). Characteristics of volunteers and nonvolunteers in psychological experimentation. *Journal of Consulting Psychology,* **22,** 475–479.

Maslow, A. H. (1942). Self-esteem (dominance feelings) and sexuality in women. *Journal of Social Psychology,* **16,** 259–293.

Maslow, A. H., and Sakoda, J. M. (1952). Volunteer-error in the Kinsey study. *Journal of Abnormal and Social Psychology,* **47,** 259–262.

Matthysse, S. W. (1966). Differential effects of religious communications. Unpublished doctoral diss., Harvard University.

Maul, R. C. (1970). NCATE accreditation. *Journal of Teacher Education,* **21,** 47–52.

May, W. T., Smith, H. W., and Morris, J. R. (1968). Consent procedures and volunteer bias: A dilemma. Paper read at Southeastern Psychological Association, Roanoke, April.

May, W. W. (1972). On Baumrind's four commandments. *American Psychologist.* **27,** 889–890.

Mayer, C. S., and Pratt, R. W., Jr. (1966). A note on nonresponse in a mail survey. *Public Opinion quarterly,* **30,** 637–646.

McClelland, D. C. (1961). *The Achieving Society.* Princeton, N. J.: Van Nostrand.

McConnell, J. A. (1967). The prediction of dependency behavior in a standardized experimental situation. *Dissertation Abstracts,* **28,** (5-b), 2127–2128.

McDavid, J. W. (1965). Approval-seeking motivation and the volunteer subject. *Journal of Personality and Social Psychology.* **2,** 115–117.

McDonagh, E. C., and Rosenblum, A. L. (1965). A comparison of mailed questionnaires and subsequent structured interviews. *Public Opinion Quarterly,* **29,** 131–136.

McGuire, W. J. (1966). Attitudes and opinions. *Annual Review of Psychology,* **17,** 475–514.

McGuire, W. J. (1968a). Personality and attitude change: An information-processing theory. In A. G. Greenwald, T. C. Brock, and T. M. Ostrom Eds., *Psychological Foundations of Attitudes,* New York: Academic Press.

McGuire, W. J. (1968b). Personality and susceptibility to social influence. In E. F. Borgatta and W. W. Lambert, Eds., *Handbook of Personality Theory and Research.* Chicago: Rand McNally.

McGuire, W. J. (1969a). Suspiciousness of experimenter's intent. In R. Rosenthal R. L. Rosnow, Eds., *Artifact in Behavioral research.* New York: Academic Press.

McGuire, W. J. (1969b). The nature of attitudes and attitude change. In G. Lindzey and E. Aronson, Eds., *The Handbook of Social Psychology,* rev. ed., Vol III. Reading, Mass.: Addison-Wesley.

McLaughlin, R. J., and Harrison, N. W. (1973). Extraversion, neuroticism and the volunteer subject. *Psychological Reports,* **32,** 1131–1134.

McNemar, Q. (1946). Opinion-attitude methodology. *Psychological Bulletin,* **43,** 289–374.

McReynolds, W. T. and Tori, C. (1972). A further assessment of attention-placebo effects and demand characteristics in studies of systematic desensitization. *Journal of Consulting and Clinical Psychology,* **38,** 261–264.

Meier, P. (1972). The biggest public health experiment ever: The 1954 field trial of the Salk poliomyelitis vaccine. In J. M. Tanur, Ed., *Statistics: A Guide to the Unknown,* San Francisco: Holden - Day, Pp. 2–13.

Menges, R. J. (1973). Openness and honesty versus coercion and deception in psychological research. *American Psychologist,* **28,** 1030–1034.

Meyers, J. K. (1972). Effects of *S* recruitment and cuing on awareness, performance, and motivation in behavioral experimentation. Unpublished master's thesis, Ohio State University.

Milgram, S. (1965). Some conditions of obedience and disobedience to authority. *Human Relations,* **18,** 57–75.

Milgram, S., Bickman. L., and Berkowitz. L. (1969). Note on the drawing power of crowds of different size. *Journal of Personality and Social Psychology,* **13,** 79–82.

Miller, A. G. (1972). Role playing: An alternative to deception? *American Psychologist,* **27,** 623–636.

Miller, B. A., Pokorny, A. D., Valles, J., and Cleveland, S. E. (1970). Biased sampling in alcoholism treatment research. *Quarterly Journal of Studies on Alcohol,* **31,** 97–107.

Miller, S. E. (1966). Psychology experiments without subjects' consent. *Science,* **152,** 15.

Milmoe, S. E. (1973). Communication of emotion by mothers of schizophrenic and normal young adults. Unpublished doctoral diss., Harvard University.

Minor, M. W., Jr. (1967). Experimenter expectancy effect as a function of evaluation apprehension. Unpublished doctoral diss., University of Chicago.

Minor, M. W. (1970). Experimenter-expectancy effect as a function of evaluation apprehension. *Journal of Personality and Social Psychology,* **15,** 326–332.

Mitchell, W., Jr. (1939). Factors affecting the rate of return on mailed questionnaires. *Journal of the American Statistical Association,* **34,** 683–692.

Moos, R. H. and Speisman, J. C. (1962). Group compatibility and productivity. *Journal of Abnormal and Social Psychology,* **57,** 190–196.

Mosteller, F. (1968). Association and estimation in contingency tables. *Journal of the American Statistical Association,* **63,** 1–28.

Mosteller, F., and Bush, R. R. (1954). Selected quantitative techniques. In G. Lindzey, Ed. *Handbook of social psychology,* Vol. I. Cambridge, Mass.: Addison-Wesley.

Mulry, R. C. and Dunbar, P. (n.d.). Homogeneity of a subject sample: A study of subject motivation. Unpublished manuscript, University of Indiana.

Myers, T. I., Murphy, D. B., Smith, S., and Goffard, S. J. (1966). Experimental studies of sensory deprivation and social isolation. Technical Report 66–8, Contract DA 44–188–ARO–2, HumRRO, Washington, D.C.: George Washington University.

Myers, T. I., Smith, S., and Murphy, D. B. (1967). Personological correlates of volunteering for and endurance of prolonged sensory deprivation. Unpublished manuscript.

Neulinger, J., and Stein, M. I. (1971). Personality characteristics of volunteer subjects. *Perceptual and Motor Skills,* **32,** 283–286.

Newberry, B. H. (1973). Truth telling in subjects with information about experiments: who is being deceived? *Journal of Personality and Social Psychology,* **25,** 369–374.

Newman, M. (1956). *Personality differences between volunteers and nonvolunteers for psychological investigations.* Doctoral diss., New York University School of Education. Ann Arbor, Mich: University Microfilms, No. 19, 999.

Niles, P. (1964). The relationship of susceptibility and anxiety to acceptance of fear-arousing communications. Unpublished doctoral diss., Yale University.

Norman, R. D. (1948). A review of some problems related to the mail questionnaire technique. *Educational and Psychological Measurement,* **8,** 235–247.

Nosanchuk, T. A., and Marchak, M. P. (1969). Pretest sensitization and attitude change. *Public Opinion Quarterly,* **33,** 107–111.

Nottingham, J. A. (1972). The *N* and the out: Additional information on participants in psychological experiments. *Journal of Social Psychology,* **88,** 299–300.

Nunnally, J., and Bobren, H. (1959). Variables governing the willingness to receive communications on mental health. *Journal of Personality,* **27,** 38–46.

Oakes, W. (1972). External validity and the use of real people as subjects. *American Psychologist,* **27,** 959–962.

Ohler, F. D. (1971). The effects of four sources of experimental bias: Evaluation apprehension, cueing, volunteer status, and choice. *Dissertation Abstracts International,* **32,** (5-A), 2800.

O'Leary, V. E. (1972). The Hawthorne effect in reverse: Trainee orientation for the hard-core unemployed woman. *Journal of Applied Psychology,* **56,** 491–494.

Olsen, G. P. (1968). Need for approval, expectancy set, and volunteering for psychological experiments. Unpublished doctoral diss., Northwestern University.

Ora, J. P., Jr. (1965). Characteristics of the volunteer for psychological investigations. Technical Report, No. 27, November. Vanderbilt University, Contract Nonr 2149 (03).

Ora, J. P., Jr. (1966). Personality characteristics of college freshman volunteers for psychological experiments. Unpublished master's thesis, Vanderbilt University.

Orlans, H.,(1967). Developments in federal policy toward university research. *Science,* **155,** 665–668.

Orne, M. T. (1959). The nature of hypnosis: Artifact and essence. *Journal of Abnormal and Social Psychology,* **58,** 277–299.

Orne, M. T. (1962a). On the social psychology of the psychological experiment: With particular reference to demand characteristics and their implications. *American Psychologist,* **17,** 776–783.

Orne, M. T. (1962b). Problems and research areas. In *Medical Uses of Hypnosis,* Symposium 8, April. New York: Group for the Advancement of Psychiatry.

Orne, M. T. (1969). Demand characteristics and the concept of quasi-controls. In R. Rosenthal and R. L. Rosnow, Eds., *Artifact in Behavioral Research.* New York: Academic Press.

Orne, M. T. (1970). Hypnosis, motivation, and the ecological validity of the psychological experiment. *Nebraska Symposium on Motivation,* **18,** 187–265.

Orne, M. T. (1971). The simulation of hypnosis: Why, how, and what it means. *International Journal of Clinical and Experimental Hypnosis,* **19,** 183–210.

Orne, M. T. (1972). Can a hypnotized subject be compelled to carry out otherwise unacceptable behavior?: A discussion. *International Journal of Clinical and Experimental Hypnosis,* **20**, 101–117.

Orne, M. T. and Scheibe, K. E. (1964). The contribution of nondeprivation factors in the production of sensory deprivation effects: The psychology of the "panic button." *Journal of Abnormal and Social Psychology,* **68**, 3–12.

Orne, M. T., Sheehan, P. W., and Evans, F. J. (1968). Occurrence of posthypnotic behavior outside the experimental setting. *Journal of Personality and Social Psychology,* **9**, 189–196.

Orne, M. T., Thackray, R. I. and Paskewitz, D. A. (1972). On the detection of deception: A model for the study of physiological effects of psychological stimuli. In N. S. Greenfield and R. A. Sternbach, Eds., *Handbook of Psychophysiology.* New York: Holt, Rinehart and Winston.

Ostrom, T. M. (1973). The bogus pipeline: A new *ignis fatuus? Psychological Bulletin,* **79**, 252–259.

Pace, C. R. (1939). Factors influencing questionnaire returns from former university students. *Journal of Applied Psychology,* **23**, 388–397.

Page, M. M. (1968). Modification of figure-ground perception as a function of awareness of demand characteristics. *Journal of Personality and Social Psychology,* **9**, 59–66.

Page, M. M. (1969). Social psychology of a classical conditioning of attitudes experiment. *Journal of Personality and Social Psychology,* **11**, 177–186.

Page, M. M. (1970). Role of demand awareness in the communicator credibility effect. *Journal of Social Psychology,* **82**, 57–66.

Page, M. M. (1971a). Effects of evaluation apprehension on cooperation in verbal conditioning. *Journal of Experimental Research in Personality,* **5**, 85–91.

Page, M. M. (1971b). Postexperimental assessment of awareness in attitude conditioning. *Educational and Psychological Measurement,* **31**, 891–906.

Page, M. M. (1972). Demand awareness and the verbal operant conditioning experiment. *Journal of Personality and Social Psychology,* **23**, 372–378.

Page, M. M. (1973). On detecting demand awareness by postexperimental questionnaire. *Journal of Social Psychology,* **91**, 305–323.

Page, M. M. and Lumia, A. R. (1968). Cooperation with demand characteristics and the bimodal distribution of verbal conditioning data. *Psychonomic Science,* **12**, 243–244.

Pan, Ju-Shu, (1951). Social characteristics of respondents and non·respondents in a questionnaire study of later maturity. *Journal of Applied Psychology,* **35,** 120–121.

Parlee, M. B. (1974). Menstruation and voluntary participation in a psychological experiment: A note on "volunteer artifacts." Unpublished manuscript, Radcliffe Institute, Cambridge, Mass.

Parten, M. (1950). *Surveys, Polls, and Samples: Practical Procedures.* New York: Harper.

Pastore, N. (1949). *The Nature–Nurture Controversy.* New York: King's Crown Press.

Pauling, F. J., and Lana, R. E. (1969). The effects of pretest commitment and information upon opinion change. *Educational and Psychological Measurement,* **29,** 653–663.

Pavlos, A. J. (1972). Debriefing effects for volunteer and nonvolunteer subjects' reactions to bogus physiological feedback. Paper read at Southern Society for Philosophy and Psychology, St. Louis, March–April.

Pellegrini, R. J. (1972). Ethics and identity: A note on the call to conscience. *American Psychologist,* **27,** 896–897.

Perlin, S., Pollin, W., and Butler, R. N. (1958). The experimental subject: 1. The psychiatric evaluation and selection of a volunteer population. *American Medical Association Archives of Neurology and Psychiatry,* **80,** 65–70.

Philip, A. E. and McCulloch, J. W. (1970). Test–retest characteristics of a group of attempted suicide patients. *Journal of Consulting and Clinical Psychology,* **34,** 144–147.

Phillips, W. M., Jr. (1951). Weaknesses of the mail questionnaire: A methodological study. *Sociology and Social Research,* **35,** 260–267.

Politz, A., and Brumbach, R. (1947). Can an advertiser believe what mail surveys tell him? *Printers' Ink,* June 20, 48–52.

Pollin, W., and Perlin, S. (1958). Psychiatric evaluation of "normal control" volunteers. *American Journal of Psychiatry,* **115,** 129–133.

Poor, D. (1967). The social psychology of questionnaires. Unpublished bachelor's thesis, Harvard College.

Price, D. O. (1950). On the use of stamped return envelopes with mail questionnaires. *American Sociological Review,* **15,** 672–673.

Pucel, D. J., Nelson, H. F., and Wheeler, D. N. (1971). Questionnaire follow-up returns as a function of incentives and responder characteristics. *Vocational Guidance Quarterly,* **19,** 188–193.

Quay, H. C., and Hunt, W. A. (1965). Psychopathy, neuroticism, and verbal conditioning. *Journal of Consulting Psychology,* **29,** 283.

Raffetto, A. M. (1968). Experimenter effects on subjects' reported hallucinatory experiences under visual and auditory deprivation. Paper presented at the Midwestern Psychological Association meeting, Chicago, Ill.

Ramsay, R. W. (1970). Introversion-extraversion and volunteering for testing. *British Journal of Social and Clinical Psychology,* **9,** 89.

Raymond, B., and King, S. (1973). Value systems of volunteer and non-volunteer subjects. *Psychological Reports,* **32,** 1303–1306.

Reid, S. (1942). Respondents and non-respondents to mail questionnaires. *Educational Research Bulletin,* **21,** 87–96.

Remington, R. E., and Strongman, K. T. (1972). Operant facilitation during a pre-reward stimulus: Differential effects in human subjects. *British Journal of Psychology,* **63,** 237–242.

Resnick, J. H., and Schwartz, T. (1973). Ethical standards as an independent variable in psychological research. *American Psychologist,* **28,** 134–139.

Reuss, C. F. (1943). Differences between persons responding and not responding to a mailed questionnaire. *American Sociological Review,* **8,** 433–438.

Richards, T. W. (1960). Personality of subjects who volunteer for research on a drug (mescaline). *Journal of Projective Techniques,* **24,** 424–428.

Richter, C. P. (1959). Rats, man, and the welfare state. *American Psychologist,* **14,** 18–28.

Riecken, H. W. (1962). A program for research on experiments in social psychology. In N. F. Washburne, Ed., *Decisions, Values and Groups.* Vol. II, New York: Pergamon. Pp. 25–41.

Riegel, K. F., Riegel, R. M., and Meyer, G. (1967). A study of the dropout rates in longitudinal research on aging and the prediction of death. *Journal of Personality and Social Psychology,* **5,** 342–348.

Riggs, M. M., and Kaess, W. (1955). Personality differences between volunteers and nonvolunteers. *Journal of Psychology,* **40,** 229–245.

Ring, K. (1967). Experimental social psychology: Some sober questions about some frivolous values. *Journal of Experimental Social Psychology,* **3,** 113–123.

Robins, L. N. (1963). The reluctant respondent. *Public Opinion Quarterly,* **27,** 276–286.

Robinson, R. A., and Agisim, P. (1951). Making mail surveys more reliable. *Journal of Marketing,* **15,** 415–424.

Rokeach, M. (1966). Psychology experiments without subjects' consent. *Science,* **152,** 15.

Rollins, M. (1940). The practical use of repeated questionnaire waves. *Journal of Applied Psychology,* **24,** 770–772.

Rose, C. L., (1965). Representativeness of volunteer subjects in a longitudinal aging study. *Human Development,* **8,** 152–156.

Rosen, E. (1951). Differences between volunteers and non-volunteers for psychological studies. *Journal of Applied Psychology,* **35,** 185–193.

Rosenbaum, M. E. (1956). The effect of stimulus and background factors on the volunteering response. *Journal of Abnormal and Social Psychology,* **53,** 118–121.

Rosenbaum, M. E., and Blake, R. R. (1955). Volunteering as a function of field structure. *Journal of Abnormal and Social Psychology,* **50,** 193–196.

Rosenberg, M. J. (1965). When dissonance fails: On eliminating evaluation apprehension from attitude measurement. *Journal of Personality and Social Psychology,* **1,** 28–42.

Rosenberg, M. J. (1969). The conditions and consequences of evaluation apprehension. In R. Rosenthal and R. L. Rosnow, Eds., *Artifact in Behavioral Research.* New York: Academic Press.

Rosenhan, D. (1967). On the social psychology of hypnosis research. In J. E. Gordon, Ed., *Handbook of Clinical and Experimental Hypnosis.* New York: Macmillan, Pp. 481–510.

Rosenhan, D. (1968). Some origins of concern for others. *Educational Testing Service Research Bulletin, no.* **68–33.**

Rosenhan, D., and White, G. M. (1967). Observation and rehearsal as determinants of prosocial behavior. *Journal of Personality and Social Psychology,* **5,** 424–431.

Rosenthal, (1965). The volunteer subject. *Human Relations,* **18,** 389–406.

Rosenthal, R. (1966). *Experimenter Effects in Behavioral Research.* New York: Appleton-Century-Crofts.

Rosenthal, R. (1967). Covert communication in the psychological experiment. *Psychological Bulletin,* **67,** 356–367.

Rosenthal, R. (1969). Interpersonal expectations: Effects of the experimenter's hypothesis. In R. Rosenthal and R. L. Rosnow, Eds., *Artifact in Behavioral Research.* New York: Academic Press.

Rosenthal, R., and Rosnow, R. L. (1969). The volunteer subject. In R. Rosenthal and R. L. Rosnow, Eds., *Artifact in Behavioral Research.* New York: Academic Press.

Rosenzweig, S. (1933). The experimental situation as a psychological problem. *Psychological Review,* **40,** 337–354.

Rosenzweig, S. (1952). The investigation of repression as an instance of experimental idiodynamics. *Psychological Review,* **59,** 339–345.

Rosnow, R.L. (1968). One-sided versus two-sided communication under indirect awareness of persuasive intent. *Public Opinion Quarterly,* **32,** 95–101.

Rosnow, R. L. (1970). When he lends a helping hand, bite it. *Psychology Today,* **4,** no. 1, 26–30.

Rosnow, R. L. (1971). Experimental artifact. In *The Encyclopedia of Education,* Vol. III. New York: Macmillan and Free Press.

Rosnow, R. L., and Aiken, L. S. (1973). Mediation of artifacts in behavioral research. *Journal of Experimental Social Psychology,* **9,** 181–201.

Rosnow, R. L., Goodstadt, B. E., Suls, J. M., and Gitter, A. G. (1973). More on the social psychology of the experiment: When compliance turns to self-defense. *Journal of Personality and Social Psychology,* **27,** 337–343.

Rosnow, R. L., Holper, H. M., and Gitter, A. G. (1973). More on the reactive effects of pretesting in attitude research: Demand characteristics or subject commitment? *Educational and Psychological Measurement,* **33,** 7–17.

Rosnow, R. L. and Robinson, E. J. Eds., (1967). *Experiments in Persuasion.* New York: Academic Press.

Rosnow, R. L., and Rosenthal, R. (1966). Volunteer subjects and the results of opinion change studies. *Psychological Reports,* **19,** 1183–1187.

Rosnow, R. L., and Rosenthal, R. (1970). Volunteer effects in behavioral research. In K. H. Craik, B. Kleinmuntz, R. L. Rosnow, R. Rosenthal, J. A. Cheyne, and R. H. Walters, *New Directions in Psychology,* Vol. IV. New York: Holt, Rinehart and Winston.

Rosnow, R. L., and Rosenthal, R. (1974). Taming of the volunteer problem: On coping with artifacts by benign neglect. *Journal of Personality and Social Psychology,* **30,** 188–190.

Rosnow, R. L., Rosenthal, R., McConochie, R. M., and Arms, R.L. (1969). Volunteer effects on experimental outcomes. *Educational and Psychological Measurement,* **29,** 825–846.

Rosnow, R. L, and Suls, J.M. (1970). Reactive effects of pretesting in attitude research. *Journal of Personality and Social Psychology,* **15,** 338–343.

Ross, J. A. and Smith, P. (1965). Experimental designs of the single stimulus, all-or-nothing type. *American Sociological Review,* **30,** 68–80.

Ross, S., Trumbull, R., Rubinstein, E., and Rasmussen, J. E. (1966). Simulation, shelters, and subjects. *American Psychologist,* **21,** 815–817.

Rothney, J. W. M., and Mooren, R. L. (1952). Sampling problems in follow-up research. *Occupations,* **30,** 573–578.

Rubin, Z. (1969). The social psychology of romantic love. Unpublished doctoral diss., University of Michigan.

Rubin, Z. (1973a). Disclosing oneself to a stranger: I. Effects of reciprocity, anonymity, sex roles, and demand characteristics. Unpublished manuscript, Harvard University.

Rubin, Z. (1973b). *Liking and Loving: An Invitation to Social Psychology.* New York: Holt, Rinehart and Winston.

Rubin, Z. (In press). Disclosing oneself to a stranger: Reciprocity and its limits. *Journal of Experimental Social Psychology.*

Rubin, Z., and Moore, J. C., Jr. (1971). Assessment of subjects' suspicions. *Journal of Personality and Social Psychology,* 17, 163–170.

Ruebhausen, O. M. and Brim, O. G. (1966). Privacy and behavioral research. *American Psychologist,* 21, 423–437.

Salzinger, K. (1959). Experimental manipulation of verbal behavior: A review. *Journal of General Psychology,* 61, 65–94.

Sarason, I. G., and Smith, R. E. (1971). Personality. *Annual Review of Psychology,* 22, 393–446.

Sarbin, T. R., and Allen, V. L. (1968). Role theory. In G. Lindzey and E. Aronson, Eds., *The Handbook of Social Psychology,* rev. ed. Vol. I. Reading, Mass.: Addison-Wesley.

Sarbin, T. R., and Chun, K. T. (1964). A confirmation of the choice of response hypothesis in perceptual defense measurement. Paper presented at the Western Psychological Association meeting, Portland, Ore.

Sasson, R., and Nelson, T.M. (1969). The human experimental subject in context. *The Canadian Psychologist,* 10, 409–437.

Schachter, S. (1959). *The Psychology of Affiliation.* Stanford: Stanford University Press.

Schachter, S., and Hall, R. (1952). Group-derived restraints and audience persuasion. *Human Relations,* 5, 397–406.

Schaie, K. W., Labouvie, G. V., and Barrett, T. J. (1973). Selective attrition effects in a fourteen-year study of adult intelligence. *Journal of Gerontology,* 28, 328–334.

Schappe, R. H. (1972). The volunteer and the coerced subject. *American Psychologist,* 27, 508–509.

Scheier, I. H. (1959). To be or not to be a guinea pig: Preliminary data on anxiety and the volunteer for experiment. *Psychological Reports,* 5, 239–240.

Schofield, J. W. (1972). A framework for viewing the relation between attitudes and actions. Unpublished doctoral diss., Harvard University.

Schofield, J. W. (1974). The effect of norms, public disclosure, and need for approval on volunteering behavior consistent with attitudes. Unpublished manuscript, Harvard University.

Schopler, J. (1967). An investigation of sex differences on the influence of dependence. *Sociometry, 30,* 50–63.

Schopler, J., and Bateson, N. (1965). The power of dependence. *Journal of Personality and Social Psychology, 2,* 247–254.

Schopler, J., and Matthews, M. W. (1965). The influence of the perceived causal locus of partner's dependence on the use of interpersonal power. *Journal of Personality and Social Psychology, 2,* 609–612.

Schubert, D. S. P. (1964). Arousal seeking as a motivation for volunteering: MMPI scores and central-nervous-system-stimulant use as suggestive of a trait. *Journal of Projective Techniques and Personality Assessment, 28,* 337–340.

Schultz, D.P. (1967a). Birth order of volunteers for sensory restriction research. *Journal of Social Psychology, 73,* 71–73.

Schultz, D. P. (1967b). Sensation-seeking and volunteering for sensory deprivation. Paper read at Eastern Psychological Association, Boston, April.

Schultz, D. P. (1967c). The volunteer subject in sensory restriction research. *Journal of Social Psychology, 72,* 123–124.

Schultz, D. P. (1969). The human subject in psychological research. *Psychological Bulletin, 72,* 214–228.

Schwirian, K. P. and Blaine, H. R. (1966). Questionnaire-return bias in the study of blue-collar workers. *Public Opinion Quarterly, 30,* 656–663.

Scott, C. (1961). Research on mail surveys. *Journal of the Royal Statistical Society,* Ser. A, **124,** 143–195.

Seeman, J. (1969). Deception in psychological research. *American Psychologist,* **24,** 1025–1028.

Sheridan, K., and Shack, J. R. (1970). Personality correlates of the undergraduate volunteer subject. *Journal of Psychology, 76,* 23–26.

Sherman, S. R. (1967). Demand characteristics in an experiment on attitude change. *Sociometry, 30,* 246–260.

Sherwood, J. J., and Nataupsky, M. (1968). Predicting the conclusions of negro–white intelligence research from biographical characteristics of the investigator. *Journal of Personality and Social Psychology, 8,* 53–58.

Shor, R. E., and Orne, E. C. (1963). Norms on the Harvard Group Scale of Hypnotic Susceptibility, Form A. *International Journal of Clinical and Experimental Hypnosis, 11,* 39–47.

Short, R. R., and Oskamp, S. (1965). Lack of suggestion effects on perceptual isolation (sensory deprivation) phenomena. *Journal of Nervous and Mental Disease,* **141**, 190–194.

Shuttleworth, F. K. (1940). Sampling errors involved in incomplete returns to mail questionnaires. *Psychological Bulletin,* 37, 437 (Abstract).

Siegman, A. (1956). Responses to a personality questionnaire by volunteers and nonvolunteers to a Kinsey interview. *Journal of Abnormal and Social Psychology,* **52**, 280–281.

Siess, T. F. (1973). Personality correlates of volunteers' experiment preferences. *Canadian Journal of Behavioural Science,* **5**, 253–263.

Sigall, H., Aronson, E., and Van Hoose, T. (1970). The cooperative subject: Myth or reality? *Journal of Experimental Social Psychology,* **6**, 1–10.

Sigall, H., and Page, R. (1971). Current stereotypes: A little fading, a little faking. *Journal of Personality and Social Psychology,* **18**, 247–255.

Sigall, H., and Page, R. (1972). Reducing attenuation in the expression of interpersonal affect via the bogus pipeline. *Sociometry,* **35**, 629–642.

Silverman, I. (1964). Note on the relationship of self-esteem to subject self-selection. *Perceptual and Motor Skills,* **19**, 769–770.

Silverman, I. (1965). Motives underlying the behavior of the subject in the psychological experiment. Paper read at American Psychological Association, Chicago, September.

Silverman, I. (1968). Role-related behavior of subjects in laboratory studies of attitude change. *Journal of Personality and Social Psychology,* **8**, 343–348.

Silverman, I. (1970). The psychological subject in the land of make-believe. *Contemporary Psychology,* **15**, 718–721.

Silverman, I., and Kleinman, D. (1967). A response deviance interpretation of the effects of experimentally induced frustration on prejudice. *Journal of Experimental Research in Personality,* **2**, 150–153.

Silverman, I., and Margulis, S. (1973). Experiment title as a source of sampling bias in commonly used "subject-pool" procedures. *Canadian Psychologist,* **14**, 197–201.

Silverman, I., and Shulman, A. D. (1969). Effects of hunger on responses to demand characteristics in the measurement of persuasion. *Psychonomic Science,* **15**, 201–202.

Silverman, I., and Shulman, A. D. (1970). A conceptual model of artifact in attitude change studies. *Sociometry,* **33**, 97–107.

Silverman, I, Shulman, A. D., and Wiesenthal, D. L. (1970). Effects of deceiving and debriefing psychological subjects on performance in later experiments. *Journal of Personality and Social Psychology,* **14**, 203–212.

Silverman, I, Shulman, A. D., and Wiesenthal, D. L. (1972). The experimenter as a source of variance in psychological research: Modeling and sex effects. *Journal of Personality and Social Psychology,* **21**, 219–227.

Silverman, I. W. (1967). Incidence of guilt reactions in children. *Journal of Personality and Social Psychology,* **7**, 338–340.

Sirken, M. G., Pifer, J. W., and Brown, M. L. (1960). Survey procedures for supplementing mortality statistics. *American Journal of Public Health,* **50**, 1753–1764.

Smart, R. G. (1966). Subject selection bias in psychological research. *Canadian Psychologist,* **7a**, 115–121.

Smith, M. B. (1973). Protection of human subjects—Ethics and politics. *APA Monitor,* **4**, 2.

Smith, R. E. (1969). The other side of the coin. *Contemporary Psychology,* **14**, 628–630.

Solomon, R. L. (1949). An extension of control group design. *Psychological Bulletin,* **46**, 137–150.

Sommer, R. (1968). Hawthorne dogma. *Psychological Bulletin,* **70**, 592–595.

Speer, D. C., and Zold, A. (1971). An example of self-selection bias in follow-up research. *Journal of Clinical Psychology,* **27**, 64–68.

Spiegel, D., and Keith-Spiegel, P. (1969). Volunteering for a high-demand, low-reward project: Sex differences. *Journal of Projective Techniques and Personality Assessment,* **33**, 513–517.

Spielberger, C. D. and DeNike, L. D. (1966). Descriptive behaviorism versus cognitive theory in verbal operant conditioning. *Psychological Bulletin,* **73**, 306–326.

Stanton, F. (1939). Notes on the validity of mail questionnaire returns. *Journal of Applied Psychology,* **23**, 95–104.

Staples, F. R., and Walters, R. H. (1961). Anxiety, birth order, and susceptibility to social influence. *Journal of Abnormal and Social Psychology,* **62**, 716–719.

Star, S. A., and Hughes, H. M. (1950). Report on an educational campaign: The Cincinnati plan for the United Nations. *American Journal of Sociology,* **55**, 389–400.

Stein, K. B. (1971). Psychotherapy patients as research subjects: Problems in cooperativeness, representativeness, and generalizability. *Journal of Consulting and Clinical Psychology,* **37**, 99–105.

Steiner, I. D. (1972). The evils of research: Or what my mother didn't tell me about the sins of academia. *American Psychologist,* **27**, 766–768.

Straits, B. C., and Wuebben, P. L. (1973). College students' reactions to social scientific experimentation. *Sociological Methods and Research,* **1**, 355–386.

Straits, B. C., Wuebben, P. L., and Majka, T. J. (1972). Influences on subjects' perceptions of experimental research situations. *Sociometry,* **35**, 499–518.

Streib, G. F. (1966). Participants and drop-outs in a longitudinal study. *Journal of Gerontology,* **21**, 200–209.

Stricker, L. J. (1967). The true deceiver. *Psychological Bulletin,* **68**, 13–20.

Stricker, L. J., Messick, S., and Jackson, D. N. (1967). Suspicion of deception: Implications for conformity research. *Journal of Personality and Social Psychology,* **5**, 379–389.

Stricker, L. J., Messick, S., and Jackson, D. N. (1969). Evaluating deception in psychological research. *Psychological Bulletin,* **71**, 343–351.

Stricker, L. J., Messick, S., and Jackson, D. N. (1970). Conformity, anticonformity, and independence: Their dimensionality and generality. *Journal of Personality and Social Psychology,* **16**, 494–507.

Stumberg, D. (1925). A comparison of sophisticated and naive subjects by the association-reaction method. *American Journal of Psychology,* **36**, 88–95.

Suchman, E. A. (1962). An analysis of "bias" in survey research. *Public Opinion Quarterly,* **26**, 102–111.

Suchman, E., and McCandless, B. (1940). Who answers questionnaires? *Journal of Applied Psychology,* **24**, 758–769.

Suedfeld, P. (1964). Birth order of volunteers for sensory deprivation. *Journal of Abnormal and Social Psychology,* **68**, 195–196.

Suedfeld, P. (1968). Anticipated and experienced stress in sensory deprivation as a function of orientation and ordinal position. *Journal of Social Psychology,* **76**, 259–263.

Suedfeld, P. (1969). Sensory deprivation stress: Birth order and instructional set as interacting variables. *Journal of Personality and Social Psychology,* **11**, 70–74.

Sullivan, D. S., and Deiker, T. E. (1973). Subject–experimenter perceptions of ethical issues in human research. *American Psychologist,* **28**, 587–591.

Swingle, P. G., Ed. (1973). *Social Psychology in Natural Settings: A Reader in Field Experimentation.* Chicago: Aldine.

Tacon, P.H.D. (1965). The effects of sex of E on obtaining Ss for psychological experiments. *Canadian Psychologist,* **6a**, 349–352.

Taffel, C. (1955). Anxiety and the conditioning of verbal behavior. *Journal of Abnormal and Social Psychology,* **51**, 496–501.

Taub, S. I., and Farrow, B. J. (1973), Reinforcement effects on intersubject communication: The scuttlebutt effect. *Perceptual and Motor skills,* **37,** 15–22.

Teele, J. E. (1962). Measures of social participation. *Social Problems,* **10,** 31–39.

Teele, J. E. (1965). An appraisal of research on social participation. *Sociological Quarterly,* **6,** 257–267.

Teele, J. E. (1967). Correlates of voluntary social participation. *Genetic Psychology Monographs,* **76,** 165–204.

Thistlethwaite, D. L., and Wheeler, N. (1966). Effects of teacher and peer subcultures upon student aspirations. *Journal of Educational Psychology,* **57,** 35–47.

Thomas, E. J., and Biddle, B. J. (1966). The nature and history of role theory. In B. J. Biddle and E. J. Thomas, Eds., *Role Theory: Concepts and Research.* New York: Wiley.

Tiffany, D. W., Cowan, J. R., and Blinn, E. (1970). Sample and personality biases of volunteer subjects. *Journal of Consulting and Clinical Psychology,* **35,** 38–43.

Toops, H. A. (1926). The returns from follow-up letters to questionnaires. *Journal of Applied Psychology,* **10,** 92–101.

Trotter, S. (1974). Strict regulations proposed for human experimentation. *APA Monitor,* **5,** 1, 8.

Tukey, J. W. (1970). *Exploratory Data Analysis: Limited Preliminary Edition.* Reading, Mass.: Addison-Wesley.

Tune, G. S. (1968). A note on differences between cooperative and non-cooperative volunteer subjects. *British Journal of Social and Clinical Psychology,* **7,** 229–230.

Tune, G. S. (1969). A further note on the differences between cooperative and non-cooperative volunteer subjects. *British Journal of Social and Clinical Psychology,* **8,** 183–184.

Underwood, B. J., Schwenn, E., and Keppel, G. (1964). Verbal learning as related to point of time in the school term. *Journal of Verbal Learning and Verbal Behavior,* **3,** 222–225.

Valins, S. (1967). Emotionality and information concerning internal reactions. *Journal of Personality and Social Psychology,* **6,** 458–463.

Varela, J. A. (1964). A cross-cultural replication of an experiment involving birth order. *Journal of Abnormal and Social Psychology,* **69,** 456–457.

Verinis, J. S. (1968). The disbelieving subject. *Psychological Reports,* **22,** 977–981.

Vidmar, N., and Hackman, J. R. (1971). Interlaboratory generalizability of small group research: An experimental study. *Journal of Social Psychology*, **83**, 129–139.

Vinacke, W. E. (1954). Deceiving experimental subjects. *American Psychologist*, **9**, 155.

Wagner, N. N. (1968). Birth order of volunteers: Cross-cultural data. *Journal of Social Psychology*, **74**, 133–134.

Wallace, D. (1954). A case for-and against - mail questionnaires. *Public Opinion Quarterly*, **18**, 40–52.

Wallace, J., and Sadalla, E. (1966). Behavioral consequences of transgression: I. The effects of social recognition. *Journal of Experimental Research in Personality*, **1**, 187–194.

Wallin, P. (1949). Volunteer subjects as a source of sampling bias. *American Journal of Sociology*, **54**, 539–544.

Walsh, J. (1973). Addiction research center: Pioneers still on the frontier. *Science*, **182**, 1229–1231.

Ward, C. D. (1964). A further examination of birth order as a selective factor among volunteer subjects. *Journal of Abnormal and Social Psychology*, **69**, 311–313.

Ward, W. D. and Sandvold, K. D. (1963). Performance expectancy as a determinant of actual performance: A partial replication. *Journal of Abnormal and Social Psychology*, **67**, 293–295.

Warren,-J. R. (1966). Birth order and social behavior. *Psychological Bulletin*, **65**, 38–49.

Waters, L. K., and Kirk, W. E. (1969). Characteristics of volunteers and nonvolunteers for psychological experiments. *Journal of Psychology*, **73**, 133–136.

Webb, E. J., Campbell, D. T., Schwartz, R. D., and Sechrest, L. (1966). *Unobtrusive Measures: Nonreactive Research in the Social Sciences*. Chicago: Rand-McNally.

Weber, S. J., and Cook, T. D. (1972). Subject effects in laboratory research: An examination of subject roles, demand characteristics, and valid inference. *Psychological Bulletin*, **77**, 273–295.

Wechsler, D. (1958). *The measurement and appraisal of adult intelligence*, 4th ed. Baltimore: Williams and Wilkins.

Weigel, R. G., Weigel, V. M., and Hebert, J. A. (1971). Non-volunteer subjects: Temporal effects. *Psychological Reports*, **28**, 191–192.

Weiss, J. H. (1970). Birth order and physiological stress response. *Child Development*, **41**, 461–470.

Weiss, J. H., Wolf, A., and Wiltsey, R. G. (1963). Birth order, recuitment conditions, and preferences for participation in group versus non-group experiments. *American Psychologist,* **18**, 356 (Abstract).

Weiss, L. R. (1968). The effect of subject, experimenter and task variables on subject compliance with the experimenter's expectation. Unpublished doctoral diss. S.U.N.Y., Buffalo.

Weiss, R. F., Buchanan, W., Altstatt. L., and Lombardo, J. P. (1971). Altruism is rewarding. *Science,* **171**, 1262–1263.

Weitz, S. (1968). The subject: The other variable in experimenter bias research. Unpublished manuscript, Harvard University.

Wells, B. W. P., and Schofield, C. B. S. (1972). Personality characteristics of homosexual men suffering from sexually transmitted diseases. *British Journal of Venereal Diseases,* **48**, 75–78.

Welty, G. (n.d.). The volunteer effect and the Kuhn-McPartland Twenty Statements Test. Unpublished manuscript.

White, H. A., and Schumsky, D. A. (1972). Prior information and "awareness" in verbal conditioning. *Journal of Personality and Social Psychology,* **24**, 162–165.

White, M. A., and Duker, J. (1971). Some unprinciples of psychological research. *American Psychologist,* **26**, 397–399.

Wicker, A. W. (1968a). Overt behaviors toward the church by volunteers, follow-up volunteers, and non-volunteers in a church survey. *Psychological Reports,* **22**, 917–920.

Wicker, A. W. (1968b). Requirements for protecting privacy of human subjects: Some implications for generalization of research findings. *American Psychologist,* **23**, 70–72.

Wicker, A. W., and Bushweiler, G. (1970). Perceived fairness and pleasantness of social exchange situations: Two factorial studies of inequity. *Journal of Personality and Social Psychology,* **15**, 63–75.

Wicker, A. W., and Pomazal, R. J. (1970). The relationship between attitudes and behavior as a function of specificity of attitude object and presence of a significant person during assessment conditions. Unpublished manuscript, University of Illinois.

Williams, J. H. (1964). Conditioning of verbalization: A review. *Psychological Bulletin,* **62**, 383–393.

Willis, R. H. (1965). Conformity, independence, and anticonformity. *Human Relations,* **18**, 373–388.

Willis, R. H., and Willis, Y. A. (1970). Role playing versus deception: An experimental comparison. *Journal of Personality and Social Psychology,* **16**, 472–477.

Wilson, P. R. and Patterson, J. (1965). Sex differences in volunteering behavior. *Psychological Reports,* **16**, 976.

Winer, B. J. (1968). The error. *Psychometrika,*, **33**, 391–403.

Wolf, A. (1967). Personal communication. Oct. 21.

Wolf, A., and Weiss, J. H. (1965). Birth order, recruitment conditions, and volunteering preference. *Journal of Personality and Social Psychology.* **2**, 269–273.

Wolfensberger, W. (1967). Ethical issues in research with human subjects. *Science,* **155**, 47–51.

Wolfgang, A. (1967). Sex differences in abstract ability of volunteers and nonvolunteers for concept learning experiments. *Psychological Reports,* **21**, 509–512.

Wolfle, D. (1960). Research with human subjects. *Science,* **132**, 989.

Wrightsman, L. S. (1966). Predicting college students' participation in required psychology experiments. *American Psychologist,* **21**, 812–813.

Wuebben, P. L. (1967). Honesty of subjects and birth order. *Journal of Personality and Social Psychology,* **5**, 350–352.

Wunderlich, R. A., and Becker, J. (1969). Obstacles to research in the social and behavioral sciences. *Catholic Educational Review,* **66**, 722–729.

Young, F. W. (1968). A FORTRAN IV program for nonmetric multidimensional scaling. *L. L. Thurstone Psychometric Laboratory Monograph,* No. 56.

Zamansky, H. S., and Brightbill, R. F. (1965). Attitude differences of volunteers and nonvolunteers and of susceptible and nonsusceptible hypnotic subjects. *International Journal of Clinical and Experimental Hypnosis.* **13**, 279–290.

Zeigarnik, B. (1927). Das Behalten Erledigter und Unerledigter Handlungen. *Psychologische Forschung,* **9**, 1–85.

Zimmer, H. (1956). Validity of extrapolating nonresponse bias from mail questionnaire follow-ups. *Journal of Applied Psychology,* **40**, 117–121.

Zuckerman, M., Schultz, D. P., and Hopkins, T. R. (1967). Sensation-seeking and volunteering for sensory deprivation and hypnosis experiments. *Journal of Consulting Psychology,* **31**, 358–363.

Index of Names

Subject Index